The Consultant's Guide to Proposal Writing

THIRD EDITION

The Consultant's Guide to Proposal Writing

How to Satisfy Your Clients and Double Your Income

THIRD EDITION

Herman Holtz

John Wiley & Sons, Inc.

New York • Chichester • Weinheim • Brisbane • Singapore • Toronto

This book is printed on acid-free paper. ♾

Copyright © 1998 by Herman Holtz. All rights reserved.

Published by John Wiley & Sons, Inc.
Published simultaneously in Canada.

This publication is designed to provide accurate and authoritative information in regard to the subject matter covered. It is sold with the understanding that the pub-lisher is not engaged in rendering professional services. If professional advice or other expert assistance is required, the services of a competent professional person should be sought.

Library of Congress Cataloging-in-Publication Data:

Holtz, Herman.
    The consultant's guide to proposal writing : how to satisfy your
clients and double your income / Herman Holtz. — 3rd ed.
      p.   cm.
    Includes index.
    ISBN 0-471-24917-3 (hardcover : alk. paper)
    1. Proposal writing in business. 2. Business consultants.
I. Title.
HF5718.5.H63   1998
808'.066658—dc21   98-22811
                                           CIP

Printed in the United States of America.

10 9 8 7 6 5 4 3 2

Writing is a lonely profession. The daily routine is just the writer and the keyboard. We cherish the quiet atmosphere, but unbroken solitude becomes oppressive, and many of us seek periodic relief from that deadly silence. The computer provides an avenue of relief that is also a supporting influence via discussion groups we call "mailing lists." That is a loosely organized network of people with some common interest, who stay in touch with each other and conduct discussions via e-mail.

I sponsor such a list. I call it "Scribes" because it is for freelance writers of all descriptions. My exchanges with others on the list break that deadly solitude, but they do more than sustain my morale: They help me as a writer, too, for our basic mission is to be there for each other. I am deeply indebted to all who participate and contribute to the list. It would be impractical for me to attempt to list here all the subscribers to the list, and it would be unfair to the rest of them if I were to name just a few. I therefore dedicate this book to all my Scribe listmates without naming any individually. May you continue to find success as freelance writers and enjoy being writers as much as I do.

Preface

We are all witness to and a great many of us participants in the most astonishing high-tech revolution yet, one that continues without apparent pause. Startling changes have come about in a very few years with the appearance of almost revolutionary new technologies and products. One especially prominent and pervasive new development is the online phenomenon that now includes the Internet as its principal focus. In reviewing the second edition of this book to determine what is outdated and must be replaced with current information for the third edition, I have a sense of searching through the artifacts of an ancient civilization: The changes are that profound, and the proposal-writing tools of only a few years ago, when the second edition was published, seem that archaic now.

The online avenue of trade and communication and the changes it has brought about have affected all the marketing activities associated directly and indirectly with proposal writing, even the learning of and acquiring proposal and bid solicitations for. We have most certainly not achieved the paperless society—not yet, at least—but much of the transmission of paper by conventional mail has most certainly yielded to electronic transmissions via online systems. I now read the *Commerce Business Daily* on my computer screen and often find that I am reading not only the synopsis of a planned procurement, but I am reading the RFP also because the solicitation says, "This Request for Proposals (RFP) constitutes the only solicitation; proposals are requested and NO WRITTEN SOLICITATION WILL BE ISSUED." This is followed by citation of and reference to relevant regulations of the Federal Acquisition Regulations (FAR), greatly reducing the amount of information needed in the RFP.

Proposal writing has become an important element in marketing—not only in marketing to federal, state, and local governments, but increasingly in everyday commerce, as well. The special survey of independent consultants conducted for this new edition of *The Consultant's Guide to Proposal Writing* clearly revealed that increase. In fact, respondents to my survey reported that they do not always refer to their sales presentations as proposals, nor are their proposals always written presentations, but are oral presentations in some cases. And some respondents pointed out that they delivered at least some of their presentations online, via e-mail and attachments to e-mail messages. In fact, one respondent favored me with a complete copy of one of his presentations (sans client names and costs, of course).

The typical business proposal used in commerce may present complete details of the proposed project, but it includes far less ancillary information than do proposals responding to government RFPs. It is not usually necessary to offer a client in commercial business as much information as is required by government agencies, which normally stipulate what information is required, unlike the corporate client seeking proposals. Too, in commercial practice, what is called a proposal is often merely a brief written summary and confirmation of what has been discussed and agreed to in earlier face-to-face meetings and discussions with clients. In government contracting, even if such meetings, discussions, and verbal agreements have taken place, all details must be documented in a proposal that will be incorporated by reference in the resulting contract.

Despite these considerations, and allowing for differences, the proposal written for a government contract is an excellent model generally for a proposal to any client. In my own applications, I have tended to follow that model for all proposals, with the philosophy that it is better to provide more information than is required than to risk being nonresponsive by not having enough. Therefore, much of this book is based on that proposal model, although as an independent consultant you are quite likely to need only relatively simple and informal proposals most of the time and may well find a simpler format to be a more suitable model for your needs.

One other important difference between proposals pursuing government contracts and those addressed to clients in the private sector is this: Government policy in soliciting contracts is basically the encouragement of competition and equal opportunity. Thus, proposals written to government agencies are almost always competitive, despite the frequent use of "selected sources" (noncompetitive procurement), when such procurement is justified. A great many independent consultants and other self-employed specialists win much of their business through recommendations and contracting with "old" clients. Thus, they often write proposals without having direct competition. That makes a significant difference in approach.

Aside from the still increasing use of proposals as a marketing tool in all markets, the use of fax, computer disks, the Internet, and e-mail have come to play important roles in proposal writing and activities connected with proposal writing, such as research and issuance of requests for proposals. Some of these developments tend to simplifying and expediting the processes, but they also bring up new concerns and complications.

There are other consequences of the growth of proposal writing. For one, proposal consulting has taken its place as one of the many independent consulting specialties offered to proposal writers as support. These are time- and labor-saving services, making life easier and proposal processes vastly less time consuming and less costly. Standard Form 129, Application for Bidders List (an application to be placed on the bidders list), is not as widely used as it was once because there are simpler, faster, easier ways to be listed now, but some agencies still invite the submission of this form. When I wanted a copy of this form, I had to search about the government Web sites a bit, but I soon found a place to download forms, and I was able to print out on my own printer an exact copy of the official form, whereas a few years ago I would have had to get a printed copy from a government procurement office.

Technology also plays other important roles in proposal development and production. With today's equipment, found in even the smallest offices now, proposals are easily produced with elaborate formats and the appearance of formally printed documents, even with color printing, graphs, charts, and other illustrations of professional quality.

What is delivered to clients today is not always paper, either, with CDs, floppy disks, and e-mail often constituting or supplementing proposals, and with oral proposals called for in some situations.

To add to the change, there has been a definite trend toward simplifying the procurement systems overall and using well-established commercial trade practices where it is practicable, including the use of credit cards for informal and spontaneous purchasing at commercial outlets. A noticeably larger percentage of procurements are today being effected through sealed bids and Requests for Quotation and Purchase Orders, by Selected Source (noncompetitive) procurements, and by other speeded-up procedures and processes.

The change is almost incomprehensible to one schooled in older methods. I started marketing to government agencies when my major reliance for market research was the daily paper edition of the *Commerce Business Daily*. It was then available at the annual fee of $15. Studying that little daily catalog of government wants and business opportunities was a morning chore I pursued with great zest, knowing that once in a while I would find a contract opportunity that was exactly right for our organization and for which we could be a strong competitor. Deterioration of traditional mail services and most other services threatened to make that a less and less practical way to find those opportunities, as deliveries of the CBD (the inevitable contraction of the publication's name) became erratic and uncertain: Friday's edition might arrive the following Wednesday and Wednesday's edition the next Monday, while the annual subscription fee climbed to three figures and continued rising even then.

That publication is now part of the abundance of marketing information available at my desk with the punch of a few keys. Overall, today's abundance of marketing information online—on the computer screen, that is—is almost overwhelming. It is with ease that you may find and request copies of various solicitations electronically (by fax and e-mail) and even have them delivered electronically in some cases. But even easier, today many of the announcements in the CBD are themselves both synopses of requirements and complete solicitations. If you are viewing them on-screen, you may print them out directly as the full and official RFP.

And yet, much as so many things have changed, much remains the same, in essence, for the purpose is still marketing. The change has been far more in the technologies that affect relevant market research and production of proposals than in the development of proposal content and proposal strategies. Most that is fundamental and basic is as it was, in that respect. It is the means, not the ends, that have been primarily affected by change; the ends remain the same: Clients still want proposals for the same reasons, and proposal writers labor at their development for the same reasons. The client seeking to have work done by anyone always has at least two concerns in general: One concern is for the practicality of the solution and services offered; the other for the capability and the reliability of anyone being considered as a possible supplier. The client seeks any reassurance that he or she may put trust in the consultant retained, so that single word, *trust,* sums up a major purpose of proposals and Requests for Proposals. Clients seek suppliers in whom they can place their trust, and proposal writers offer information designed to inspire that trust and win contracts.

The basic premise on which both the original and second editions of this book were based was that many consultants recognize the importance of proposals in marketing and need a guide to help them produce more effective proposals. The success of the book in both editions substantiated the premise and inspired the writing of this third edition to report on changes that affect proposal writing and to guide the reader into the changed environment of proposal writing. However, whereas the intended readers of the original and second editions were all independent consultants for whom proposal writing could be an important marketing activity to sell their consulting services, this third edition adds several other readers to its intended audience: It adds that growing class of proposal consultants, those independent consultants for whom proposal-writing support service is their chosen field of specialization, for one. It adds also those independent consultants for whom the addition of proposal-writing support to the services they offer clients is a viable option. And it adds those writers who want to learn more of proposal writing as one of the services they will offer their clients.

Despite the many changes, the federal government is still a commanding market for consulting services—perhaps even greater than ever, with the Department of Defense still the largest government market. However, the third edition of *The Consultant's Guide to Proposal Writing* will introduce and focus on many new and important developments directly relevant to proposal writing. You and others interested in improving your proposal skills, and thereby increasing your marketing success, need to know about these.

Despite new developments and changes, the opening statements of the preface to the original edition of this book are as valid and timely today as they were more than a decade ago when I first wrote them:

If there is one skill that I have found to be utmost in importance to the success of the typical independent consultant, it is skill in marketing: the ability to win clients and contracts. And if there is one ability that I have found to be utmost in importance to achieving that skill in marketing the consultant's services effectively, it is the ability to develop winning proposals—that task which we all so often refer to erroneously as "proposal writing."

However, even the development (writing) of effective proposals is only one element of proposal-related ability. Another element is probably of equal importance and perhaps of even greater importance. Many consultants who do write adequate proposals fail to utilize them effectively, and so do not draw full benefits from their proposal-writing skills. Helping you become fully aware of and fully dedicated to maximizing your success through wise and faithful practice in both areas is therefore a major objective of this book.

The technological marvels have already revolutionized the efficiency with which we can research the market for opportunities and respond to those we find attractive. They have and will continue to improve the physical quality of the proposals we write—their typefaces, their bindings, and their illustrations. Technology is a boon to marketing communications. Modern online facilities enable us to learn of more market opportunities and learn of them more swiftly than ever. We communicate more swiftly and conveniently among ourselves, with our clients, and with our prospective clients. But the need to write and market skillfully with our proposals, the true measure of proposal quality, has not changed: That quality depends as much as ever on our skills, creativity, and cleverness.

Unfortunately, many consultants still groan at the mere thought of writing a proposal, as also observed in the preface to that first edition. The still expanding technologies of the computer age make writing much easier, of course, in the sense of physical exertion. Modern word processors, with their spell checkers and other refinements, come close to actual thinking, or so it often seems as the software makes corrections and does so much of the writing task for us.

Especially there is a great deal of relief in the wealth of still growing online facilities. They have even eclipsed the advances in desktop computers generally, although those advances have been almost revolutionary also and have made the online explosion possible. Use of the

Internet would not be a practical possibility for most of us without the great leaps in memory and storage capabilities of today's computers.

Even in my own case (and I am fortunate enough to actually *enjoy* writing and rewriting), this has made writing a much easier and more pleasant task. I wrote the first edition of this book on a CP/M computer, using an early WordStar (3.0) word processor software program, which those familiar with early desktop computers will recognize as virtually a Stone Age system in both software and hardware—almost primitive by today's standards. A mere handful of years—only four—and two computers later, I used what was then one of the latest and fastest desktop computers available, one using the 386 chip with 2MB of RAM and a "large" 65MB hard disk. And this, in 1997, is written on my fourth computer, one that is already dated and verging on obsolescence because it has "only" 16MB of RAM and "only" a 730MB hard disk! (I am at a loss to even guess at what kind of system I shall be using to write the fourth edition.)

Many of the techniques and tactics I explain and recommend have become infinitely easier to use because of the greatly enhanced capabilities of modern computers. To be quite accurate, the enhancements and enlarged capabilities are really the result of enormously improved software, but the new software is possible only because of great leaps in hardware capabilities—increases in memory, speed, and storage. Hardware and software are interdependent: Each depends for its success on advances made by the other. However, the net result is that the computer is more and more a true labor-saving device, and marketing success in today's milieu depends in some part on the quality and modernity of your high-tech equipment. You are well advised to try to keep your equipment up to date. Learn to use all the relevant software. Build your computer libraries and files carefully and thoroughly; they will soon become your most powerful tool for creating effective proposals. In fact, writing proposals will become far easier, after a time, not only because of your developing experience and skill, but even more because of your expanding resources in computer files. And, by all means, learn to take advantage of the online facilities you can reach via the Internet to support and simplify your proposal writing. (I will discuss these in the appropriate chapters, of course.)

Learning to use the various types of software is also most important. It was only after I had been tapping away at a keyboard for a time, using little but word processing software, that I began to realize that word processing software is not the only kind of software a proposal writer needs and can use gainfully. In addition to the word processors, there are spelling checkers, thesauruses, grammar checkers, outliners, database managers, spoolers, file managers, key redefiners, spread-sheet programs, communications software, readability-measurement and -enhancement programs, and even others to help you. In fact, whereas most of these were separate programs a few years ago, most of the modern word processors include many of these programs. It was once necessary to learn each type of software through long and often painful experience. Today, most of the major programs have special tutorials and pull-down menu systems that make the learning process much easier and, perhaps even more significant, provide automated functions and so much on-the-spot guidance that they reduce the need to learn the program.

The computer and all that is connected with it make life easier for everyone when used wisely and well, and that includes the authors of winning proposals.

Herman Holtz
Silver Spring, Maryland, 1998

Contents

headlines. Three basic kinds of presentation strategy. Dramatic, striking proposal copy. Another device: storyboarding.

List of Figures

An Orientation
in Proposals

> A request for a
> proposal is an
> invitation to make a
> sales presentation,
> and that is a
> marketing
> opportunity, even a
> unique marketing
> opportunity, if you
> take full advantage
> of it.

Competitive versus
Noncompetitive Marketing
Situations

In time, most of us develop a number of steady clients, clients with whom we enjoy good business relationships and mutual trust, so that they call on us whenever they need our services. They may or may not ask for a proposal each time in these cases, but usually they do not seek competitive bids, so we have no competition, as long as our price and schedule are acceptable to the client.

Of course, this is not the case where the client has no favored consultant but is trying to evaluate prospective consultants for their capability and dependability. The client is trying to make a good choice by asking a number of consultants for competitive quotes or proposals. It is thus a much different situation from the first one postulated. It is this situation that we are addressing here: writing proposals in competition with other consultants who have been invited to submit proposals for some stated need.

1

Why Do Clients Want Proposals?

Understanding clients' typical problems and concerns in such circumstances is especially helpful in writing proposals. Understand, first of all, that in retaining a consultant who is a stranger, a client perceives risks to his or her business. The client does not know whether the services of the consultant who is retained will be good, bad, or indifferent in quality and usefulness. The client seeks to find the *right* consultant, one who merits trust and will provide the most beneficial services. But not all clients are skilled in how to find and select the most suitable consultant for the need. Not all clients even recognize immediately the need to seek consultant help, much less how to judge who is the best consultant for a given need.

It is equally true that not all clients understand and appreciate the value of using proposals to help them find the right consultants. Some clients always request proposals, but some request proposals only when they plan a large project, and some rarely or even never request proposals at all.

Helping clients learn the value of using proposals is usually to your advantage and ought to be a part of your marketing strategy. Instead of proposing to only those who ask for proposals, you can take the initiative by asking clients to accept unsolicited proposals from you as a follow-up to initial contacts, once you qualify the prospect—verify that there is both serious interest in getting help and an ability to retain you. This approach will pay off by providing more opportunities for you, resulting in more effective marketing of your services.

Of course, this approach may suggest to clients the idea of inviting others to submit proposals, creating competition. That should not dismay you. It should give you an advantage if you do a good job of proposal writing. It also eliminates some competitors, for many consultants cringe at the thought of writing anything, but especially proposals, and do not respond to requests for proposals, so it may reduce competition in the end.

Most clients embrace the proposal method of seeking out consulting services once they understand the value of using proposals. Clients will normally come to see that having consultants submit proposals is an effective way to build a base of information upon which they can make an evaluation and select the best consultant for their purposes. Well used, the RFP—request for proposals—is the most effective tool for the task—most effective for both parties, requester and proposer. The proposals submitted provide the information necessary for your sales arguments and for the client's decision. (If you or any other consultant fails to respond effectively, that fact is itself useful information for the client in reaching a decision.) Let's look first at some specific client concerns.

Technical/Professional Capabilities

The client seeking a consultant has two critical concerns. The first and usually more compelling one is concern for the importance of what the client needs to accomplish. Often it is a matter of the welfare and perhaps even the survival of the client's organization. But even a thriving business must steer clear of undue and unnecessary risks. The client is gambling more than money in retaining a consultant. On the results of your work and recommendations, the client may undertake major projects and spend large sums of money in marketing campaigns, reorganization, purchase of capital items, or any of many costly and risky undertakings. To be effective, you must inspire the client's confidence in you.

There is also the personal stake of the executive who retains you or on whose advice you are retained. This individual may or may not be the proprietor or chief executive of the organization, but his or her personal position and career are also at stake. An unfortunate decision can destroy a position and a career. (I can recall a difficult situation I once faced because my client had previously had a bad experience with another consultant of a name closely resembling mine, and he was reminded of it unpleasantly whenever my name was mentioned.)

So there are both general business and personal concerns of clients—risks, as well as benefits—involved in retaining consultants, which highlights the importance of requesting and evaluating proposals to reach a decision. Inevitable, therefore, is the critical importance to the client of identifying and assessing every proposer's capabilities.

What Are "Capabilities"?

In light of these concerns, it is easy to understand why the alert client seeking a consultant looks for hard evidence of each consultant's capabilities. The client in the cosmetics field seeking a marketing consultant is probably going to want some clear and convincing evidence that you offer not only general marketing capabilities, but capabilities in marketing cosmetics. True or not, many clients believe that marketing capability is not easily transferable from one industry to another, but that their own marketing problems are unique and require correspondingly specialized marketing experience. Further, the client will certainly want some clear and convincing evidence that those claimed marketing capabilities are genuine.

THE QUESTION OF PERCEPTION

This does not mean that the client is necessarily correct in these beliefs. The fact that you have never marketed cosmetics before does not preclude your producing a highly effective marketing plan for the cosmetics client. But that is not the point. The point is that this client *perceives* cosmetics marketing experience as a necessary qualification and will therefore scan proposals for evidence of that specific experience. The validity of the client's premise is another matter. You are always at the mercy of the client's perception.

Experience, both in general (e.g., marketing) and in specific fields (e.g., cosmetics), represents certain capabilities. But these are general capabilities, and there are other items that must be listed, such as the applications in the field. Think in terms of what you can *do*, specifically, for the client—the following, for example:

- Develop general marketing strategies.
- Write advertising copy.
- Devise packaging alternatives and recommendations.
- Conceive special promotional campaigns and plans.
- Conduct market surveys.
- Scout and analyze competition.
- Make presentations to the top officials of the client organization.
- Train staff people in the client organization.
- Design and recommend distribution systems.
- Segment the market and plan strategies and promotions for each segment.
- Devise and conduct research.

THE QUESTION OF COMPETENCE

The capabilities listed are one thing. But there is another aspect to the question of capabilities. There is the matter of technical/professional competence. Even given that you can point to specific experience in the many tasks and disciplines in the field of interest, the client wants to know how competent you are in these things. The client will soon enough learn that experience per se is not sufficient; even inept practitioners can often point to a great deal of experience in the field. (Or is that *exposure,* rather than experience, and are they the same thing? Posing and answering that question—e.g., "Exposure versus experience" or "Exposure is not experience"—may be the basis for a sales argument.) The client will want to see evidence that you have an acceptably high degree of competence and are good enough at the required tasks. Here are some items of information that help the client judge your competence and capability:

- Formal education and academic record
- Understanding of the client's problem or need, as evidenced in the proposal
- Proposed solution or approach to the solution
- Track record: verifiable history of success at the tasks
- Outstanding accomplishments: remarkable successes, innovations
- Other noteworthy and relevant achievements
- Career history: former employers, positions, clients
- Honors and awards
- Testimonials from former employers and/or clients

Other Benefits to the Client

Not all clients realize it at first, but there is another substantial benefit they can derive from requesting and reviewing proposals. This benefit makes it worthwhile for the client to encourage the greatest number of responses, despite the time and energy required to review a large number of proposals. The client benefits by being presented with multiple analyses of his or her requirement from a variety of specialists, offering a variety of views and approaches. This furnishes the client a valuable data bank and often a better insight into his or her real needs.

Obviously, you and other consultants who submit proposals are not going to carry out a complete and detailed analysis of the problem in your proposals, but you must do at least some preliminary analysis and propose at least a general approach to solving the problem. If the client has done a good job of writing the statement that explains the problem, the proposals submitted usually provide the thoughtful client a wealth of insight and expert preliminary advice. Even if many of the proposals are of little or no direct benefit in this regard, many will contain valuable information. In fact, it is rarely that the proposals submitted, individually and collectively, do not represent a greater knowledge of and insight into the client's problem than the client had originally. That is a bonus for the client, which alone is worth the cost of preparing the request and reading the proposals, aside from the enormously expanded base of knowledge that it gives the client to help in selecting a consultant.

This is not to say that the client is deliberately seeking free consulting services, although this is what the client gets, in effect. But that is an inevitable result—and not a loss to you. Many businesspeople find it necessary to furnish free samples to prospective buyers. To prove your abilities, you must demonstrate them somehow. On the other hand, the cynical use of an RFP to get free analyses is not unknown, unfortunately, and you must use judgment in deciding how much to reveal in your proposals and presentations. (Mercifully, the practice of deliberately picking your brains to euchre you into giving away your services is fairly rare, and most prospects are sincere in requesting proposals and asking for certain information.)

How Much Do You Have to Give Away?

Aside from the possible hazard of giving prospects—people who are not yet clients—so much information in your proposals that you are giving away the store, there is the matter of cost to you. Proposal writing is time-consuming and is therefore costly marketing. Time is both the most costly resource you have and your chief commodity. From that viewpoint alone you must make a judgment as to how much you should reveal in a proposal—how much, that is, is necessary to win the contract. That is all that you ought to give away.

There is no formula for measuring that. You must provide the prospect with enough information to prove your case and win the contract, but no more. But deciding how much is enough is purely judgmental, and you must base it on your own estimate. One guideline to help you judge this is a list of at least five elements that the effective proposal must include:

1. Evidence of your clear understanding of the client's problem
2. An approach and program plan or design that appears to the client well suited to solving the problem and likely to produce the results desired
3. Convincing evidence of your qualifications and capability for carrying out the plan properly
4. Convincing evidence of your dependability as a consultant or contractor
5. A compelling reason overall for the client to select you—a winning strategy

Each of these will be discussed in much greater detail as we proceed. In fact, the remainder of this book will be devoted primarily to discussing these items and how they are implemented, as well as how, where, and when to utilize proposals as a prime marketing tool. However, some discussion is needed here before we address these items in painstaking detail.

Understanding of the Client's Problem

An amazingly large number of proposals convey the distinct impression that the writer of the proposal did not understand the problem. In some cases, the writer truly did not understand the problem. Sometimes the consultant, eager for business, is stretching things a bit too far, making a try for a contract and project that is not really in his or her field. Sometimes the consultant has been in too great a hurry to write the proposal and has not given enough thought to the expressed need—has not studied the need at length and planned thoroughly enough to offer a convincing presentation. Often, however, the prime weakness is simply careless writing. That is, the consultant understands the problem all right and has a worthy approach, but fails to demonstrate that understanding and explain the virtues of the approach and proposed plan or design.

Don't expect the client to study your program and analyze it to perceive your merit and that of your program; it won't happen without your help, even if the client has the technical capability to appreciate your design without your guidance. You have to lead the client through your arguments to your conclusion. Unless your proposal establishes and demonstrates your understanding of the need clearly in the introductory portion (and in terms that do not require a great deal of technical expertise or mental gymnastics to understand), the client may decide that time is better spent on the next proposal. Often as many as two out of three proposals are disqualified and discarded as a result of the first reading or even a partial reading.

Program Plan or Design

The part of the proposal that establishes your understanding of the client's problem should bridge logically into a discussion of your program plan or design. That discussion must convince the client that yours is the best approach and the best design or plan for satisfying the client's need.

This is a place to sell your ideas, a critical area: Unless you manage to convince the client here that you offer what is probably the best plan, you will have already lost. Here you are going to need both sales ability and rationale.

Your Qualifications and Capability

Proposing, explaining, and selling a plan or design as the best one is one thing. Proving that you have all the necessary qualifications for carrying out the plan or implementing the design is another thing. And establishing those qualifications beyond reasonable doubt is only partially dependent on establishing your own technical and professional credentials.

Part of those qualifications is specific experience that relates directly to the need. General experience that does not relate directly may not be acceptable to the client. Some projects require certain resources, such as access to special equipment, laboratories, or clerical labor; people to do field surveys; and other necessities. There is also the matter of other professionals whom you may require to support you for larger projects or special tasks. Vague or general assurances that you have access to necessary resources and/or associates or others you can turn to are not acceptable as proof of needed resources. The typical client is likely to want some solid and specific evidence of adequate and assured availability of any necessary resources, including supporting professionals when the project obviously requires such support.

Dependability

Dependability of a contractor is always a concern. A client who has previously had experience with someone who was less than totally dependable will worry about dependability. A superb project plan or design, with a superbly qualified consultant to carry out the plan, can still founder quite easily if the consultant is not highly conscientious and dedicated to the project. Dedication is as important a consideration as that of technical/professional capability. All clients want assurance that they may depend upon you if they award you the contract, but promises and pledges alone are not enough to provide that assurance. Something more substantial than soothing syrup is needed.

Winning Strategy

There are numerous strategies possible in proposal writing, all of which we will discuss. However, there is always the question of the major strategy, the winning strategy (also referred to as capture strategy or main strategy, to distinguish it from other, subordinate strategies) upon which you base your entire argument and hope of capturing the contract.

To put this another way and clarify the meaning immediately, the winning strategy is your explanation to the client of why the client should award the contract to you.

In simple terms, sales techniques are based on giving prospects reasons for doing business with you. The proposal is not a solicitation or entreaty and should not be written as a plea. It is a sales presentation and should be presented as an offer to do something for the client. But don't expect the client to find reasons for accepting your offer; you must do your own selling. You must furnish the reasons, make the client see why it is in his or her own best interests to accept your offer. That is what strategy is all about—the right reasons and the way to present them for greatest effect.

The Evolution of Strategy

Strategy was mentioned last in this series of five elements of effective proposals, but in fact all of the other four items are closely linked to this last-named item and even stem from it. Strategy should drive the entire proposal. In fact, the evolution of strategy, for even the simplest and most informal proposal, should be along the lines of Figure 1.

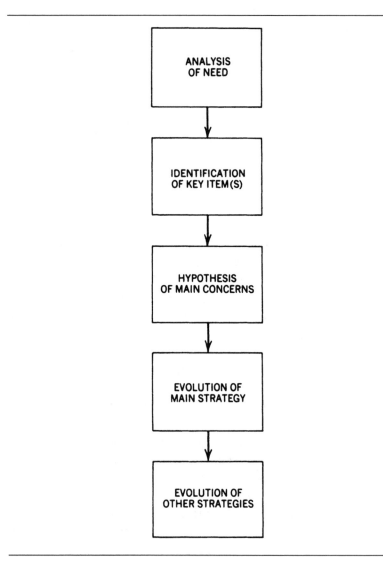

Figure 1   First steps in devising a strategy for a proposal.

Following is an introduction to the basic steps in strategy development. (See Figure 1.)

You begin by analyzing the client's need, based on the client's own description of the need, as filtered and interpreted through your own knowledge and experience, plus any independent observations you have been able to make. Then you define the client's need in your own terms, which may or may not coincide and agree with the client's identification.

As a result of this beginning analysis, you form a hypothesis of what are the primary concerns that drive the client and inspired the request for proposals, offering you the opportunity that every RFP offers. Your success in evolving an effective main strategy is usually tied closely to the accuracy with which you are able to hypothesize the client's major "worry items."

The major beginning steps are, then, to identify the problem, decide what are the key points of the problem and the basic reason for seeking consulting help, and hypothesize the client's chief worries, at least tentatively. You can now begin to devise some sort of main strategy, one that addresses the client's principal worries, of course, while furnishing the client some assurance that the need will be entirely satisfied.

You should understand, at this point, that strategy does not include or embrace those first four items enumerated earlier in this discussion. Those are obligatory items that must be present in each and every proposal, whereas the strategy is something unique, developed especially for the individual proposal and based on the circumstances surrounding that proposal.

Understand also that the process is not entirely linear or sequential, as charts and other presentations describe it, but is an iterative process with many iterations. It is necessary to idealize the process—project it as though it were the orderly and sequential process described—to show the logical progressions. In most proposals of even modest size, the developing and writing of a proposal involves many feedback loops, trial fits, and modifications. There is the assembling of tentative theories or hypotheses, testing them, discarding some, reshaping others, and otherwise molding the plans and approaches until a final approach and a design are settled on. And this is usually as true for the proposal written by a single individual as it is for the proposal written by a large team of consultants.

The foregoing concerns the evolution of the main, or capture, strategy primarily. But inevitably there are several other proposal elements for which strategies must be evolved, areas that may or may not coincide with or support the main strategy. The other elements include at least these:

- Program strategy
- Cost strategy
- Presentation strategy
- Competitor strategy

You should concern yourself with each of these in any proposal you write, although the main strategy will usually coincide with only one of these—usually the program strategy or the cost strategy— although it may be that your chief challenge will be to outshine your competitors. Still, each of these areas makes its own contribution to the client's decision, and the surest way to be successful is to be thorough in attending to all details and so maximize the odds in your favor. Hasty and careless proposals rarely win anything.

Formal versus Informal Proposals

The chief difference between formal and informal proposals is size and format. Logically, the presentation of information and ideas follows the same sequence in each, but the formal proposal is usually submitted for a sizable project as a discrete document, with headlines, cover and title page, and other such publication formalities. The informal proposal, however, is usually in the form of a letter of several pages. (It is often referred to, therefore, as a *letter proposal.*) The fact of its being a letter does not change the philosophy of the proposal. Whatever has been or is said later about the formal proposal applies to letter proposals equally. It is a letter proposal because the project is a small one and does not merit a formal proposal.

A Recommended Proposal Format

A note here: Although I am about to present and recommend my own proposal format, there are other formats. In Chapter 13, I will suggest to you several Web site addresses where you may find other suggested formats, some for special purposes, such as grants and other funding and, in one case, unsolicited proposals.

Occasionally a client will mandate a proposal format, specifying the order in which information is to be presented, as well as precisely what information is required. This is fairly rare, however; usually, the client explains what information is required, but leaves the format up to you. Government RFPs, for example, are usually highly specific in what information is required, but are usually flexible on format, especially when the project is of modest size, one that can be handled by an independent consultant.

I recommend a general proposal format (Figure 2), with brief explanations following those items for which such explanation is required. (Later discussions will be based on the presumption of this format and will elaborate extensively on these brief introductory explanations.) The reasons for the recommendation of this particular format are several:

1. It was developed over years of practical experience with proposals.
2. It reflects many useful practices of others observed over the years.
3. It is similar to or compatible with many mandated formats.
4. It is a logical development of ideas and information.
5. It is quite flexible, adaptable to most needs and readily modified or expanded.
6. It works. I and many of my clients have used it successfully many times over many years.

This is a four-part format, which can be easily expanded to five or even more parts, as the occasion requires. In some cases, such expansion is desirable and beneficial, even required. It is readily adaptable to the multivolume approach required for some large proposals. We will discuss these matters later, as each subject and the need for each discussion arises, when we explore the various needs and situations under which you must or should offer a proposal.

I call each part a *section* and use generic or descriptive titles and sideheads (I offer only a few such sideheads; most proposals of any size will use many more), and I number them with Roman numerals

SECTION I: INTRODUCTION

ABOUT THE OFFEROR

UNDERSTANDING OF THE REQUIREMENT

SECTION II: DISCUSSION

THE REQUIREMENT

ANALYSIS

APPROACH

SECTION III: PROPOSED PROJECT

PROJECT ORGANIZATION

MANAGEMENT

PLANS AND PROCEDURES

STAFF

DELIVERABLE ITEMS

SCHEDULES

RESUME(S)

SECTION IV: QUALIFICATIONS AND EXPERIENCE

RELEVANT CURRENT AND RECENT PROJECTS

RESOURCES

MISCELLANEOUS

FRONT MATTER

APPENDIXES

Figure 2   General proposal format.

in the example here. Of course, in the actual case you can call them *chapters,* name and number any way you please, and make whatever changes you wish. Those are superficial matters that do not affect the outcome. The sideheads listed define the general order and logic of the presentation. There will be more detailed coverage later, with examples, but here are some brief expansions.

Section I

The first section should be brief, since it is only introductory, and I recommend only two subsections, although you may, of course, use additional subject headings, as you will see when we discuss specifics and furnish concrete examples.

The first subsection has three aims: (1) to introduce yourself briefly (who and what you are—name and field of specialization), (2) to give some very brief idea of your credentials and experience to establish your qualifications quickly (perhaps the names of a well-known client or two), and (3) to offer something that captures attention and arouses early interest, motivating the reader to keep turning pages, wanting to know more.

The second subsection should demonstrate your understanding of the client's requirement, but since it is to be brief, summarize that requirement and identify its *essence,* discriminating between essential need and extraneous details. That demonstrates true understanding.

Section II

There should be a direct transition from that statement of understanding to the first sentences of Section II. Section II starts by expanding on that discussion of the requirement to explore and probe all aspects of it, bringing the reader aboard with regard to your analyses and rationale. This leads to the clearly defined, logical approach with which this section should end. This is a section for proving your approach and selling it to the client.

Section III

This is where you present your plans for implementing that approach. It is a natural transition from Section II, and the major headings listed are essentially self-explanatory. (Again, you may wish to add subheadings.) Moreover, this is not necessarily the order in which these subjects will be presented, but all should be included in this section. It is usually this section, however, that is split into two or three sections or even separate volumes for major proposals, offering the subject of management separately and sometimes listing deliverables and schedules separately. This section is, in effect, the specification of the service for which you offer to contract.

Section IV

The major headings of this section are also generally self-explanatory, may be added to and/or supported with subheadings, and may be presented in an alternate order, if your sense of order is different from that suggested here. These are, however, the typical subjects.

Miscellaneous

There are several other elements referred to under that general heading of front matter; they will be discussed later in more detail. Typical front matter for a formal proposal includes a title page, a table of contents, an executive summary, a frontispiece, a response matrix, and possibly even other items.

Many proposals have an appendix, or even several appendixes. These will also be discussed later.

Application of Format to Letter Proposals

We have, of course, not been discussing huge proposals for major projects, such as are so often requested by government agencies, but proposals fitting the capabilities of independent consultants. Even then, however, there are occasions calling for a formal proposal and occasions calling for a brief, informal proposal.

The chief difference between the formal and informal (letter) proposal is that the latter will not have a title page, table of contents, and other such features, but will be entirely in a letter format, although it may identify itself as a proposal. It should, however, have a narrative introduction, a discussion, a proposed program (or procedures), and qualifications of the offeror. It may, in some cases, have limited front matter—principally a summary—and even an appendix.

Bear another important fact in mind always: Don't wait to be asked for a proposal, formal or otherwise. Whenever you believe that you have a serious prospect or a prospect with a serious need, and you think that you know enough of the need to offer a proposal, do so. It may be best not to ask the client for permission to do so, in some cases: If you ask and are refused, you can't submit a proposal, but if you do not ask, you are free to follow up an initial contact with a letter that is actually a proposal!

The Proposal Is a Unique Sales Opportunity

The first question raised in this chapter was why clients want proposals. The answer to that question also discussed why you should want to write proposals—because each is a sales opportunity, but, even more significant, it is a unique sales opportunity: There is no other occasion quite as ideal to demonstrate to a prospective client what you can do for him or her. Other kinds of presentations offer opportunities to present your capabilities, but only in proposals and/or follow-up formal oral presentations do you get the opportunity to present a thought-out analysis and plan specific to a prospective client's stated needs. That is one of the chief reasons to create opportunities to write proposals by offering them voluntarily, as a standard marketing practice.

CHAPTER 2

What It Takes to Write
a Good Proposal

A good proposal is one that wins the contract. But there are other measures of proposal quality, and it is certainly necessary to examine and understand these other measures, if you are to become an expert in writing and using proposals.

Is It Really Proposal *Writing?*

The proposals presented here to discuss principles of proposal development are written presentations, relying principally on text, so it is natural enough that we refer to *proposal writing.* Yet, what is the significance of that word *writing* in this use? How important is the skill of writing in the production of a successful—contract-winning—proposal?

We looked at this briefly from the client's viewpoint, to judge what the client expects or should expect, and why the client wants or should want proposals as a key to selecting a consultant. Understanding the client's needs and purposes is a guide: It tells us why we write proposals, how we should write them, what should be in them, how we should use them, and what we should expect them to do for us. Briefly, and as one government contracting officer put it, the client's purpose in requesting proposals is to select the best possible consultant, with the best possible plan, to be completed in the shortest possible time, at the lowest possible cost.

That idealized procurement goal assumes that the client has a true insight into his or her need and that the several qualities specified are not mutually exclusive, as they often are. Sometimes the client knows or thinks he or she knows precisely what the problem is and how it must be solved. But the client is too often aware of symptoms only and does not recognize that these are only symptoms and do not define the problem. *You* must then determine what the problem or need really is.

Whichever the case, you must counsel the client honestly, not necessarily for moral reasons only, but also because it is necessary. Too, if you must correct the client's analysis of his or her problem, you must do so diplomatically, so that you do not give offense. Tact is essential in all marketing.

In short, you must manage somehow to be several things in writing proposals, and the writer's hat is only one of the several you must wear. You must also be a marketer, sales expert, diplomat, analyst, subject-matter expert, designer, and perhaps even one or two other things. A deficiency in even one of these areas or functions can easily cost you the contract, but never lose sight of the fact that your proposal must be *persuasive*. Steve Wilson, an independent and busy proposal consultant based in the Washington, D.C., area, observes, for example, that lately he is finding that the record of "past performance is as important as price" in writing the most persuasive proposal.

Skills Needed to Write Winning Proposals

I rank the following, in this descending order of importance, as the major skills required to turn out proposals that win contracts:

1. Marketing and sales skills
2. Analytical and creative skills
3. Subject-matter expertise
4. Writing skills

This does not say that any of these are unimportant or that this is the priority of importance in all situations. At times, one of these skills or talents is paramount, at least for the moment, but all make their contributions. Strength in all is necessary, and weakness in any may prove fatal. Nor should writing be underrated, despite these observations. Writing is important as the vehicle for implementing these other skills effectively by skillful integration of all. However, it is true enough that, despite some exceptions, even the most skillful writing alone rarely wins proposal competitions, while marketing and sales skills alone have often carried the day, even with weaknesses in the other areas. Hence, the significance of the estimated rank ordering, the chief purpose of which is to establish an appreciation of all the several skills and capabilities that make up successful proposal *writing*. It is usually the best proposal, not necessarily the best consultant, that wins the contract.

New Influences

There have been many relevant new developments in the past few years, and three major ones stand out as compelling influences related to proposal writing:

1. The explosive growth in sophistication and capabilities of the desktop computer and its software
2. The almost complete dominance of the personal computer (pc) as the desktop computer of choice, and the equal dominance of Windows as the modern operating system of the PC
3. The impact of cyberspace—the Internet, Web sites, e-mail, and other online activity

The early PC, with word processing software, revolutionized office routines for producing business documents almost immediately, as a direct threat to the continued existence of the typewriter. It also began to revolutionize writing itself in many ways—especially proposal writing. But today's PC hardly resembles the early models and offers many kinds of help in proposal development other than word processing. The modern computer with up-to-date software, the Windows operating system, and the online revolution of the Internet mandate the writing of the third edition of this book. (The Macintosh computer is still alive and favored by many, but has continued to decline in market share, so the PC is the major player, and it is our reference here.) But there have also been changes in the markets where proposals are a major marketing tool. For one, where the government markets were the major arenas for proposal competitions in years past, proposals are more and more a marketing tool in the private sector, and that is another reason this new edition is needed.

Marketing and Sales Skills

A later chapter will be dedicated to sales and marketing, but it is virtually impossible to discuss even the basics of proposal writing without some reference to sales and marketing activities. This discussion is thus inevitably a preview of that later chapter, although the focus here will be on sales activity more than marketing and will not go much beyond principles.

SOME TYPICAL KINDS OF FUMBLES

Whatever else it may be, a proposal is first and foremost a sales presentation. One of the most common causes of proposal failure is failing to recognize this. Here are a few examples of proposals written to other objectives and thus failing to become winners:

1. The Aggressive/Defensive Proposal. Some consultants write proposals with a focus on the terms they demand. They tend often to have a tone of aggressiveness and defensiveness, even of paranoia. These writers tend also to hedge promises and commitments with numerous escape clauses, casting doubt on the client's integrity and intentions to deal honorably.

2. The Loud-Claims Proposal. Some consultants appear to labor under an inability to distinguish claims and laudatory self-appraisals from sales arguments. Their proposals contain few facts and are characterized principally by hyperbole, heavy with adjectives and superlatives alleging the writer's great accomplishments, highly respected place in the profession, and marvelous abilities. The strategy apparently is to overwhelm the client by outshouting all others.

3. The "Me Too" Proposal. Some proposals appear to mumble only that the writer can do the job as well as anyone, so why not make the award to that proposer. Such proposals almost inevitably succumb to the competition of other proposals that are based on legitimate sales arguments and strive to be originals rather than carbon copies.

4. "I'm Not Really Sure I Know What You Want" Proposal. One common type of writer, usually a neophyte in proposal writing, believes that the client knows exactly what he or she wants to see proposed and that the client will award the contract to the fortunate writer who succeeds in guessing exactly what that is. This consultant is very much afraid that whatever he or she proposes will not be exactly what the client wants, and therefore the consultant is completely evasive and general, never says anything very concrete, and especially never commits the offer to a detailed plan of action or even a clear-cut analysis of the problem. (In fact, this is the underlying reason for many "me too" proposals.)

5. The "Whatever It Is, I Will Do It" Proposal. A variant of the preceding example is the proposal that says or clearly implies that the writer is not at all sure what the client wants done, but whatever it is, the proposer will take care of it and do a great job.

6. The Canned-Solution Proposal. Some consultants have one or two canned solutions, old reliable standards they offer every potential client, no matter what the client specifies as the need. And some of this genre even have preprinted proposals, with a few blanks for the client's name and address and other minor variables. They manage to win an assignment once in a while, when the need happens by chance to coincide with the canned solution, but it doesn't happen very often.

THE PROBLEM'S IMPORTANCE TO THE CLIENT

All of these approaches and their variants ignore the client's interest. They reflect indifference to the client's need, intended or not, and suggest that the consultant who writes them doesn't really care what the client's problem is and does not care enough to devote much study and thought to the proposal. Whether the cause for all these almost-certain-to-lose approaches is fear, laziness, indifference, arrogance, or plain ignorance of what it takes to win, all radiate the same message: Just give me the money and I'll do whatever it is you want done, but your problem does not merit much of my time before I have a contract.

Of course, the problem is important to the client, who would not be seeking or even considering consulting help if the problem were not important. It is therefore a fatal error to convey any suggestion, directly or indirectly, that you low-rate the importance of the problem. To avoid this, you must be deeply conscious of the client's feelings and respect the seriousness of the problem. To write anything effectively, but especially to write a successful sales presentation, you must be able to perceive the problem from the client's perspective, to understand and even actually feel the client's concerns and earnest desires. That is the essence of selling. Your own perceptions are of no importance here; only the client's perspectives matter: Everyone acts in his or her own self-interest. The client does not care what you want, except as your wants are necessary or are an avenue to achieving his or her own wants. The way to sell anything is to identify what the client wants and then show the client how to satisfy that want through what you offer.

Analytical and Creative Skills

NEEDS AND WANTS

Marketing people sometimes refer to needs and wants as though they were different things. They are not. *Want* meant "lack of," in an earlier time (e.g., "for want of a nail . . .") but is used today to mean "desire," whereas *need* is generally used to refer to a necessity. Practically, when a client decides to want (desire) something, that want becomes a need, and the sales/marketing problem is one of how to persuade the client that the best or most direct way to satisfy the need is to accept your offer. Simple? It is that simple—and yet that complex.

A common failure in marketing is failure to identify the client's need *as the client sees it*. You cannot sell the client something the client truly does not want—does not identify as his or her need, that is, or as the best way to satisfy the need. That may seem to be a hairsplitting point, but it often makes the difference between success and failure in the marketplace.

Let us suppose that the client has announced a perceived need for a better inventory-control and -management system to replace the one currently in use. The client's objection to the existing system is that it is wasteful of warehouse space and capital, with too much stock of slow-moving items. Several consultants have offered proposals. All offer more or less standard or classical solutions to the problem through computer control, basing ordering of inventory on complex calculations involving required lead time for ordering, history of traffic in the item, current orders, anticipated orders, and estimates based on trend lines and projections. All of those approaches or solutions appear suitable enough for satisfying the client's perceived need, as the client's request for proposals defines or identifies that need. You, however, do not accept the client's definition of need without question, but you study it carefully to either validate the definition, as described in the RFP, or amend and correct it before writing your own proposal. You decide that the client's definition of need is a bit shallow and needs more careful thought. You redefine it accordingly and offer a different approach, one that is considerably more sophisticated than the one just described and better suits the need as you perceive it.

Sensible though others' approaches are, they are conventional and conservative, while your approach is more modern, in step with the newest technology. You recommend the addition of equipment and software to enable the client to track the supply situation in real time and order items accordingly, via computer-to-computer connections, which will reduce the lead time by days and thus reduce total costs for the client. You might even propose a study of suppliers to identify those equipped for advanced computer-to-computer monitoring and ordering, thus maximizing efficiency and paving the way for a turn-key project.

The client now decides that this—ordering all inventory via computer to reduce the lead time and minimize the time items reside and age in storage—is really the need. For all practical purposes, you are now the only consultant offering the right solution, the one that satisfies the real need that you have now persuaded the client to perceive.

In one sense, you have created a need—a new need—by showing the client a better way. (Many marketing and sales successes are the result of skillful "education" of the client, helping the client discover the "truth" about his or her need.) But in another sense, there is no such thing as a new need, for basic needs never change. Only the ways of satisfying those basic needs change.

Many new products and new services struggle for success in the marketplace. Some manage to become large successes after a long time. Some become only modest successes, no matter how long they struggle for position in the marketplace. And some never find success.

On the other hand, some become instant successes. Television is an example, as are videocassette recorders, desktop computers, pocket calculators, and xerographic copying machines. However, all those other xerographic copying machines that had to use specially treated paper cast hardly a shadow in the wake of Xerox® because only that latter company could make its copies on plain paper, at least until its protective patents finally expired years later.

The *need*, then, was defined by the public in all cases. We can argue that the invention of TV created a need for TV, but the need for home entertainment always existed, and TV was one of a long series of steadily improving means of home entertainment, the latest of which is the videocassette recorder-player, and the predecessor of which was the radio.

Copiers that required specially treated paper were modest successes because plain-paper copying was a dramatically better way to satisfy the need for copying: It was swift, convenient, and produced copies of steadily improving fidelity, until the most modern copier models produced copies that sometimes were even better than the originals. So Xerox was immensely successful, in contrast to its rivals. (None of the earlier types of office copiers had been very convenient or efficient, and they were hardly an improvement over carbon paper. They succeeded in finding acceptance, for a time, because nothing better was available to satisfy the need for copying. But they all disappeared from view almost literally overnight when xerographic copying on a practical basis made its appearance.)

Examine the apparent need, then, in terms of (1) what the basic and classic need it represents really is, and (2) how you can satisfy that need in some better way than it has ever been satisfied before or, at least, a better way than your competitors are likely to offer. And "better" can mean faster, cheaper, more convenient, more reliable, or other "better."

MARKETING/SALESMANSHIP CONSIDERATIONS

One of those ingenious home-workshop inventors, Fred Gris, had a great idea early in his career. (He created many successful inventions before and since.) He invented a solution to a problem that vexes a great many of us: He devised a way to make the ketchup flow easily out of that traditional narrow-necked bottle. And so off he went to sell his invention to the leading manufacturer of ketchup, convinced that his fortune was assured.

To his dismay, he found himself all but thrown down the stairs by the horrified officials of that firm when they heard his proposition. They could not get him off their premises fast enough. Later, disappointed and disillusioned, Gris philosophized that he had learned his lesson: He would henceforth offer clients only what they wanted, not what they needed.

Brilliant and imaginative inventor that he is, he was slightly off target in his ruminations about a lesson learned. The ketchup manufacturer's whole advertising and marketing campaign is based on that "slowest ketchup in the west" theme. Gris's invention would have totally destroyed that carefully crafted and slowly built-up image of quality, which was based on the message that the thicker the ketchup, the higher its quality. From a marketing and sales viewpoint, the ketchup executives not only did not need that new invention, they needed to bury it as quickly as possible, as a direct threat to their existence or at least to their commanding position in the ketchup market.

Lesson: To write a good proposal, you must have a good understanding of marketing, and you must understand the client's view of what he or she perceives as a need, although that may not be what *you* think the client needs.

CREATIVITY

Finding or devising a new and better way to satisfy a need is a creative process and should be recognized as such. The nature of creativity is a discussion for another chapter, but mention of a basic principle or two about the subject is needed here because one of the characteristics required to write a really good proposal is creative imagination.

First of all, creativity is rarely, if ever, the result of a truly new or revolutionary idea. Instead, it is generally a new combination of ideas, an extrapolation of what is already known. TV owes its basic circuits and technology to the earlier radio sciences, for example, but it did not become a practical reality until the picture tube was added as the means for displaying the output of the system. (Early models used unsatisfactory devices called "flying spot scanners.") But the picture tube was not a new invention either. It was an adaptation of the cathode-ray tube used in a laboratory instrument, the oscilloscope. Nor was the transistor a brand-new idea, since its predecessor devices and basic technology go back to 1870 at least. And today's chip, which has sent the vacuum tube to Valhalla, was born from transistor technology. So the modern personal computer is a new combination of radio, TV, early computer, telephone, and other technology. Creativity is, thus, largely a matter of reassembling known ideas into new combinations and new patterns or adapting established ideas, devices, and methods to new uses.

One of the obstacles to creativity—an inhibiting factor, that is—is the all-too-human resistance to change. Giving up familiar ways that are comfortable and accepting the hazard of the unknown raises a sense of insecurity for many, especially those who are experts in what is already known. Thus Thomas Edison, Louis Pasteur, Charles Kettering, and many others were assailed for their "ignorance" and "stupidity" in attempting to achieve what the experts "knew" were "impossible" goals—the incandescent electric light, proof that microorganisms do not evolve spontaneously out of inert matter, and the automobile self-starter, respectively. And these are only three of literally hundreds of such possible citations, not the least of which was Admiral William Leahy's confident assertion that the atomic bomb would never detonate, which he qualified with the assurance that he spoke as an expert on explosives, something totally unrelated to atomic energy.

It requires a sturdy and dedicated individual to proceed in the face of such sneering, condescending condemnation by those reputed to be well-known experts. Courage is not the least of the characteristics that enable creative individuals to press on with their efforts. The courage to challenge conventional wisdom and be unshaken by criticism, no matter the source, is almost a prerequisite for creative success. On the intellectual side, however, success also requires deep and broad knowledge of one's field and related areas.

Subject-Matter Expertise

A great many breakthroughs are based on original ideas by individuals who are not regarded as qualified experts in the fields of the breakthrough and are, in fact, sniffed at somewhat disdainfully as amateurs. If Thomas Edison were starting out today, he probably could not get a job as a scientist or engineer in any organization and probably would have trouble even being hired as a lab swipe. When I was employed at Philco-Ford's government communications and weapons division some years ago, the engineer there with the greatest number of patents to his name (some 65 patents) had never seen the inside of a college. Moreover, the engineer who was designing some of the most sophisticated secure-communications digital devices was likewise from the "old" (noncollege) school and, moreover, did not know how to draw a functional logic diagram or utilize Boolean algebra for his designs, but drafted everything laboriously in complicated electronic circuit diagrams.

This is not to deny the advantages of formal education and experience. It is to point out that it is the knowledge and ability per se, no matter how and where acquired, that make the difference. (And perhaps ignorance of what is "impossible" helps, too.) You can hardly be creative without knowing what you are doing and examining the problem or need objectively, no matter what others say or think. Kettering was himself quoted as saying that education was "all right" if one did not permit it to interfere with thinking. (Nor does this denigrate or make light of the instinctual urges, which are probably the logic of the subconscious mind, that inspire many acts of creativity.)

Today, because the desktop computer is a reality and has invaded offices everywhere, from the most elaborate corporate headquarters to the most humble at-home office, millions of individuals have been adding computer skills to their repertoires, many even becoming outstandingly expert in the various computer arts and sciences.

Being computer knowledgeable, if not expert, is not a necessity for proposal writing, but it is certainly a great asset in many ways. Take only the example cited earlier of the proposal for solving inventory-management problems by offering an entirely new approach. Conceiving that technical strategy could stem only from an appreciation of computer capabilities. The author of that idea was able to formulate an imaginative new approach only because she had learned something of what can be done in this new computer age, especially in routine and efficient computer-to-computer communication available literally at the press of a button.

Writing Skills

Finally we come to that subject of writing per se, which has been relegated to last place, despite the term *proposal writing*. The main significance of writing skill is this: Writing is the means by which we implement and exploit all that other work that has gone into devising a program and a set of sales/marketing strategies. Strategy has two parts, the concept and the implementation. The latter is a function of the writing: Ineffective writing means ineffective strategy, and even ineffective design.

Consider, for example, that situation postulated earlier where you did not settle for the client's description of the need, but decided to study the need in some depth—to validate the need or, if you could not validate it, refine the client's definition. Having decided that the client had not probed deeply enough in defining the need, you redefined it in your proposal and offered what you thought was the best possible solution.

Handled properly in your written presentation, this can be the basis for a powerful strategy. It demonstrates your own sincerity and perceptiveness, and possibly even a superior approach and greater ability than other proposers have demonstrated. It also virtually compels the client to study all other proposals to see how they measure up by comparison. It is also a competitor strategy: If you do a proper selling job and convince the client that yours is the way to go, you knock out most—and maybe all—of your competitors without making a direct reference to any. In Chapter 8, which deals with writing persuasively, I will suggest wordings and arguments to maximize these effects without knocking competitors.

The success of the strategies you devise will be dependent on the quality of your writing. That does not refer to literary elegance or grammatical perfection, but to the persuasiveness of your prose and the clarity of your communication. Readers will not struggle to understand what you write. If what you write is not clear, the reader will usually sigh and go on. We will discuss the factors that enable you to achieve persuasiveness, too, in Chapter 8. We will discuss the use of the computer and certain types of software, including but not restricted to word processors, to help you achieve great impact with your writing.

Developing the Necessary Skills

The first step in developing and/or honing existing skills in these areas is to recognize and accept the need to do so. All good writing is rewriting: Even the most expert professional writer accepts that as the secret of writing well. One of the greatest benefits of using a computer for writing: It encourages rewriting because it makes rewriting easier to do than ever before.

A major purpose of this book is, in fact, to help you in developing or further developing your skills in the several areas necessary for proposal success, even in that of the subject-matter knowledge. And I propose to begin in perhaps that very area where you may believe that you do not need my help. But before we get into these discussions, let me point out that you will find that some of these areas are actually closely intertwined and that dividing them into separate discussions in earlier paragraphs was a purely mechanical device to make certain points. In the following discussions, I will not make any great effort to so separate the topics, so that you can see their close interrelationships.

I freely acknowledge that you almost certainly are already far more expert in your own technical or professional field—that field or those fields in which you specialize as a consultant—than I am, intend to be, or could be. I can therefore not impart to you any subject-matter knowledge per se, nor do I intend to try to do so.

On the other hand, do you really know as much as you should about your own field and—think carefully about this—other, closely related fields? Are you keeping up with your field? Reading at least some of the literature? Active in a relevant association or two? In touch with others in your field? Attending conferences and conventions? Making at least occasional contributions to the literature, even if that is only a trade journal or two? Do you think that you need to know more about what is happening currently in your field and related subjects? And do note the earlier remarks about getting fully on board in the matter of the modern desktop computers. That is a horizontal field we all must become at least literate in. (But any consultant today ought to be more than merely literate in computers.) And, finally, are you taking full advantage of the research and other information-furnishing assets of the current age?

If you are not answering yes to at least a few of these queries, you are in danger of becoming a dinosaur in your field. The world won't wait for you to catch up; you have to keep up, even if that means running a good bit of the time. If you are not more expert, more imaginative, more enterprising, and more dedicated to your profession than are most of the nine-to-five workers in your field, you are badly handicapped in becoming a really good proposal writer. (Yes, really good proposal writers are a special breed because they work at it.)

Your creative output is related quite closely and in some proportion to your information input. But that input does not occur automatically as a result of reading the daily literature of your field. You need to be a good researcher, too, to be a good writer and, especially, to be a good proposal writer. You need to make yourself aware of all the sources of information available to you, many of them databases accessible by computer and, today, the vast reaches of the Internet. But seeking existing information is only one ingredient necessary to create new ideas. Another required ingredient is introspection—thinking about things in general, about what they mean and how they can be best understood.

Creative people are people constantly in quest of more and/or new information about a great many things, but they are also quite aware that the information they seek may not exist anywhere. That is, they may have to generate that information themselves through creative thinking. Professor Charles H. Townes, for example, was reportedly ruminating on a park bench when he conceived the maser (microwave amplification by stimulated emission of radiation) and, soon after and more significantly, the laser (light amplification by stimulated emission of radiation), the latter a revolutionary scientific breakthrough. However, he had been working on the problem with other scientists for a long time and had been gathering relevant information and pondering the problems during all that time, as had the others, before his introspection finally produced the seminal inspiration that represented the breakthrough. The point of some earlier discussions was that new and better ways themselves create new needs. That is, you can address a client's stated need in either or both of two ways:

1. Study the need itself, as defined by the client, and decide whether that is the true definition of the need or whether you must redefine it. That is, decide what is the true need, the end result that the client really wants.

2. Accept the client's definition and study the various ways to satisfy the stated need (achieve the end result) and identify the best way, redefining the need in terms of that best way.

In many cases, it is that second approach that works best and that we really use. Here is an example of how that might work.

The client says he or she wants a rapid-delivery service. But, restricted in thinking by his or her perception of reality—the delivery services available, that is—the client does not define the need beyond such a term as "fastest possible delivery," when in fact the client really wants to be able to deliver documents to the opposite coast on the same day. The obvious method is express air service, which can do the job within 12 hours. But there is another way, one that can do the job in a fraction of that time: electronic mail— e-mail—a method using the Internet system. E-mail does not replace all other forms of mail, but it is far more effective and efficient for many uses. It becomes a need by the simple virtue of its availability. If the client did not know that it was possible, the proposer who explains and proposes it creates a new need by simply making the client aware of the possibility.

But wait: There is also fax (facsimile) transmission, which is even better than e-mail for some purposes because it is as fast and far simpler (any layperson can do it, using a stand-alone fax machine, whereas e-mail requires skill in using a computer). That changes the need further.

Note that what changes the need here is not the creation of a method not heretofore available, but simply making the client *aware* of that method. If the client does not know that the method (fax) exists, educating the client changes the client's definition of need. It is not truth itself but the client's perception of truth that makes the difference. Is fax, then, the final answer? Not necessarily. Depending on the size and nature of the delivery, fax may be better or not as good for the given case, so there must be consideration of all the factors.

Technological, economic, and marketing or business factors are involved in evaluating the basic options. How can you write an effective proposal if you are not reasonably knowledgeable in all areas?

A Master Strategy

The education of a client is a general master strategy available in many proposal situations. Sometimes you can devise a totally different and better way to satisfy a need simply by knowing much more than the requester knew. You often succeed then in changing the rules—writing your own, in essence. This means that you have actually succeeded in changing the specification of the need, invalidating all proposals that limit themselves to responding to the need as defined in the RFP. And if no competitor knew of or made the effort to develop a new and better way, or was forthright enough to educate the client accordingly, you often would wind up with a clear field.

There is a qualifier in all this, however: For practical purposes (as a winning strategy, that is), your new and different innovation is better only if the client agrees that it is better. Your allegation that it is better does not automatically make it so in the client's perception. To change the definition or specification of need, you must succeed in persuading the client to agree with your definition. That is, you must *sell* that idea to the client.

Moreover, you must never assume that the client can or will easily see for himself or herself that your solution is by far the best one; you must explain your rationale carefully, making sure that the reader is able to follow your reasoning completely. For even if the client is knowledgeable enough to make the analysis without your help—and that may or may not be so in any given case—there is no reason for the client to go to that much trouble. To expect that is to expect the client to do your selling job for you. It won't happen. And finally, aside from all this, there is at least one other consideration: The probability is that the client, like most other people, almost instinctively resists new and different ideas and is not likely to hasten to embrace your new and different idea unless you succeed in your persuasive arguments for it.

Most people are not visionary at all, and they tend to reject new ideas, especially those that are revolutionary and call for casting out old ideas and old prejudices. Alexander Graham Bell was unable to sell his telephone to Western Union, whose officials thought the idea of people talking to each other over a wire was ridiculous. (Of course, they also saw the telephone as contrary to their interests.)

Kodak and IBM, among others, reportedly were offered and rejected the new xerographic copying invention that tiny Haloid Corporation embraced and that sparked its growth into today's giant Xerox Corporation. Those who rejected Chester Carlson's invention could not foresee much of practical value in this idea of xerographic copying. Thomas Watson, head of IBM, which was later to become by far the leading mainframe computer firm in the world, was originally highly unenthusiastic about computers. In 1943 he estimated a world market for computers to be about five buyers.

There are, of course, legions of similar stories. The platitude about the better mousetrap is a myth. The world will not beat a path to your door, no matter how good your mousetrap is, unless you manage to sell it to the world. Do not be misled by the occasional exceptions. Exceptions to all rules are inevitable, but they do not invalidate the principle.

Evidently, almost no one is immune to the human tendency to wear blinders. Ironically, even those who ought to know better out of their own experience have the same frailty: As late as 1922 Edison expressed the opinion that radio was a passing fad. Lee DeForest, inventor of one of the most basic breakthroughs in radio (the "audion" tube) and considered to be at least one of the parents of

radio, assured any who would listen that TV was probably a technical possibility but could never be a practical success because it was
not feasible commercially or financially. And H. G. Wells, acclaimed
writer of visionary science fiction novels, predicted that submarines
would succeed in nothing but suffocating their crews to death.

The tendency of most of us to resist new ideas is in some proportion to how different or revolutionary those new ideas are. Those
ideas with which we are most uncomfortable are those that require
us to discard the familiar notions and opinions we already hold, so
we are far more resistant to revolutionary change than we are to evolutionary change. The latter are new ideas we can accommodate side
by side with those we already hold or by minor modification of the
latter, instead of requiring us to cast them out totally. We are also
uncomfortable with new ideas that we do not really understand and
so tend to reject ideas for that reason as well.

The means for presenting and selling new and different ideas to
clients must take these principles into consideration also, to avoid
traumatizing the client with new ideas that he or she will find
extremely difficult to accept. There are several means for so doing,
and in a later chapter we will explore some means for coping with
these problems successfully, but the principles should be borne in
mind as we proceed next to discuss the various kinds of strategies
that can be and should be embodied in most proposals.

CHAPTER 3

The Development of Effective Strategies

The General Anatomy of Strategy

In marketing, as in war, strategy is a prime factor of success and failure. And as in military matters, discriminating among the many possible strategies and tactics to identify that one most likely to effect success is much more art than science.

It is not easy to define the word *strategy*. Even lexicographers have difficulty with it. They tend to cast its definition in terms of artifices for conducting war. In a more general sense, however, strategy is whatever principles you employ in choosing methods or procedures that you believe will lead to success. In this case, we are discussing methodologies for inducing prospective clients to find our proposals more persuasive than those of our competitors, so we can win the contracts for which we are competing. But that is an oversimplification too, which is why I prefer the word *goal* to the word *objective*. *Goal* suggests the long-term target, whereas *objective* suggests the short-term or immediate target—an important distinction.

The Goal versus the Objective

Contracts for which you must submit proposals are not normally one-call sales, but require you to progress successfully through a series of several steps to win the sale. That makes winning the contract at stake in the usual proposal contest a general goal, rather than a direct objective. Except for small contracts, proposal competitions rarely result directly in contract awards. In most proposal contests, and especially in the case of the large contracts, proposal evaluations are followed by calls for oral presentations, for best and final offers, for discussions, and for other kinds of negotiations or preliminaries to negotiations. Typically, the process for all but the smallest purchases entails distinct phases:

1. Selection of the most suitable candidates to be invited to submit proposals and compete; issuance of the request
2. Reading and evaluation of proposals, selecting all nominally acceptable as "within the competitive range"
3. Follow-up discussions, oral presentations, best and final offers by selected proposers, and narrowing and rank ordering of candidates
4. Negotiations leading to the award of a contract

These phases may be formal or informal, organized or spontaneous, but they are the typical sequence of events. In most cases, the evaluation is a preliminary step to the final choice. The proposal is thus a mechanism for narrowing the field to the acceptable candidates, from whose number the client will eventually choose a contractor.

In the case of large contracts, the several phases or steps are likely to be formal ones, with top-ranked proposers invited to attend discussion of their proposals ("orals") and often also invited to make formal presentations ("dog and pony shows"). This usually includes an invitation to submit relevant amendments to both the technical proposal and the cost proposal. (The latter is a not too subtle suggestion that paring the price is invited and likely to be helpful.)

In the case of small contracts, these may be brief, informal procedures, via letter, fax, telephone, or, today, e-mail, but the effect is the same: proposal follow-up to reach final decisions.

Identifying the True Strategic Approach

This clearly implies two broad strategies: For the small contract, the broad strategy is pursuit of a direct contract award, whereas in the case of the large contract, the strategy is logical pursuit of an invitation to a best-and-final offer and meeting as the main objective.

A go-for-broke win strategy, conceived in the hope of winning the contract directly and immediately on the basis of the proposal itself, may thus be a mistake, distracting you from what ought to be your true objective: getting over a first hurdle and in line for the next procedure. A true win strategy anticipates the several phases and the needed responses to each.

Theoretically, you cannot know whether the client will choose a winner without that usual postproposal activity; there are exceptions. But, should the client bypass those usual postproposal steps, having based your main strategy on the objective of getting into that next-stage phase will not hurt you in any way. The reverse is not true. Shooting for a direct win means a go-for-broke attack, and that can hurt you because it leaves you unprepared for the next phase. You may need to save something for that encore.

The Advantage of Face-to-Face Presentation

Even the preceding rationale is not the entire essence of the matter. Being restricted to writing alone to make their presentation is a handicap to many marketers, who firmly believe that they can do a far more effective marketing job in face-to-face discussions with prospective clients. For them, the most important objective of their proposal-writing effort is to win the opportunity for such discussions—to "get to the table," as many put it.

This is probably true for everyone. There are some advantages in making a written presentation, and there are others in an oral presentation, such as the psychological one of achieving a second-step commitment by the client. For most of us, the ideal is often the combination of both: the powerful written presentation, followed by the face-to-face meeting and discussion. It is so much in your interest to do this, that the wise marketer of consulting services does not even try to guess whether the client will issue an invitation to orals or other discussions. Instead, if you are such a marketer, you will do everything possible to induce the client to find a meeting necessary. You will set a clear objective of inducing the client to call for proposal follow-up, and you will structure and design your win strategies to include this objective as the first step.

The objective is nothing by itself. You need some kind of plan to put your strategy to work and produce that result, as the following consultants did (two of many such cases).

CASE HISTORY NUMBER 1

An organization overwhelmed with mail requesting highly technical information regarding its activities in wind energy utilization devices invited consultants to propose a program for handling that overload. One consultant responded that handling the overload was not the major problem, but preparing to handle future overloads without contracting the work out was the true problem for the client. He could solve that and enable the organization to handle the heavy mail problem in-house with a design strategy he had developed and which he would gladly disclose.

Obviously the organization's officers could not afford to do other than hear him out, and so they invited him to make an oral presentation. He did so and was awarded a contract of far greater scope than originally contemplated.

CASE HISTORY NUMBER 2

Invited to devise an on-the-job training program for technicians, a training-systems consultant proposed such a radically new and different approach to the design of the system that the client could hardly help but ask the consultant to visit and explain her ideas. The consultant, a wise marketer, had deliberately withheld key details of her plan, while issuing a clear invitation to request a formal presentation of the plan. She knew she had piqued the client's curiosity enough to ensure that she would be asked to appear and be cross-examined by the client's staff.

Devising Strategies

A successful strategy is often the result of inspiration. That is a more or less subconscious process. But we cannot afford to be at the mercy of uncertain and unpredictable inspiration and subconscious processes, nor to accept any premise that requires such fortuitous circumstances for the development of effective strategies. We must have something much more dependable and controllable, something that can be employed methodically and produce effective strategies on demand. We must therefore find those elements that are the basis for all successful strategies. But there are several strategic arenas in which our proposals must compete, and these subdivide into major and minor strategies. Let's first have a quick look at these. However, note this: The most effective strategy is one suggested by the client, one built around whatever appears to be of the greatest importance to the client. The search for a strategic approach must therefore be based on a quest to identify the client's prime concerns and priorities, even when the client has not consciously stated these. Always be watchful for clues to these.

The Major Strategies

It is necessary to have a master strategy (known variously as capture strategy, main strategy, win strategy, etc.), but there are at least four other major strategic concepts to consider, as well as some others that we will discuss here, too. First, however, a few introductory thoughts about these major strategies, suggested by the identifying names assigned them:

- Technical or program strategy
- Cost strategy
- Competitive strategy
- Presentation strategy

The win strategy must be a sharply focused one. It is usually one of these, but never all of these; the remaining strategies are supporting, but must never eclipse or upstage the main strategy. At the same time, these strategies may be linked in some manner, and the linkage must be clear. It may even be essential to the strategy.

For example, if your win strategy is one of offering the lowest costs, you must prove that you can do the job properly at the promised lowest costs, and that may entail showing how your innovative and clever technical or program strategy makes the low cost possible. Most effective win strategies have cause-and-effect links to more than one of these, but one clear strategy must dominate. The process of deciding what that strategy is to be should be a major objective of the preliminary requirements identification and analysis.

Whatever the specific situation, it is essential that you decide on your elected win strategy as early in the proposal process as possible, because it has such a great effect upon all elements of the proposal—the program design strategy, the presentation strategy, and perhaps even the competitive strategy. But you also need the flexibility to modify or even change your win strategy if later developments suggest that as a wise move. Therefore, identify your tentative win strategy as early as possible, but review it frequently and do not hesitate to refine and sharpen it continuously.

Identifying a Win Strategy

The main (win) strategy many inexperienced marketers employ is to try to utilize and maximize all the strategic ideas in a kind of "buckshot" approach. This is based on the hope that the more buckshot or strategic attacks scattered by the proposal, the more likely it is that some will strike the target in a vital spot and thus produce some kind of salutary effect.

Alas, it rarely happens. Trying to be all things results in a dissipation of your effort. You scatter not only your strategic ammunition but you also scatter your energies. The lack of clear focus, that vague meandering around the subject without ever coming to grips directly with it, is characteristic of many unsuccessful proposals. That weakness reflects the lack of commitment to a main strategy as a base for the proposal. It is probably the reason for failure of about two thirds of all proposals.

To be maximally effective and become a decisive factor, strategy must have a clear focus, and that must be on something for which you believe the client has concern. It cannot help your cause to argue the technical merits of your proposed method or the virtues of your specialized experience when the client has shown major concern for costs only. You must have decided which is the most critical concern of the client, crystallize your strategy to address that concern, and suspend your entire presentation from that superstructure. If you decide that the client is especially concerned with keeping the cost low, you must seek means for doing so in every aspect of the program you propose, while developing evidence to demonstrate that the cost saving is not at the expense of performance and quality. The reader should never have the slightest doubt as to exactly what your principal argument is. Nor should you.

There is, of course, always a hazard in the decision that commits you to a specific strategy: the hazard that you will make the wrong decision and waste all your efforts in pressing home the wrong strategy. It is undoubtedly that danger that impels so many proposers to try "polypharmacal" proposals, offering many kinds of medicine to cure the client's ills.

The danger of making the fatal error is real. But the proper approach to avoiding that error is to do that which is necessary to identify the proper win strategy. It is far more a matter of doing the right thing than one of avoiding the wrong thing.

This is not to say that the many other strategies are not to be utilized. They can and should make their own contributions. But they should be most definitely in supporting roles, linked to the main strategy, and clearly subordinated to it. Let's take a look at each of these.

Technical/Program Strategy

Technical or *program strategy* includes such matters as your approach to the solution of the client's problem, satisfaction of need, characteristics of design, procedures prescribed, materials to be used, special features, innovative ideas, and use of specialists/special resources. These may have direct effects and be closely linked, even in cause-and-effect relationships, with such other matters as costs and schedules.

Cost Strategy

Cost is rarely the sole consideration and often not even the chief consideration in the client's choice, but cost is never unimportant. Cost strategy is always possible because cost is rarely an absolute term or an absolute quantity. Cost is relative, of many kinds, and with many qualifiers—for example, acquisition costs, maintenance costs, installation costs, support costs, and total cost of ownership or life-cycle costs. The true cost must take all into account, and a higher acquisition cost may mean a lower total ownership cost.

In many cases it is simply not possible to determine what the final true costs will be or, perhaps more significant, even who the low bidder is among all the proposers or bidders. In this inescapable anomaly there are the conditions for the development of cost strategies and arguments for your position.

Competitive Strategy

It is a competitive world, and you are rarely fortunate enough to be the only consultant invited to propose. In most cases you are one of at least several—frequently many—able consultants vying for the contract.

No matter how capable you are or how well you write, it is likely that at least some of your competitors are as able as you and write as well as you. To believe that none of your competitors approach you in competence or capability for presenting their credentials is unrealistic. Remember at all times that, with only occasional exception, the client judges the capabilities and competence of the proposers primarily by what they say in their proposals and how credible those statements appear to be. Ergo, as far as the client is concerned,

Proposal quality = consultant quality

True or not and justified or not, this is the client's perception. That means that you must have some kind of competitive strategy so that you help the client find reasons to rate your proposal higher than those of competitors. In fact, competitive strategy should ideally be based on one prime factor that somehow dramatizes the issue in your favor.

Presentation Strategy

Your proposal is a sales presentation. Many presentation strategies—techniques that can make your proposal more effective by increasing its impact, capturing the client's attention in some special way, or otherwise maximizing the benefits by various artful methods—are possible. Presentation strategy is not usually decisive, but don't underestimate the contribution to success that a good presentation can make. It is often in the presentation that the other strategies are implemented successfully, where they might otherwise not have an effect on the outcome.

Strategies in a Minor Key

Many problems require the development of minor strategies to cope with them successfully. In fact, these strategies deserve a special category: *assets and liabilities strategies.*

You are not often so perfect for a requirement that your qualifications represent 100 percent assets and zero liabilities with regard to the requirement. More often, you must weigh your assets and liabilities vis-à-vis the requirement in evolving some kind of strategy. However, aside from the question of a win strategy and those other major strategic factors, there is the question of exploiting your assets and overcoming your liabilities.

For example, suppose you must write a proposal to offer your services in an area where you have little or no specific experience to present as your technical/professional qualifications. How can you cope with this? Some requirements may clearly call for the services of a sizable team, one considerably larger than your own staff. How do you satisfy the client that you can meet this need successfully and without risking failure? A requirement may be for services primarily in your field, but still require special capabilities for some aspect of the project—special qualifications you do not possess. How can you overcome this liability?

On the other hand, you also need to evolve strategies for maximizing the benefits of your assets. If you have extraordinary experience or other resources that are directly relevant to the client's need, you can benefit from exploiting these as an advantage over competitors. But you will gain the benefits of exploiting them properly only by utilizing specific strategies to do so. It won't come about spontaneously.

How Important Are the Minor Strategies?

These latter strategies are referred to as "minor" strategies only because they generally affect only relatively minor matters. But that is not always the case. Often that strategy that began life as the solution to some apparently minor asset or liability begins to assume more and more importance as the proposal evolves, and sometimes it becomes the pivot upon which success turns. One small firm (total staff of four), for example, was among those invited to submit proposals to create and present a training program for a large firm managing a federal (Energy Department) facility in Idaho. The problem was that the schedule was exceedingly difficult to meet because it was a "needed yesterday" requirement. However, this small firm pursuing the contract happened by chance to have an unusual asset:

It had a proprietary program on the shelf that was so close to what was needed that it could be adapted to the need with only a few days' work. This asset translated into both a probably unique ability to meet the impossible schedule and a cost advantage. However, the schedule advantage was all that was required to win the job easily: No one else could offer a firm guarantee to meet the schedule. Thus the proposal focused the entire sales argument on this, and this became the win strategy.

Other Objectives

Here are a few other kinds of objectives you might find it useful to consider in various proposal circumstances:

- Persuade the client to modify the statement of work.
- Make the client perceive unusually splendid qualifications in you.
- Persuade the client to see extraordinary assets in your proposed design.
- Sell the client a different (and better) approach than the request suggests.
- Sell the absolute need for some unique resource you offer.
- Alert the client to the hazards of the project.
- Convince the client that any cost in excess of that which you estimate is sheer waste and totally unnecessary.

Of course, there are thousands of other possible objectives, each clearly defining or implying a strategy, which may be a win strategy or only a subordinate strategy. In either case it is necessary to do more than merely state the allegation of the objective. Strategy is the means of persuading the client to agree with the statement, to perceive the situation as you perceive it. Flat statements are not enough to do the job; they represent opinion or claims, not demonstrated facts or what the client will accept as facts.

If you wanted to alert the client to possible hazards of the project, you might validate your allegation (and so implement your strategic objective) by citing case histories, published papers, public statements of prominent authorities, or simple logical analysis. And to add weight to your arguments, you might even reproduce some of the relevant published material, drawings, photographs, or other supporting materials.

The Opposite Poles of Strategy

There are two angles of attack open to you as a proposal strategist; we might call them the positive and negative approaches. In the positive mode, you might try to better your position by boosting yourself and what you have to offer. In the negative approach, you try to better your position by trying to knock your competitors out. In some cases you might use one or the other of these two general approaches, but more commonly you will employ both. Both are entirely legitimate in this competitive world—even that one of attacking competitors and doing your level best to discredit them in the eyes of the client.

Positive Strategy: Gain

Most of what we have discussed is geared to boosting your own image and ideas. This approach is based on the promise of gain. It argues that this proposal offers the client the greatest gain of all the courses open for whatever reason the basic strategy dictates, such as better schedule, lower cost, greater dependability, or other such boon.

Obviously, this approach claims that you offer more gain—for example, better results—than do your competitors in general, although it never knocks competitors directly. The implication that competitive offers and competitive capabilities are inferior to your own is subtle or low-key. Of course, all of us have come to expect that every advertisement and sales presentation will necessarily make the claim of superiority of product or service. We would be dumbfounded at any presentation that neglected to make such a claim.

The strategies underlying these kinds of presentations do not qualify as competitive or competitor strategies. They are not aimed directly or indirectly, except in that most general sense, at invalidating competitive claims, and therefore they represent only one of the two basic strategic orientations. But it is possible to draw a bead on competitors without appearing unethical or in violation of good taste.

Negative Strategy: Fear

Boosting your own position at the direct expense of competitors, while avoiding the stigma of directly knocking competitors, calls for delicacy. Probably the most effective way to do this is to use fear motivation. One method is to combine the gain motivation with the provision of a worry item and present this with a twist: You alert the client to the problems and even disasters that are possible (perhaps even probable) unless certain measures are taken, certain capabilities are at hand, certain resources are available, certain foresight is present, and so on. Of course, you are the only proposer with that foresight, offering whatever you say is necessary to avoid disaster.

Now in that latter sentence lies the root of the strategy. For it to be effective, it must meet certain conditions:

1. The problems or disasters predicted must be legitimate (believable) eventualities. (That is, you must identify real possibilities and make them believable.)

2. They must be things your competitors are not likely to think of or point out to the client in their own proposals (or your solutions must be better).

3. You must provide some credible evidence of your own unique capabilities to cope successfully with the projected problems.

That latter condition is the hardest to satisfy, inasmuch as probably all or nearly all the proposers in any given proposal competition are competent providers of whatever consulting services are required. And to succeed with the first two items but fail totally with the last one is to probably make yourself appear somewhat foolish but, worse still, give your competitors more of a boost than a kick. Therefore, give careful thought to that aspect of this strategy. But here is a bit of guidance in that matter.

If you have some special and unique or unusual asset, such as a helpful proprietary resource or some highly specialized experience, you can probably make that the basis of your claim. If you do not have that kind of advantage, there is always one other way to address this, a way that has proved to be successful many times. Base your claim on the need for foresight and advance planning, pointing out that you are now demonstrating that foresight and advance preparation. Be sure that you have identified real potential problems that probably no one else will think of or probably will not mention in their own proposals.

In short, the essence of this technique is to find or create the worry item that is a legitimate concern and provides some special advantage over competitors in terms of the image you present in your proposal.

Image Strategy and Capability Brochures

The image you strive to create for yourself is itself a strategic approach, one on which you normally base all your marketing effort. And one place you try to create that image is in your brochures, especially that type of brochure that is known in some circles as a *capability brochure.*

For many consultants, the capability brochure is virtually a standard proposal, often used as a major element of or basis for the consultant's proposals. Of those consultants surveyed in gathering material for this edition, 60 percent reported that they employed brochures and other boilerplated material as major portions of their proposals, and only 25 percent reported that each of their proposals was a completely custom-written original.

A well-designed capability brochure is itself based on a major strategic concept, usually one that strives toward creating a specific image for the consultant. Computer Programming Services, Inc. (CPS), a computer consultant in Prairie Village, Kansas, supplied a sample of its capability brochure, which the company uses as an integral part of its proposals. The basic strategy underlying the firm's posture is quite evident in that brochure. It is a clear message that the firm sells absolutely no proprietary products, neither hardware nor software, but offers only custom services to clients. The firm has therefore no commitments to any proprietary products, and for that reason has no difficulty being completely impartial and objective in its recommendations to clients—that is, the stated firm policy with regard to proprietaries enables the company to truly represent its clients and its clients' best interests.

In many situations, the capability brochure is a necessity for gaining access to a client's bidders list. Some clients wish to restrict the list of those from whom they receive bids and proposals to ensure that they are received from only well-qualified consultants, and so they require that the aspirant first submit a capability statement of some sort to qualify as a bidder or proposer. Thus the capability brochure may be a direct or an indirect marketing necessity.

The capability brochure is an excellent idea for anyone offering custom services of any kind. It is itself a basis for many, if not all, of your proposals (depending on several factors to be discussed later). It is a guide to and aid in preparing individual proposals also: A well-designed capability brochure greatly facilitates and speeds up proposal writing. And, not the least of its virtues, it is an excellent means of establishing and promoting your professional image, as CPS does with its own brochure.

An image strategy should send a message. CPS's image is one of deliberately engineered objectivity to enable unflinching loyalty to the client. But here, as examples, are images other brochures present:

- "Quick reaction" services, available to support clients on short notice, with impossible schedules, and in emergencies of all kinds
- "One-stop" services, a resource to handle virtually every related requirement within the general field
- Unparalleled experience in the field, possibly even unique in quality of experience or capability
- Top-drawer; the ne plus ultra of such services; expensive, but the very best

Unfortunately, many of the brochures offered by consultants reflect no strategy at all, image or otherwise, but pursue the futile allegations of the consultant's superiority in all respects by self-appraisal, with generous use of superlatives and, in some cases, cute gimmicks. Obviously, the "strategy" intended here is to overwhelm the client with claims, hyperbole, and cleverness, which is, of course, no strategy at all.

As a consultant, you probably should have a capability brochure of some kind, and it should most definitely be based on some strategy or USP (unique selling point) designed to create a distinctive and suitable image for you. That image should be the one that you wish to present generally, but it should also be the underpinning for not only your proposals specifically but for all your marketing presentations.

Theme

The strategy underlying brochures and proposals has still another aspect, a related subject to consider. The subject is *theme*.

Theme is a word that has several meanings and yet is a difficult concept to define in terms of what it means in proposals and other sales presentations. It is closely related to strategy and should reflect strategy. Properly used, it is also a reinforcement and continuous reminder to the client of your image and of your strategy. And if we have trouble defining theme briefly, we can at least study some examples.

A company proposing to design for the Department of Defense an airplane that could be used by both the Air Force and the Navy decided that its proposal theme was to be "an aerodynamic solution to an aerodynamic problem."

A competitor offered its own proposal, presenting its own technical arguments for its proposed design, and used the theme "commonality."

The first company used a theme that appealed to logic, assuming that the client accepted the technical arguments for its design and claims of superior technical/scientific aeronautical engineering expertise. The second company used a theme that appealed to emotions, assuming that the DoD had a truly great desire to achieve commonality.

The first proposer, using the "aerodynamic solution to an aerodynamic problem" as its chief argument, was striving to project the image of an organization of superlative technical expertise and unflagging devotion to scientific integrity, offering what it insisted was the only design that made aeronautical sense.

The second proposer focused its efforts on an image of total devotion to the client's primary goal, taking the position that its technical/scientific competence was a given, with no need to argue it, since the company was well known in its field. The strategy was to portray a project and staff so committed to the client's desired end goal, commonality, that it never took its eye off that target, not for a single page.

In another case, the client had asked for a computer/data processing service that was difficult enough to supply at best. Briefly, the request called for a contractor to supply on demand the services of any of a vast number of computer specialists, each with different expertise in computer languages, machines, kinds of programs, and job functions.

The proposal request suggested that the successful proposer would need to be an organization with all such experts on staff, readily at hand. This would obviously have slanted the requirement toward only the largest of the computer service companies.

One proposer decided that it could not make its strongest possible presentation if it were based on that suggested modus operandi, since that approach denied the proposer the opportunity to take advantage of its strengths as an organization. The proposer was sure that it could do the job very well and make a strong argument for itself with a different approach from that suggested by the client's RFP. The firm therefore took the sensible course of exploring ways of meeting the requirement through employing methods that would take advantage of its own strengths. And, accordingly, the firm pursued the proposal presentation along the following lines:

1. The firm first isolated the desired result, focused on it, and pointed out that the suggested method was only one of several ways to achieve the desired result and satisfy the requirement.

2. The firm argued against the suggested approach, pointing out its weaknesses, that even if there were a company or two large enough to have all the cited kinds of experts on staff (which was itself a doubtful supposition), there was no guarantee that the one expert required for any given task would always be available immediately, when needed. Quite the contrary, chance being so often perverse, that expert would probably be the only one of that kind in the company and would be already engaged several thousand miles away on another assignment.

3. The firm suggested another approach, using its own large rosters of consultants (its primary business was the provision of technical/professional temporaries) and argued for it.

4. The firm expressed its conviction that this was an even more responsive proposal than one offering the suggested solution because this would guarantee the same result, which it said was the true test of responsiveness, and would be a more efficient, more dependable, and less costly approach.

The strategy was thus for the proposer to take advantage of its strength by changing the rules of the game, thus invalidating the suggested approach and denying competitors the advantages of their strengths.

The theme was that success depended on the contractor's total capabilities and not on any specific design of the system of services. It was a theme that reflected the proposer's basic strength as a leading provider of technical/professional temporaries, with an already-in-place staff accustomed to filling such requirements every day. It was a most successful approach.

In still another case, the client wanted to contract with an electronics firm for the design and manufacture of a teleprinter, which would include many of the elements and capabilities of a desktop computer and the printer used with such computers. One proposer, anticipating that most, if not all, competitors would propose systems consisting of separate components interconnected by cables, proposed a teleprinter unit enclosed in a single housing as a monolithic unit. This proposal used that word *monolithic* as a recurring theme and USP in discussing design pros and cons, arguing for the advantages of its own design versus the disadvantages and weaknesses of a design requiring separate units interconnected by cables.

It proved an effective device, helping greatly to support the major strategy, which was superiority of design. The client agreed and became convinced that it reflected an important idea and was indicative of superior design.

Designing Strategies from Strengths

In a later chapter we will get into specific tools, methods, and procedures, even offering forms, for developing strategies, and you will then find that we have barely penetrated the outer skin of the subject here. But in the meanwhile, remember, if you have not already perceived this for yourself, that one of the basic approaches to developing a win strategy is to first identify clearly the end result the client seeks. Then take an inventory of all your strengths and weaknesses—assets and liabilities—vis-à-vis the requirement. Next, study all the possible ways to achieve the desired end result. Finally, select a way that enables you to utilize your own greatest strengths as a consultant, while remaining an effective way to achieve the desired result. And then devise the arguments to sell that approach to the client.

In the next chapter we are going to probe that subject of selling your approach to the client, and we will probe much more deeply into the nature of persuasion generally as the essence of sales and marketing and into the specific dos and don'ts of sales activities.

Some Basics of Sales and Marketing

Despite the mystique with which some have surrounded sales and marketing, the fundamental principles are quite easy to understand and are in themselves a basic explanation of human behavior in sales situations.

Needs, Wants, and the Gentle Art of Persuasion

There are many immutable truths in selling. They apply to all kinds of selling under all kinds of circumstances. They are truths that apply to all kinds of persuasion, and that is what selling is, of course: an act of persuasion. Sometimes the buyer is persuaded by an effective sales presentation, sometimes simply by the appearance of the item, sometimes by a description of it, sometimes even by curiosity. But selling is always an act of persuasion, even if the buyer is motivated by self-persuasion. If you wait for prospective clients to persuade themselves, however, you will certainly miss a great many sales you should have been able to make. Thus, to understand selling at its fundamentals, it is necessary to understand the art of persuasion.

We all want to believe that we are totally rational animals, logical thinkers, behaving according to the dictates of reason. We do, but with an abundance of exceptions. We are, indeed, reasoning entities, trying to be logical in our decisions and actions. However, our emotional reactions and impulses get in the way. Instead of reason overpowering emotion, too often it is the reverse. Consciously or unconsciously, we submit to emotion, to biases. We rationalize our decisions to reassure ourselves that there was logic behind what we did or decided. Who has not, for example, bought something on impulse and regretted it later in what salespeople refer to as "buyer's remorse"?

We usually try to rationalize those decisions we made and we discard or reverse those decisions and conclusions only if and when we are unable to rationalize them satisfactorily. This is especially true in sales situations: When television receivers first appeared shortly after World War II, for example, they were quite expensive, as new luxuries tend to be. A few people bought receivers, but most of us felt unable to afford this new delight, much as we wanted it. The cost prevented us from acting on that emotional desire to have this new toy. Many of us even rationalized that it was smart to wait until TV was "perfected" before buying a set. We were reluctant to admit even to ourselves that we could not afford something we wanted.

On the other hand, many who may have strained their financial resources wanted TV enough, even at those high original prices, so that they managed to persuade themselves that they could afford it or that they really needed it.

Bear this emotional influence in mind, in connection with sales and marketing. It is there at all times, playing a role. Understanding this is essential to selling, including the development of successful proposals, for it applies to the business world as much as to our private affairs.

Only a few pages ago we discussed the subject of needs and wants briefly, pointing out that a need is usually perceived as an absolute requirement that we recognize through pure objective reason, whereas a want is something we desire, although it may not be an absolute requirement. For example, owning my own word processing system was a perceived need for me, as a writer, and was the reason I bought my first personal computer, but the word-counting program, the spooler software, the A-B switch and modem, and many other additions to my first, relatively primitive, system, were expensive wants that were not real needs. (I did write many books, proposals, articles, and other things on a typewriter before I owned a computer and word processor.) But once I decided to want them I had no difficulty convincing myself that they were needs. So while I regarded all of these as needs, before I bought them they were wants, and as long as I felt unable to afford them I persuaded myself that they would not really be of much use to me. My reasoning changed abruptly, however, when circumstances enabled me to afford what I wanted. I had no difficulty then in reframing that want as an absolute need, a need that had to be satisfied without further delay.

In fact, there is no practical difference between a want and a need for marketing purposes. They are the same. The want becomes a need instantly when the individual succeeds in rationalizing the want—or when the effective sales presentation induces the client to make the rationalization.

That is the essence of all selling: Identify and stimulate the want and provide or support the rationalization. The means for doing so are varied and are what sales and marketing are all about.

What Is a Need?

Sales experts sometimes identify two different kinds of needs, naming one a "felt" need and the other a need that has been created. In general, this concept attempts to distinguish between the buyer who sets out deliberately to buy something he or she has already perceived as a need and the buyer who is persuaded to recognize or feel a need. Thus the idea of creating a need assumes that an effective sales presentation can induce a prospect to want an item. There are two things wrong with this idea:

1. There is ample evidence around that efforts to create needs by persuading uninterested prospects to become interested are almost always wasted. In fact, it is a truism that you cannot really sell a prospect anything in which the prospect does not have some interest, even if that is an unconscious interest.

2. Basic needs are really never new and have never changed throughout the course of human history. We have the same basic needs our ancestors had, even when they were living in caves.

The Felt Need

Some products and services are instant successes. Commercial radio and TV caught on with the public very quickly, as did movies, the personal computer, air travel, xerographic office copiers, express mail and package services, fast-food establishments, and a great many other things. That means that members of the public quickly decided that they had a need for these new things.

Can Needs Be Created?

It might be said that these new developments created new needs by the simple fact of their availability. Obviously, one could not have a need (as marketers use the term) for something that did not exist and was not even dreamed of. So it is valid to think of the rapid acceptance of new items as reflecting a need that had been heretofore unfilled and probably even unperceived.

On the other hand, there is another way to explain the swift success of these and many other new creations: It is possible that these items succeeded almost instantly because they satisfied felt needs that had never been satisfied before or they satisfied those felt needs in a far better way than they had ever been satisfied before.

Radio, TV, videocassette recorder-players (VCRs), and compact discs players are popular home entertainment devices. They were new and better ways of satisfying a long-standing need for entertainment, especially in the home, and they were embraced quickly by the public. Witness how these relatively new home entertainment devices have replaced theater attendance, public band concerts, public lectures, and many other older forms of pastime for adults. Computers gained acceptance quickly, despite their great cost, but the earlier acceptance and popularity of small calculators was almost an explosion. And if there is any doubt as to whether there has been a long-standing need for better means of making calculations, consider the Chinese abacus and how long it has been in existence.

The message here is plain enough, even as it was suggested earlier: First determine what the client really wants—the truly basic want, that is, for that is the real need—and then show the client a better way to satisfy that need. If you can persuade the client to accept your argument that yours is truly a better way, success is almost inevitable.

Clients Do Not Always Recognize a Felt Need

Oddly enough, in the face of all that I have said here, the client's felt need is one that is often not felt consciously, but only unconsciously. As many people have observed, they "know it when [they] see it," but presumably not until then. Consciously, they feel only a vague discontent, an unrest, an awareness that something is needed, and yet are unable to actually "put [their] finger on it." It is a sensation somewhat akin to that of trying to recognize a face you know you ought to recognize or recall a name you know that you should know, some knowledge that probably lies deeply in your subconscious, but won't appear on command.

This comes through often in proposal requests and statements of work written by clients, as they describe what they are unable to identify clearly enough to specify in detail. It is readily apparent in such cases that the client is troubled and feels a need for help (that is indeed the universal reason for using the services of a consultant), but often the help needed includes help in deciding what the problem is.

Good Proposals Help Clients Identify Their Needs

Your proposal itself is a direct benefit to the client, if it is truly a good proposal. Often the client is unable to actually identify and define the problem accurately, and sometimes the client is not able to even describe the symptoms with any great accuracy or in detail. That makes your analysis of the client's work statement and interpretation of the need most important and a service to the client. This alone—the effective preliminary analysis and need identification or the lack of it—is often the difference between successful and unsuccessful proposals. If you do such an effective job of making that identification and defining the problem that the client reading your proposal reacts mentally, "Yes, yes! That's it exactly!," you are striking a nerve, a major achievement in any sales effort.

Many Clients Need Education

There is often a need for client education. Educating the client—selectively, in terms of the immediate problem and its solution—is often the key to a successful main strategy. Of course, this must be done judiciously. Often enough the client would not care to admit such a need as this and may even feel defensive about it. It's important to be aware of this, for obvious reasons, and exercise a great deal of diplomacy in administering the necessary education. But that aside, never underestimate the importance of the education, and quite often it is most needed by clients who appear to have the least need for it! Witness my own case, vis-à-vis buying a computer and word processor:

With a fairly extensive technological background in modern electronics, including much experience with mainframe computers in a variety of major applications, I was sure that I fully understood the significance of personal computers and word processing. I thought myself to be in an especially privileged position in this respect. Moreover, as the already successful professional writer of a large number of books and other publications, I was sure that I had a realistic grasp on what word processing would and would not mean to me as a writer. I thought it would be pleasant and convenient to work with this new technological miracle, and I planned to do so eventually, but I didn't think that the use of word processing would contribute much to my efficiency or effectiveness as a writer. In fact, I was convinced that it would not greatly increase my productivity, since I was already making free and effective use of all the time- and labor-saving cut-and-paste techniques I had learned in my years in the technical-publications industry and had even developed a few special techniques and tactics of my own. I was thus able to keep the labor of retyping revised manuscript copy to a minimum. I therefore did not see how this new system could do very much to increase the quality or reduce the labor of my writing, since I already did what I believed to be an at least adequate amount of self-editing, rewriting, and revision, while minimizing the production labor required.

I was wrong on all counts. I didn't find out how wrong I was until I began to use a word processor. And the chief reason I decided that I could afford a word processor when I did was that I was beginning to write books about computers and their use, and I found it embarrassing, as well as ludicrous, to do so without having a system of my own.

I believe that I would have somehow managed to buy one much earlier had I been properly educated by someone in what a word processor would really do for me—had I somehow gained a more accurate and insightful grasp of what word processing really is. In fact, when I did buy a system, after fairly extensive research, I bought one featured in full-page advertising in the *Writer's Digest,* that enduring journal of freelance writing that I have read for a great many years.

(I think it was at that point, when I read that advertising, that I began to suspect that perhaps word processing offered more for the professional writer than I had previously believed.)

Incidentally, inasmuch as word processing is reported as by far the most popular use of and outstanding reason for buying personal computers, it soon struck me as odd that so few manufacturers and distributors of computers focused any significant portion of their advertising efforts on media and means for reaching writers and explaining the true benefits to the writer. This reveals quite clearly a shortcoming of many marketers in failing to understand what business they are in.

What Business Are You In?

In conducting seminars in proposal writing, I sometimes ask my attendees, "What business are you in?" I get such answers as these:

"We provide accounting services."

"We are marketing consultants."

"I am an interior designer."

"I teach people how to use their computers."

"We help clients design their office systems."

All these answers suffer from the same fault: Each definition is focused on "we" or "I" and describes what the consultant sells or wishes to sell. None reflects what the client wishes to buy or even shows awareness of or concern for what the client wants.

The railroads represent the classic case cited so often to illustrate the point. Becoming "fat, dumb, and happy," the prosperous railroad magnates sneered at change and stubbornly insisted that they were in the railroad business, even as they watched their dwindling freight business going to the huge tractor trailers multiplying on the growing network of superhighways, while their vanishing passenger business was flowing to the growing number of airports, large and small. Only when they had begun to founder did they begin to reshape their thinking, but it was too late then to salvage more than a shadow of their former industry.

The problem is that each of us tends to think in selfish terms, in terms of what we want rather than in terms of what the client wants. We even rationalize that what we want is what the client ought to want. And even when the subject of educating the client arises, most of us—at least until we come to know better through getting a proper education in the subject ourselves—believe that educating the client means making the client understand why what we want is what he or she ought to want.

Of course, this is getting it all backward. It is we who should want what the client wants. It is we who should—must—offer what the client wants and must identify and define our business in those terms. Even today, many do not understand what the railroads were or should have been selling. Some people who ought to know better believe that the railroads were actually in the transportation business. But that is wrong too because even that is a bit too abstract to come to real grips with what customers want and so to properly orient and focus marketing appeals. It is not "transportation" per se that customers want to buy, as they perceive their wants, but it is *satisfying* their own customers (getting their goods delivered) and getting themselves to wherever they want to go as quickly and as comfortably as possible. Customers want these services provided efficiently, speedily, safely, comfortably, conveniently, and economically.

Airlines offer much greater speed in actual transit time than do railroads, but they do not offer as much convenience in many respects, due primarily to the remote locations of airports and the hassle of transportation to and from those airports. Nor do airlines always offer greater speed in total travel time, especially in short hauls of a few hundred miles where passengers spend much more time traveling to and from airports than they do in the air. Rail travel, in portal-to-portal terms, is often as rapid as air travel, as well as much more convenient, more comfortable, and less expensive. Had the railroads focused on those advantages and concentrated on increasing them, they would almost surely have retained much of their passenger business, especially the short-haul business. And had they thought out and maximized the advantages they could offer in freight forwarding—delivering the goods to customers—they would have kept much more of their freight business than they did. But the railroads failed to even think out marketing strategies, much less do anything to put them to work. At least they did not do so until the damage was done, when it was too late to salvage very much, even with the help of the federal government and heavy subsidies, as the government struggles to prop up this white elephant that has become a dinosaur.

Nothing has changed very much. Not everyone has learned from that classic case, and many of us are making those same kinds of mistakes today, albeit on a smaller scale and in less dramatic industries.

The business you are in has nothing to do with what you want. It has everything to do with what the client wants. And in a very large sense we are all in the same business: helping clients. The differences among us are in how we help clients, or perhaps more accurately, in what help clients need.

To help you to gain a firm grasp on this and apply it to your own case, try your hand at the exercise presented in Figure 3. The idea here is to first study the typical consulting services numbered as 1 to 10, and then match up those services with the kinds of benefits suggested in the second part of the figure by writing in the number(s) of each kind of service you believe can be fairly represented as offering that/those benefit(s). Of course, some of the services offer more than one kind of benefit or the benefit can be represented in more than one set of terms, so you should wind up with many more than ten numbers written on the lines following the list of possible benefits.

You should also, at some point, add a description of your own services and your own ideas about benefits offered by any of these services, including your own. (That is why blank lines are provided.) Conceiving of additional benefits, and words with which to express them, is an important part of this exercise, designed to compel you to think seriously about this. This is an opportunity to orient and sharpen your thought processes vis-à-vis this aspect of marketing, and the time you spend in this will be well-spent time.

Finally, go to the third part of the figure and write out a statement of the business you are in, as you now see it. Be sure that this is a statement that stresses what you do to help the client directly and in terms of final result. Do not overlook the emotional element in articulating that main benefit. Don't worry about how many words you need to make your statement, and do actually write it out. Return to it later and see whether you are still satisfied with that definition or wish to revise it, as you gain more insights into successful proposal-writing strategies and tactics.

CONSULTING SPECIALTIES

1. Marketing services
2. Interior design
3. Office systems design
4. Computer systems specialist
5. Hypnotist

6. Speech coach
7. Publications specialist
8. Conference management
9. Investment advisor
10. Real estate appraiser

11. Your own specialty(ies) _____

_____

_____

PRIMARY BENEFITS

Maximize profits _____   Reduce risk _____

Stop smoking _____   Raise efficiency _____

Save money _____   Increase sales _____

Be in style _____   Gain personal prestige _____

Avoid making a mistake _____   Improve business image _____

_____

_____

_____

THE BUSINESS YOU ARE IN

_____

_____

_____

_____

_____

Figure 3 Exercise sheet.

Note also the point made earlier that the most basic appeals and motivators are emotional ones, not rational ones. Study those benefit items and note that most have an emotional appeal—to be in style, to gain in personal prestige, to make more money, to improve one's business image.

This is not by chance. All experienced marketers and sales experts are well aware that the prime motivator is emotional and that logic and reason play necessary but only supporting roles in marketing and sales.

Motivators

Earlier you read that fear and greed are prime motivators. People act out of the desire to gain what they want and avoid what they fear. There is a great deal of evidence around that fear is probably by far the more persuasive motivator. That is itself not too surprising, when you consider the ever greater pressures of modern life and what that does to increase the sense of insecurity that most of us have to some degree. (In fact, is there anyone who is not insecure to at least some degree in this uncertain world?)

Motivators Are Emotional

Note carefully that these are emotional motivators. Study all successful advertising and especially that appearing on TV as commercials. You can easily tell which are the most successful ones: They are the ones that are repeated again and again, over a great period of time—excellent evidence that they are effective. Study these for emotional content, the common factor.

Invariably, successful advertising is addressed to the emotions, to what people are most likely to want to gain or avoid. Insurance, smoke detectors, burglar alarms, locks, security systems, safes, and many other items are sold principally through fear motivation, often with an appeal to guilt thrown in, as insurance advertisements urge prospects to remember their obligations to provide for their families even after they are gone from this sphere. Many items are sold through promises of gain—money, love, fun, prestige, and other such endowments. Sometimes advertisers manage to incorporate both kinds of motivators, as in the case of some securities advisors who promise to reduce the risks while helping you make profitable investments and even offering discounted stock brokerage fees.

Selling Motivating Benefits—What the Item Does

Note how many of these successful advertisements do not even attempt to sell the product or service directly, but instead focus the major persuasive effort on the claimed benefit directly and then describe and sell the product or service only as the means to the benefit. Rare indeed is the advertiser who makes much effort to prove its product better than anyone else's product, except to support its claims of what the product does for the buyer. Kitchen or dishwasher detergents are not of better quality per se, in the TV commercials, for example; they simply produce better results, such as literally spotless glassware and dishes that shine so that you can see your face reflected in them. And once the advertiser has established that claim of beneficial result, the time comes to support that claim with some evidence to help the prospect believe the promise of pleasing results.

"Prove" the Claim

Wherever possible, that "evidence" (which may or may not be legitimate evidence, but which the advertiser hopes the prospect will accept as evidence) is linked logically and directly to the qualities or characteristics of the product or service. For example, claims of better riding qualities in an advertiser's automobile might be supported by technical or semitechnical descriptions of the suspension system. This is the best kind of evidence, usually, and should be used when possible.

In some cases, it is not possible to link the promised blessing with the qualities of the product or with any direct claim to superiority of product. Beer is one such case. Beer advertisers rarely base their advertising on any claim of product superiority in quality. (Not only would that be almost impossible to prove, but beer drinkers couldn't care less about the technology of making beer or the logic of one method over another.) Rather, beer advertisers only suggest broadly that it's more fun to drink their beer by showing their beer being consumed in a good-times atmosphere. And, as another (and less powerful) theme, they try to portray their product as the "in" product by commercials that attempt to prove that "everyone" (or at least everyone with good taste) orders their product.

In another case, where there is no logical basis (and probably no valid basis) on which to lay a claim of superiority, the advertiser might simply claim superiority and "substantiate" that with testimonials by some public figure from the sports or entertainment world. Or, as an alternative, an actor dressed appropriately as an authority with relevance to the advertised product or service, such as in a white laboratory coat, might offer the "expert opinion."

Humans have a herd instinct, too, and tend to join the flock, rather than go it alone. Probably this is another manifestation of our common sense of insecurity, and it is used effectively in marketing. The influence of testimonials and other data that demonstrate widespread acceptance of your product or service is not entirely logical nor is it real evidence that yours is a good product or service, but it is also an emotional appeal to the human instinct to join the crowd and agree with the popular view. Possibly this is another manifestation of fear motivation, reflecting the fear many of us have to go it alone.

Sell Only What the Client Wants

I once had the opportunity to observe an outstandingly successful Fuller Brush salesman at work. His technique was quite simple. He went through his entire case of samples—he carried perhaps 30 to 40 items—showing each to the customer with a few words of introduction, watching the customer's eyes intently. If the eyes remained vacant, he went on. If he detected a spark of interest, he stopped and began to sell that item, usually with great success.

There were many other aspects to his technique, but this was the basic one and it was the one that most clearly explained this man's basic success. He understood that it was impracticable and wasteful of time to try to sell something the prospect was not really interested in, when the time could be invested much more profitably in selling something in which the prospect showed some immediate interest. His tactic was simply to find out which items stirred the prospect's interest, and to do so as quickly as possible so he could get on to the more important business of getting the maximum-sized orders for those items.

That's a universal truth. You can't sell the client what the client really does not want. The most effective tactic is to first find out what the client really wants, but remember that clients often do not know what they want or are not fully conscious of that want. ("I know it when I see it!") At least, this is often true in the sense that they do not know precisely how to identify or specify what they want and need your help in doing so.

We All Sell the Same Thing

Buyers are motivated by the desire to gain or avoid things. From the sellers' viewpoint, we all sell the same thing: help. And while that is true for everyone who sells anything, it is especially true for consultants because the desire for help is usually the conscious and direct objective of clients who go in quest of consulting services. We sell help in avoiding things, help in gaining things, help in achieving things. But even more fundamentally than that, it is not help itself that we sell, but the promise of help.

A Basic Marketing Problem

Why is it important to recognize the fact that what we sell is the promise of help? It is important because it illustrates both the basic difficulty in selling consulting services and the importance of the proposal in marketing. It is important to have a realistic appreciation of the marketing problem, with all its difficulties. Of course, selling a prospect a tangible object, even such a costly one as an automobile or a house, is far less difficult than selling any intangible, such as a service. And on that latter level there are sublevels of marketing difficulty too, for it is obviously far easier to sell mundane, workaday services such as automobile repair and accounting services than it is to sell the relatively sophisticated and mysterious services known as "consulting." And when those latter services are such that they mandate entrusting a stranger, no matter how well recommended, with confidential information and perhaps even with the welfare of a business enterprise, clients need a great deal of reassurance before they agree to undertake the risk.

In the face of this almost overwhelming need for gaining the client's complete confidence if you are to win the contract, it is not surprising that conventional advertising does not work well for consultants generally. And it explains why the proposal must be considerably more than a brochure and a quotation of price and terms. It must satisfy a number of requirements, at the minimum, including the following:

- A persuasive demonstration that you fully understand and appreciate the client's need.
- A believable promise of help that is appropriate to the client's perception of need.
- Evidence that you can and will deliver that promised help.
- Evidence that you are a dependable and trustworthy consultant.

CHAPTER 5

Gathering Market Intelligence

The Basic Sources of Information

> The effectiveness with which the consultant gathers information and the quality of the information gathered often make the difference between winning and losing the proposal competition.

The strength of any proposal depends on the quantity and quality of the information on which it is based. That is a truth about proposals generally, but especially with regard to your approaches and strategies. It's hard to imagine how you can devise effective approaches and strategies without adequate and accurate information, properly organized and properly utilized.

Much of your proposal content stems from your own knowledge, judgment, analysis, and creative imagination, but there must be other sources and other information also. In fact, your own cognitive and creative processes are also dependent on those other sources. This applies to formal and informal proposals responding to specific requests and to unsolicited proposals you submit as a follow-up to earlier marketing contacts.

Gathering intelligence for development of a successful proposal is rarely easy, but it is necessary. It requires effort, imagination, resourcefulness, and even ingenuity.

There are many potential sources of information—market intelligence—to support your proposal-writing effort. Following are some of the typical ones:

1. The RFP itself
2. Conversations with the client
3. Other client materials, such as brochures and reports
4. Other readily available public information about the client
5. Your own experience, knowledge, and judgment
6. Your proposal library and files
7. Study/analysis of the requirement and related research
8. Special methods and sources
9. The online world: cyberspace

Some of these items are self-explanatory or have been referred to earlier; others merit special consideration and discussion here.

The Client's RFP

Reading a Proposal Request

The sardonic injunction, "When all else fails, read the instructions," fits here very well because we often neglect to take advantage of the most important source of information: the original request for proposals and its work statement, whether that is ink and paper or "digital ink," the announcement made online and read on the screen of your monitor. Surprisingly often, the answers to questions that arise and the information you seek are readily at hand in those documents that make up the solicitation, but are still often overlooked or not studied seriously.

It is easy to understand why this is so. The client's statement of the requirement and other portions of an RFP are often neither well organized nor fluently expressed, and that can lead you astray. Impatient to get on with important work, you are unwilling to engage in what appears to be a waste of time because there seems to be little of value to be gained from study of the request.

That is not the only problem. You must guard against an unconscious tendency to leap to conclusions in reading the request and especially in reading what is not there. It's easy to see what you expect to see, rather than what is written there. This often leads to offering the client a ready-made solution that may be a reasonable approach but not the best one and perhaps not even the most relevant one.

Acres of Diamonds

Despite the apparent uselessness of much of the material in the solicitation, the contrary may be true. Often, after lengthy investigation into other sources, I have found that the information I needed was in the RFP after all. Quite often, the search through the formal request is a painstaking one and not at all easy, but it is often more productive than most other ways you can pursue information. More, it is almost always more reliable information than any other you gather. Time spent in studying the client's statement of requirements and what is wanted in the proposal is usually worthwhile and rarely wasted.

One of the reasons many consultants miss so much information of importance in reading the client's request is simply the tendency of consultants to satisfy themselves with a single reading of the RFP and an occasional brief review. That is rarely sufficient. The first reading of the typical RFP normally produces only a superficial understanding of the client's needs and desires. One of the benefits of preparing the checklists you will find recommended in Chapter 6 is the enforcement of a discipline in the reading, compelling you to read with great care, as you deliberately and consciously search out specific items for your lists. (Even if the preparation of the lists did nothing more than that, the time would be well spent.) Additional readings, as you study the problem and begin to develop an approach and design, have greater significance than the earlier readings because you now have specific questions and are in quest of specific information. Ergo, it is quite important to continue to reread the client's request continually, while you are developing the proposal. Each new reading tends to produce more insight.

Serendipitous Finds

Finding answers to specific questions or finding specific information you believe you need is one reason for that careful and continual study of the request. Another is that without it you might miss some important piece of information, even something that will spell the difference between success and the lack of it. Sometimes information that seemed trivial on first reading assumes great importance after you have worked on the proposal for a while and developed a much more in-depth appreciation of what you need to know. You must therefore satisfy yourself that you have extracted everything of worth to be extracted from the RFP.

Reading between the Lines

Another common mistake some consultants make in reading an RFP is assuming that anything not stated plainly is not present in the request. That is, they fail to even make the effort to read between the lines, much less do they do so effectively. Often the most valuable information is there between the lines—information that is implicit, not explicit, but still useful.

Perhaps you have to be something of a detective to do this reading between the lines well, but it is often the key to winning. If you do not tend by instinct to think deductively, train yourself to do so. You will be rewarded with a great increase in what you can infer from your reading.

Information often is or appears to be implied, rather than stated plainly. That may be due to nothing more or less than simple weakness in writing or a peculiarity in the writer's style. Some clients will simply be unable to express themselves as clearly as we would wish or will have a difficult writing style. In other cases, the subtlety is deliberate; there may be "political" considerations in the client's organization that prevent the client from writing as plainly as he or she would wish and compel the client to do little more than hint at certain facts. And sometimes there is a specific effort to hold back certain information, but the information gap is often quite apparent. The resourceful consultant will often sense that such a gap exists and may even be able to gauge what is withheld. There may be a personal bias in the client's view of a situation, also not unusual. But whatever the reasons, it is important for you to gain a clear and objective view.

Conversations with the Client

Information received verbally from the client is second in usefulness and value only to that contained in a formal written request for proposals. (In some cases it may even exceed that source in importance.) In fact, in the case of submitting an unsolicited proposal on your own initiative, there will be no formal written request, and perhaps not even a verbal one, from the client. It is especially important to have made notes of your conversations, preferably during the conversations, but certainly immediately afterward, while your recall is fresh.

It may be possible to tape-record the conversation, but be sure that the client does not object to this. Ask for permission to do so. But be aware that even when permission is given there may be a downside: Many people are much more guarded in their remarks when a tape recorder is running, and so, even with permission, recorded interview dialogue is not always as beneficial as unrecorded dialogue.

In responding to formal requests, especially with any government organization, it is a mistake to ask questions to which you do not truly need the answers. (You can almost always find a way to write your proposal without asking those questions.) You often give away more than you get by asking questions.

In the case of an unsolicited proposal or one that you are asked for informally and are the only one so invited, it is different. It is usually safe to ask questions now. However, first explore all accessible avenues of information, especially that of available client materials. It is embarrassing and often harmful to your image to have the client point out that he or she has already supplied the information you seek or that it is readily available elsewhere.

Other Client Materials

Often, regardless of other circumstances surrounding the situation, you can gain access to many kinds of client materials, such as annual reports, brochures, newsletters, and article reprints. Whatever sources you have, you ought to utilize these also and should keep such materials in your proposal library and resource files. Study all such materials to learn as much as possible about the client before deciding on proposal strategy and approach.

Other Readily Available Public Information about the Client

There are often other sources of information about the client, especially if the client is a well-established organization. There are, for example, D&B (Dun & Bradstreet) reports, listings and descriptions in various kinds of directories (e.g., the *Thomas Register, Standard & Poor's,* the *Dun & Bradstreet Million Dollar Directory,* and the *Facts on*

File Directory of Major Public Corporations), and various other public sources of information, most of them available in any well-stocked public library. (Many such publications appear also on the Internet.) These sources tell you a great deal about the client and provide valuable input and idea starters for your proposal effort. Too, if the clients are business firms, read the appropriate business periodicals, including the daily newspaper financial sections and the financial newspapers, the *Wall Street Journal* and the *New York Times.* Information offered now on the Internet is also public information, of course, and is the most convenient, most readily available, and perhaps most extensive information. (See Chapter 13 for details of various relevant Internet and Web locations.)

Your Own Experience, Knowledge, and Judgment, and Your Proposal Library and Files

One marketing resource you should have been building up from the day you entered practice is your proposal library and files. Work at maintaining this resource, as it expands and improves steadily; your proposal success should then likewise continue to expand and improve. Here are several basic elements to a proposal library:

- Swipe files
- Copies of your own proposals
- Competitors' proposals
- Competitor information
- Reference books
- Client information

Swipe Files

Cut-and-paste techniques have long existed. Once, one kept *swipe files,* a vast assortment of materials that had potential use elsewhere, in the form of sheets of typed material, clippings from newspapers and magazines, handwritten notes, and other such materials. Much of each new proposal consisted of such material arranged in some order and handed over to a secretary or typist to be typed up into a rough-draft manuscript. That was then edited, reviewed, revised, and polished for final typing or typesetting. Later, as xerographic copiers became available, original swipe files were left undisturbed, and xerographic copies were cut and pasted together.

Today, that has changed again. Much of the material included in today's swipe files is on computer disks and can be printed out for conventional cut-and-paste makeup, but can be handled far more efficiently by electronic cut and paste, such as can be done with any modern word processor. With modern scanners, even clippings and other hard copy can be translated easily into computer files.

Copies of Your Own Proposals

Those proposals you have written in the past that were successful in winning contracts are valuable as models, since they are models of success. However, that does not mean that the remaining proposals, those that did not win contracts, have no value. There is much in them that is useful. They are or have items that are salvageable for other use, and they should not be discarded, but should be filed as permanent items in your proposal library. Many contain valuable analyses and studies that will save you a great deal of time and money, and often even make it possible to write a new proposal that would not be viable if you had to write it all from scratch. But they also often contain many illustrations, tables, discussions, and arguments that you can use again and again, with or without minor modifications.

In this respect, these proposals are part of your swipe files, as well as models for future guidance, and should be so regarded. And they should be "shelved" as computer files, as well as printed copies, for the greater facility in handling and using them that this affords.

Competitors' Proposals

Opportunities arise to get copies of competitors' proposals. Take advantage of all such opportunities and study those competitive proposals. Be deeply conscious of a need to get copies of competitors' proposals, and opportunities to do so will arise.

Competitor Information

Collect information about competitors as eagerly as you collect information about clients and potential clients. Gather and store competitors' brochures, articles, newsletters, catalogs, capability statements, and other information. Be alert for materials when you attend conferences, conventions, trade shows, seminars, and other such events.

Reference Books

If you maintain an adequate library, you can carry out a great deal of your research without stirring from your desk. Everything with potential usefulness for proposal effort belongs in your library.

Client Information

Here is where you deposit those clippings about your clients and potential clients, as well as brochures, annual reports, and all other information relevant to clients and prospective clients.

Miscellaneous papers, drawings, price lists, catalogs, reports, and other such items all belong in your proposal reference files, as part of your proposal library. Give serendipity a maximum chance to happen.

Database Management

All of this material constitutes a database, which is simply a collection of related information. In this case, the database is the entire proposal library and reference files. Or it may be several databases, if you prefer to organize the material into several such sets of files, such as a competitor database, an own-proposals database, a swipe-files database, and others. You can do either, but the practical criterion is one of size: When files or sets of files—for example, databases—get too large, they become unwieldy and difficult to manage and manipulate. *Manipulate* includes such functions as adding to files, sorting them, and searching them to find what you are looking for, so for convenience and efficiency, it is probably wise to establish several database files.

Perhaps you have not thought of database management software as a writer's tool; probably most people don't regard it as such. However, it is most valuable as a research tool when you have the banks of material organized into files. Once you have built up those banks of swipe files, old proposals, competitors' proposals, resumes, current and past projects, and other such materials, they begin to become somewhat unmanageable if you must rely on your memory or random searching to find what you want. That's when you need the database management software.

Database management (DBM) programs enable you to organize your databases for searching, retrieving, manipulating, and sorting. The effectiveness of these is dependent on the wisdom of your design, for DBM software permits you great flexibility in designing the system to your own ideas and preferences. In a sense, a DBM program is clay that you may shape and mold to your own preference. Therein lies its great power.

If you design properly, you can sort files by competitors' names, by types of programs, by types of skills, or by any parameter for which you anticipate a need and provide tags. You can also print out a variety of reports, tables, and listings of various kinds, again largely dependent on your own ideas and preferences. Database management is therefore increasingly an essential for the maintenance of an effective proposal library.

Study/Analysis of the Requirement and Special Research

Naturally you will be making studies and analyses of the client's requirement. Sometimes special studies and research are required to carry out a proper analysis of the requirement. It may not be viable to do this yourself, if the effort requires an excessive investment in the proposal. As an alternative to dropping the proposal, you may wish to consider an arrangement with another consultant, one whose field enables him or her to handle the special study as a routine analysis. You can be coproposers and partners in any resulting contract, one may subcontract to the other, or you may be able to find some other mutually agreeable business arrangement.

Special Methods and Sources

There are many situations where special and even unorthodox methods of intelligence gathering are necessary to maximize your probabilities of winning. These problems call often for imagination and resourcefulness, and the contracts tend to go to those who gather the information they need.

Advertising for Information

One project called for operating a client-owned installation that employed a number of people. The grapevine reported that the client was unhappy with the incumbent contracting firm and would like to make a change, if they could find someone suitable.

The RFP, while not cryptic, was not enlightening either. It did not specify, for example, how many people were employed by the incumbent and did not furnish much information about their specialties, the total payroll the contractor would have to handle, or any of a number of other details one would usually want to have to support a proposal development.

The successful proposer ran carefully worded help-wanted advertisements, designed specifically to draw responses from those currently employed in the project and specifying that respondents must submit up-to-date resumes.

Resumes resulted in abundance, with a satisfying number coming from those working on the project in question. The resumes received were a mother lode of priceless information, but the proposer also invited some of the respondents—those who appeared to be key people and therefore knowledgeable of important details—to visit and be interviewed. These interviews produced even more useful information. The proposer reported later that she had never had more precise or more accurate information and she had little difficulty developing a powerful proposal that won the contract.

In a somewhat analogous, yet different, case, a consultant found herself invited to propose an on-site project several states away. The project required the hiring of several local people to do certain specialized work on the client's premises. Uncertain as to local rates for the kinds of specialists required in the client's area, the consultant placed advertisements in a local newspaper and arranged to travel there to conduct interviews. As a result of those interviews, she acquainted herself with the local supply of qualified labor for the project, learned what rates she would have to pay, made tentative arrangements to hire several people, and got permission to incorporate their resumes in her successful proposal.

This is not uncommon. Many small consulting firms, and even some not-so-small firms, use this method for gathering resumes of qualified individuals to be included in their proposals. In the course of doing this, the truly alert proposal writer manages to gather a great deal of useful information, even if that is not the specific reason for requesting the resumes.

Clipping Services

To avoid the time-consuming work of the reading and clipping you would have to do to build files on clients and prospective clients, you can subscribe to a clipping service. For a per-clipping fee, such agencies scan newspapers and magazines for you and clip out items you specify. (PR firms, for example, order items about their own clients, to check on their own effectiveness and to provide clients proof of results.) However, the traditional clipping service is not unaffected by the online revolution: While many such services are still based on clipping printed notices, there is a developing trend to "clipping" notices that appear online as a new form: *electronic clipping.* But that introduces a new subject: cyberspace. Cyberspace is that hypothetical "place" where information and communication exist—where, in fact, the potential for information and communication exist—via the online phenomenon. Cyberspace clips are thus relevant notices that appear in cyberspace—online, that is—as explained shortly.

The Facsimile Machine

Your resources should include a fax (facsimile) machine or fax board in your computer. (Virtually all computers sold today have a fax-modem board, so you do not need a stand-alone fax machine, although I find it a convenience to use both.) Fax enables almost instantaneous transmission of printed materials. There have been occasions when my request, transmitted by fax, brought back a magazine article or other response within an hour. On the other hand, there have been occasions when a client has sent me materials by fax for my comment, so I was able to read them and respond within an hour or two.

Fax machines have gone through the same pricing cycle that most high-tech products have, so that I paid a bargain price of $600 for my first fax machine, and when it expired I found another for "only" $300, which I still have. Today, I could buy its equivalent for about one half that price.

Fax is still a popular way to transmit messages and data quickly, despite the ready availability of e-mail. For one thing, fax is more secure from eavesdropping than is e-mail and the Internet in general. For another, one needs to be able to perform basic computer operations to send e-mail, but anyone with 20 seconds of instruction can send a fax by fax machine.

The Online World: Cyberspace

In the past few years we have experienced technology transfer on a grand scale, representing perhaps the most impressive technological development yet—an online technology, utilizing the desktop computer and the telephone. But with these and the wiring of the world, we have come full circle and created a global village, an electronic one. The online world, referred to as *cyberspace,* consists of several elements:

Electronic bulletin boards (BBSes)

Public databases

Commercial online services

Fax transmissions

The Internet, including e-mail and the World Wide Web, plus the online communications and various features described later (see Chapter 13)

Electronic Bulletin Board Systems (BBSes)

Until the last few years, electronic bulletin boards were proliferating rapidly, many based in private homes and many based in government and business offices. With the growth of the Internet, with its e-mail and Web sites, interest in the BBS as a business medium has declined, as interest in and use of Internet facilities has surged. A vast portion of all online business operations is via e-mail and the Web. For example, almost every government office has a Web site today, in addition to one or more BBSes. Log on to http://www.gcn.com (the Web site of *Government Computer News*) as one impressive Web site that offers links to a vast amount of information by and about federal, state, and local government agencies and their suppliers.

Public Databases

Public databases were growing rapidly before the Internet began to grow to what it is now. Almost every profession and industry was represented by stores of information that users could tap via their desktop computers, for fees based in large part on the length of time they required for information searches and transfers. With the growth of mountains of information on the Internet, so much of it available at no cost except the cost of being connected to the Internet, that new industry was also affected with a predictable slow-down. There are information services on the Web for which the user must pay use fees, but they represent a very small part of all the information available there.

Commercial Online Services

Probably the best-known and today the largest commercial online service is America Online. Another well-known name is CompuServe (recently joined with America Online), but there are also Prodigy and Microsoft Network. All of these offer a variety of services and provide access to the Internet as well.

The Internet

The Internet is actually a net of computers connected with each other via dedicated and dial-up telephone lines. Cyberspace is thus not an actual place, but an imaginary space represented by that net—by that potential for communication and information exchange. Every Internet address ("URL," for uniform resource locator) is actually a file in a computer somewhere in the world—the Internet is worldwide—reached by telephone line.

By far, the most used element of the online world is e-mail. E-mail is swift and inexpensive. It is so swift that it is possible to have a virtual dialogue with someone via e-mail, exchanging messages every few minutes. But e-mail is used for more than posting messages to others. It is also the medium for forums or discussion groups (*mailing lists* in Internet jargon), electronic newsletters, electronic magazines, and newsgroups. The latter, of which there are many thousands, are another kind of forum. Together, they make up what is known as the *Usenet*. E-mail is used to post messages there, so newsgroups bear some resemblance to the mailing list kind of forum referred to, but are an entirely different environment.

Using the Internet and E-mail

With the great number of electronic bulletin board systems in operation today, it is possible to reach a great many individuals rather easily and inexpensively by posting messages on a number of boards. I used this approach a number of times in researching information for projects. In one case, I wanted to conduct a survey among independent consultants and so placed a message on a number of BBSes inviting interested individuals to participate. I sent questionnaires to those who responded, and was able to do my survey without leaving my desk! (The results were part of the input information for the original edition of this book.)

The vast capability of the Internet tends to dwarf that of the many electronic bulletin boards, even those that joined in creating vast networks of bulletin boards, so that many of us who were BBS aficionados have all but deserted the BBS systems in favor of other online systems, especially the Internet and e-mail.

Relevant Uses of the Internet

Among the large number of uses you can make of the Internet, the following are especially relevant to proposal writing:

- Market research, especially finding proposal opportunities and leads that can be developed into proposal opportunities
- Receiving formal or informal requests for proposals and associated solicitation packages or "bid sets"
- Gathering intelligence to support proposal writing
- Finding and working with collaborators in proposals
- Submitting proposals

Market Research

The Internet is probably the greatest research facility yet developed, with worldwide reach into universities, databases, publications, and other sources of information. You can seek these out with the many search engines available—for example, Yahoo, Alta Vista, Lycos, Web Crawler, and Infoseek. Through these, you can find the federal and state purchasing and procurement facilities, most of which are well represented by Web sites, and those also of many local governments—cities and counties—that maintain Web sites. Government interest and participation in use of the Internet has grown quite swiftly, and most agencies have or are building their own Web sites.

Organizations in the private sector are also making increasing use of business proposals to find the most suitable contractors for the services they need, but you may use the many communication resources of the Internet to seek out potential clients by joining some of the appropriate forums and publishing an electronic newsletter, as many independent entrepreneurs do.

Gathering Market Intelligence

At least one aspect of gathering market intelligence has been greatly simplified by the use of the Internet. It has become much easier to scout the competition—to gather and read the competition's sales literature and so to get something of a fix on what they are all about. That has been made relatively easy by the growing number of Web sites: Many of your competitors will have sites of their own, and you may look them over by visiting their sites.

Actually, you can do more than that in scouting the competition: Use some of the search engines to see what competitors have been writing and thinking. If you furnish a competitor's name as a keyword or search term to a search engine, you will often find references to not only the competitor's site, but also his or her reports, posts to various forums, contributions to newsletters, and other utterances.

Getting Information for Development of Government Proposals

The problems of writing proposals to government agencies are similar to, and yet in some respects somewhat different from, those of writing proposals in the commercial markets. Doing business with government in general has many similarities to, but some differences from, doing business with organizations in the private sector.

The Freedom of Information Act

These differences and similarities apply to the gathering of intelligence, as it does to other aspects of proposal development. There is a great deal of information readily available about government agencies and their programs, and you can gather up a large library of materials, much of it free. But there is also one significant difference between intelligence gathering to develop proposals to government agencies and that to develop commercial proposals. It is mandatory for government agencies to release, on demand or of their own volition and initiative, all information that is not classified—affecting national security—and/or does not infringe on individual privacy or the right to hold certain information proprietary and confidential. That law is the Freedom of Information Act.

Under that act you have the right to demand certain information that is properly public information—bought with tax money. The following are typical items of information you can and should normally request:

- What the government is now paying for a given service (in the case of a competitive procurement to continue a service now being provided).
- The name of the incumbent contractor.
- A copy of the successful proposal. (Confidential and proprietary data will be excised from the copy you get.)
- Copies of reports and/or other documents generated earlier in the performance of the contract or related contracts.
- Records of work required and performed under the existing or earlier contracts.

In connection with these items, you can often get these even without invoking the Freedom of Information Act by visiting the agency's library and reading some of the reports and other documents on the shelves. And in some cases a visit to a Government Printing Office bookstore will produce a great deal of useful information available in publications of the Government Printing Office. (That "visit" may be via the GPO Web site.)

It should be noted, in connection with using the Freedom of Information Act, that you may run into difficulties on occasion if you do not specifically invoke the act when asking for the information. Some bureaucrats take advantage of the technicality that unless you specifically state that you are invoking that law, they still have the right to refuse the information. There are also some who will insist that the request must be in writing, so be prepared to meet this challenge, too. But remember, if you are unfortunate enough to encounter such an individual, that you are not asking for a favor; you are asking for what must be provided under the law. You have the right to insist on it.

One more caveat: Be cautious in asking for information about a project for which an RFP has been issued if you are planning to compete for that contract. You must not approach any personnel connected with the agency who issued the RFP or you may disqualify yourself as a proposer. If you have any doubts about the propriety of what you ask for, talk to the contracting officer about the information you seek. That will keep you out of trouble.

Government Publications

The Government Printing Office today has nothing free or even inexpensive. Every publication it sells in its bookstores costs money. However, every publication in its bookstores was originally ordered and paid for by a federal agency. (It is when the GPO thinks the publication to be salable to the public that it runs extra copies and stocks them in its bookstores.) In a great many cases, the agency that ordered the printing has copies available on request free of charge. If you can determine which agency ordered the printing of any publications that interest you, you can ask the agency for a copy.

You can also write or call federal agencies and ask for publications by their general nature, such as publications on purchasing and procurement. Do this with the Department of Defense, the General Services Administration, and other agencies.

Check also with the Department of Commerce and the Small Business Administration for their publications, many of which are free or sold at nominal prices.

Government Agencies Online

Before you do any of these things today, consult Internet and Web sources. There is an excellent chance that you will find what you want there without leaving your desk. Later in these pages (e.g., Chapter 13), you will find a number of suggested sources to consult, such as the well-named Federal Acquisition Jumpstation (http://procure.msfc.nasa.gov/fedproc/home.html), a virtual Rosetta stone for searching the federal government labyrinth. Of course, also query one or two of the major search engines and follow the leads they provide.

Many federal agencies operate one or more electronic bulletin boards today. However, they exist side by side with the ever more popular and rapidly growing population of Web sites, including those of federal government agencies. A comprehensive guide to these bulletin boards may be found at http://www.gcn.com, cited earlier as the Web site of the print periodical, *Government Computer News*. In fact, this site offers links to a great many federal, state, and local government facilities and information.

In the Beginning

When Is the Right Time to Market?

Success in marketing
is rarely a chance
occurrence. It comes
to those who think
ahead, plan ahead,
and *make* it happen.

The single most common cause of failure in consulting is the failure to market well. This is mostly the result of many newcomers to consulting failing to understand that consulting is not a one-call business. Consistent marketing success results only from consistent marketing effort.

What this means is that there is never a time when you can afford to neglect marketing. Most assignments result from spadework done many moons earlier. If you are the typical newcomer to the field, you began or will begin practice with a single client, or perhaps even without an initial client. Once working on your first project, you will give little or no thought to the day when you must find new clients. Instead, you wait until you finish that first assignment to begin looking for another client and another assignment. But marketing your services normally produces clients and assignments only weeks and months, sometimes many months, after the first marketing contacts. You may find yourself unable to survive while waiting to land that second client. That alone is responsible for much turnover in the ranks of independent consultants.

Prolonged idle time is not inevitable. You can minimize and even avoid it by advance planning—by prevention. The time for marketing is today and every day, from the day you decide to launch a consulting practice. As an independent consultant, you cannot afford to ever be too busy to maintain marketing activities if you want to continue to be busy. Need for continuous marketing is part of the price for success as an independent consultant. Make time for it.

Proposal writing is an important part of marketing, and one way to be a successful marketer is to review many opportunities to write proposals—more than you can or should respond to. Each opportunity then requires you to make a bid/no-bid decision.

Bid/No-Bid Decision Making

Every proposal represents a serious commitment—in fact, two commitments: One is the pledge of what you propose as a firm offer to the client. The other is the time and money you spend in writing the proposal. And often the latter is the greater commitment. While many proposals (e.g., the simple and informal letter proposals) are relatively minor efforts, many others are major undertakings, with large investments of time and money.

Those large organizations that write many major proposals and get all or most of their business this way often have formal systems for analyzing proposal opportunities and making decisions on whether to submit a proposal in each case. Many of these firms even have standard forms to document and report the results of each such analysis. Figure 4 typifies such designs and is the basis for the following discussion of bid/no-bid analytical procedures.

Analytical Procedure

The head data on the form are self-explanatory, identifying the opportunity and listing its basic characteristics. The other entry blanks merit discussion.

Such analysis is rarely cut-and-dried but is almost always linked to current conditions. The bid opportunity that you might eagerly seize on one occasion you may turn down on another occasion, depending on such variables as your current in-house workload, how urgently you need new work, and possible spin-off benefits (e.g., acquiring a new client or diversifying experience and market possibilities). Ergo, on one occasion you might invest time and money to

RFP HEAD DATA

Title: _____ Date:_____

Client: _____

Requirements summary:_____

Estimated probability of award: _____%

Formal proposal ☐   Letter proposal ☐   With pricing ☐   Separate pricing ☐

EVALUATIVE ESTIMATES

Estimated value ($): _____ Estimated bid/proposal effort (hrs.):_____

Probable competitors: _____

*Rank order (vis-à-vis other bid opportunities available now): No._____

Our major strength: _____

Our major weakness:_____

RATIONALE

*Arguments pro: _____

*Arguments con:_____

CONCLUSIONS AND RECOMMENDATIONS

Estimated win probability (%):_____ *Recommendation: bid [ ] No bid [ ]

REMARKS*

_____

* Consider all factors.

Figure 4   Bid/no-bid analysis form.

write a proposal for which you rate your chances at only 25 percent, whereas at another time you would not undertake any proposal unless you rated your prospects at 75 percent or more.

For these reasons, a relatively large section is provided at the bottom of Figure 4 for remarks, immediately following the space for your conclusions and recommendations. In that remarks section, the evaluator or evaluators record observations and recommendations. Motivation also may vary, as noted, and is not always profit for its own sake.

Measures to Increase the Likelihood of Success

The uncertainties and the transient conditions that have such profound effects on decisions are realities over which you do not always have control. However, here are a few marketing measures you can pursue that will help you to increase the odds in your favor and vastly improve your proposal batting average:

1. Do everything possible to receive a maximum number of opportunities to submit bids and proposals. The more opportunities you have, the more selective you can be in choosing only those that appear to offer the greatest possibilities for success. However, do not confine these efforts to getting yourself on as many bidders lists as possible, but take advantage of every opportunity to submit unsolicited proposals where you believe you have a fair chance of winning a contract or where the cost in time and money is relatively insignificant. Proposals that do not win contracts are not always a total waste: If they are superior proposals, they may not win a contract, but they win the client's attention and often bring other opportunities. So every well-written, well-thought-out proposal is a worthwhile marketing activity.

2. Maintain constant intelligence gathering to maximize your knowledge of competitor activities. Gather as many of your competitors' brochures as possible, and be alert to opportunities to acquire copies of their proposals.

3. Build the most extensive proposal library you can. It should include competitor literature, copies of your own proposals, useful boilerplate materials and swipe files, reference books, rosters and resumes of specialists you might need for some

projects, and whatever else might be proposal assets. And you should have a disk library, with as much material on disk files as possible. You can automate much of your proposal writing.

4. Evaluate possibilities of follow-on work with current clients so that you can consider this too in assessing your probable need for new contracts and project assignments. Try telling your clients frankly that you are planning your schedules for the future and need help in anticipating your probable workload. You may be surprised at the benefits of being honest and direct.

5. Keep in touch with clients you did work for in the past. Conditions change in client companies. People move about. Departments are reorganized. It is easy to be forgotten or over-looked, even by those who were most enthusiastic about the work you did. See to it that they do not forget you. Keep them on your mailing list for brochures, sales letters, and announcements. Call on the telephone and in person to say hello and remind them that you are still in practice and available to help solve problems.

Preparations for Proposal Writing

One common mistake in proposal writing is beginning to write too soon, writing before doing advance planning and preparation. The consequence of that haste is often a rough-draft proposal that requires more work to revise than it is possible to do in the time allowed for proposal submittal, compelling you to submit a proposal that is not your best possible presentation. And in some cases the cost of the revision is far too great with respect to the size of the contract. To minimize rewriting and revision, plan ahead before you begin writing so that you have precise objectives and planned routes to them.

Planning Essentials

The main elements and steps of planning a proposal are simply these:

1. Define the major objective.
2. Identify your approach.
3. Develop your grand strategy.
4. Prepare an itinerary (outline).

Of course, these are closely related to each other, and rarely does anyone have these fully detailed in advance when writing a proposal because the time element and the cost of proposal writing limits the amount of advance planning. But if proposal writing is to be done with any degree of efficiency and economy, some planning must be done before investing any large amount of time in serious writing efforts. But obviously, the data required to establish these elements must come from somewhere before the serious proposal writing begins.

The First Input

If you have carried out a bid/no-bid analysis and recorded your estimates, you already have some data that ought to be the first inputs for your proposal planning. Most of the items you will have recorded are useful for writing a proposal, and you should be conscious of this as you develop estimates and judgments that you record in that initial analysis. Following are notes on those items that are not self-explanatory.

DATA NEEDED

RFP Head Data   Aside from identifying the RFP, the client, and the proposal due date, here are some items of direct interest in reaching a decision:

- Kind of requirement. An accurate summary of the requirement is an important item here.
- Type of proposal required, as compared with the estimated size (dollar value) of the contract and the estimate of cost in labor hours to write the proposal, and recorded in the next item. (You might, for example, decide to write a letter proposal, even when you do not rate your chances for success very high, because the proposal is easy and inexpensive to write.)

Estimated Value   This is a measure of the size and importance of the proposal. It should thus be something of an indicator to the amount of effort and size of proposal that are justified and necessary. This is only a rough indicator, because it is only one of several ballpark estimates you will have made in analyzing the RFP, but it is a guideline.

Probable Competition Your ability to judge this depends on several factors. One is your familiarity with your special field. If you have been in your practice or working in the field for some time, you probably have a very good idea of who all the general competitors in your field are. That gives you some beginning idea of probable competitors for any given contract. If you have a great many acquaintances in your field, you may be in touch with a kind of grapevine that exists in all fields and is often a source for information. There is also the possibility that a preproposal conference was held by the client and, in attending that, you had the opportunity to observe and identify other attendees. Sometimes you can even persuade the client to tell you who else was invited to propose. Whatever the case, the information is usually useful and may affect your strategy decisions. Certainly it will affect your decisions about what competitor strategy to use.

Rank Order This calls for you to consider the other bid opportunities available and make your best estimate to rank this one in comparison with the others. This automatically also factors into the estimate the total number of bid opportunities available at the time. If this were your lowest-rated choice, for example, it would be number 35 in a field of 35 opportunities, but number 1 if there were no others available at the moment.

Major Strengths This is critically important. It may even be the basis for your grand strategy. Caution: This item refers to your major strengths vis-à-vis this contract only. It has nothing to do with other major strengths you may have. For example, you may be a computer expert, but unless the project you are pursuing entails computer work as a major element, this is not a relevant strength for this proposal. In all cases it is important to be objective. If you find it difficult to be objective about this estimate, get someone else to play devil's advocate for you.

Major Weaknesses Everything said about the major-strengths item applies to this item also. But in some respects this is even more important. Be sure that any weaknesses you perceive will not be fatal ones, and you must have some reason for believing that you can offset or overcome any weaknesses, if you decide to develop a proposal.

Arguments Pro Here you summarize the logical arguments for going ahead with the proposal and trying to win the contract even if you have found persuasive arguments con. This is a polemical exercise, recording the logical arguments for proposing without regard to the arguments against proposing or to your decision to propose or not to propose. There is a possible special consideration of a possible pro forma submittal: There are situations where a proposal that fails to win the contract pays off in direct benefits nevertheless. I can recall at least two cases, one of them my own, where the client did not choose the proposal for award, but liked it well enough to award the proposer other work without competition. A proposal submitted to introduce yourself and what you offer may be a valid reason to proceed with a proposal even when you doubt that you can win the contract.

Arguments Con This is the other side of the coin and should be recorded in the same philosophy as arguments pro.

Estimated Win Probability This, like the arguments pro and con, should be as objective as possible. It has nothing to do with your final decision or recommendation regarding development and submittal of a proposal. On the other hand, your estimate of win probability may or may not affect your final decision or recommendation.

Recommendation Here, summarize what you believe is the logical conclusion of the data you have analyzed and recorded and make your recommendation to propose or not to propose.

Remarks This area is used to supplement or explain any of the previous items or to add comments that are germane but not covered by any preceding item. Obviously, this may be supplemented by additional sheets, when necessary. The footnote is a reminder to do this also, suggesting that while some of the items can be estimated without regard to other factors, many cannot be estimated on an absolute scale but are necessarily estimated only after taking into account other items and/or specific conditions that are peculiar to the specific situation. Obviously, the final recommendation is the total of many factors considered together.

ROUGH ESTIMATES AND DRAFTS

There is a rough logic in the order in which the items are listed, but this is not necessarily the order in which you might enter your estimates and appraisals. There is nothing sacred about your initial estimates, and you may find it a wise procedure to make rough preliminary guesses first, making up an initial, rough-draft form as a

worksheet. You may revise that form several times, until you are satisfied that you have as accurate a set of estimates as possible. You
will probably make a more realistic and dependable appraisal by
doing this than by trying to create a do-or-die first effort.

UNSOLICITED PROPOSALS—DATA INPUTS

This discussion has been predicated on the assumption that a client
has issued a request for proposals, whether at the client's own initiative or as a result of your suggestion to the client to write out a
description of the requirement. However, it is not only when you
have received a written request for a proposal that you have the
opportunity to submit a proposal to a prospective client. If you are an
aggressive marketer, you are always alert for opportunities to offer a
proposal. Your input information may sometimes be only verbal
information gathered informally in conversation with the client and
perhaps from other sources, such as the client's brochures and
annual reports, from your own library and files, and/or from calls to
other people who can supply information. That does not make the
bid/no-bid analysis any less a valid and sensible procedure to follow.

Figure 4 is that of a form that is a useful guide in gathering information upon which to base a decision to write a proposal. There is
one item that may be misleading. It is this: probability of award. That
does not refer to your estimated chance for winning, but to the probability of the client awarding a contract to anyone. It raises the question of whether the prospect is serious and will, indeed, make an
award to someone or is soliciting proposals for some other reason—
for example, to get an idea of probable costs or to ask for a quotation
to see if management will approve an appropriation for the project.
On the other hand, this probability of award is usually a consideration only when the proposal is a fairly costly effort because it is possible in many circumstances to submit an informal letter proposal at
hardly more cost than that of sending the prospective client a printed
brochure. In that case, the question of how serious the client is about
making an award is of no real importance.

The Second Input

With the basic data of the bid/no-bid analysis at hand and a decision
to proceed with the proposal, specific data gathering and organization are next steps. The places from which to gather these are the

client's request and specification of work to be done, where there are such documents, and from whatever other sources you can find.

Some requests and their work statements are well organized and in logical order, but many are not. As one government proposal coordinator remarked, anyone can write an RFP but not everyone can write a good RFP. Many are vague, rambling, and almost incoherent. The same truth applies to information gathered from other sources. Sometimes you get a wealth of reliable and helpful information from other sources, but at other times the information is scanty and of doubtful accuracy or usefulness. Nevertheless, it is necessary to manage somehow to cope successfully under all these conditions and circumstances. A tool that has proved to be helpful in doing so is the checklist, which you should be developing as you study the requirement.

Figure 5 suggests one format for such a checklist. Actually, there are two or three lists: a list of items specifying requirements in the proposal itself, a list of items that must appear as elements of the proposed program, and, in some cases, a list of evaluative criteria specified by the client or inferred by you. (Federal agencies requesting proposals are required to use some set of objective criteria to evaluate and rank proposals and to tell respondents what those criteria are.) The same format may be used for all three lists, merely changing the heading in each case. Or you may prefer the design of Figure 6, which lists all the items on the same page, in parallel columns, with notes at the bottom or on a separate sheet. The

PROPOSAL REQUIREMENTS CHECKLIST

Item	Page/Par. nos.	Notes
State major project objectives	pp. 2, 11, 33–387	Milestone chart?
Describe relevant experience	p. 7, par. 2.3	List specific contracts and clients
List, describe entire staff proposed	p. 12	Needs 6 or more professionals; offer resumes of associates

Figure 5   One possible format for a proposal checklist.

REQUIREMENTS CHECKLIST

Proposal	Project	Evaluation
1. State major project objectives; pp. 2, 11, 33–37	1a. Must be in place by 30 DAA	1b. Understanding; 10 pts.
2. Describe relevant experience; p. 7, par. 2.3, pp. 8, 9	2a. Must be validated at 90/90	2b. Resumes; 20 pts.
3. List, describe entire staff proposed; p. 12	3a. Final report and manual due 120 DAA	3b. Viability of design; 30 pts.

Notes: (1) Milestone chart? (2) Specific contract clients. (3) Needs 6 or more professionals; offer resumes of associates.

Figure 6   An alternative checklist format.

advantage of this arrangement is that having the items side by side helps you to perceive correlation among the various items, a useful contribution. However, the format is not the important matter; the completeness of the listings is.

Why Use a Checklist?

There are several reasons for making and using a checklist, such as that suggested here, for even the small or informal proposal. Here are a few such reasons and the rationale:

1. For the vaguely written request, the checklist helps to bring order by revealing the focal points—what the client really requires—which are otherwise often buried in and obscured by the verbiage. It helps you to identify and define the true need of the client, even when the client is not entirely clear on just what that need is.

2. The checklist often brings anomalies to light, especially when various items are compared and correlated. These are important from more than one viewpoint: They are often the basis for identifying "worry items" and creating strategies. It is nec-

essary to identify and recognize these to design a practicable, efficient project; they are potent ammunition for developing competitor strategies, as you point out problems that competitors often miss or ignore.

3. Seeing the items arrayed in lists is a valuable aid to identify the most critical and most important points in both the project requirement and the proposal requirement.

4. Every requirement entails a deliverable item of some sort, but it is not always clear what that is to be. In fact, it is sometimes unclear whether the client knows exactly what is to be delivered. The checklist is a help in identifying this and even in helping the client understand precisely what it should be.

5. The list has another use, to be described later as a *response matrix,* a device that is instrumental in maximizing the technical rating given your proposal.

Graphic Equivalent

The generous use of graphics in proposals is a great asset for a variety of reasons (one proposal expert insists that at least one half the pages in a proposal must bear some graphic data):

1. It makes study and understanding of your proposal much easier for the client. Making things as easy as possible for the buyer is basic strategy for all sales activity.

2. Well-designed graphic devices displace more than their weight of text, making writing easier for the proposer and reading easier for the client. It also reduces the bulk of the product.

3. The right graphics can help you, the writer, gain a clearer understanding of the requirement and the best approach to satisfying it.

4. With good graphics, the writing job is made easier: It is much easier to write to graphic illustrations because explanations are made much simpler and require fewer words. The graphics also help you to get things into perspective. Thus, creating graphics before writing makes the writing easier and is useful in *preparing* to write.

In some circumstances, described later in this chapter, it is more effective to conceive one important graphic, a functional flowchart, before developing the checklists. The concept underlying this chart is that the work of the project is a flow process, a series of steps arranged in some logical sequence, wherein each step, proceeding from left to right, is a necessary prerequisite to the next step, and each next step is a step closer to the goal or objective of the entire flow. (It is essentially a storyboard of the requirement.) There is thus a "why" logic in such charts as you examine the flow from start to finish, and a "how" logic as you study it in the opposite direction.

Starting at the beginning, ask "why" of the information in the box and it should be answered by the information in the next box. In Figure 7, for example, the first box calls for the gathering of data. "Why" is answered by the next box, which explains that the data is needed to make an analysis of test procedures; why the analysis is needed is to validate the test procedures, and so on. Starting at the other end, "how" final delivery is accomplished is by getting client review and approval, which is gained by validation testing of the manual, and so on. These checks enable you to verify that your chart is complete and coherent, and to detect any deficiencies.

While not exactly an equivalent of the checklist, a well-conceived functional flowchart summarizes the project in the most efficient presentation possible—a single drawing or, in some cases, a set of several drawings—revealing all the significant steps of the project together with the logic of the design and delineation of the extremes, from the starting first step to the final step and the final deliverable items.

In fact, the functional flowchart of the project often comes to the client as a revelation, providing a much deeper insight into the requirement than the client had before and often revealing that the consultant has a clearer view than the client. The presentation of a really good functional flowchart is thus an impressive performance, and the client is often somewhat awed by the consultant's demonstrated vision, which can pierce to the heart of the requirement.

Figure 7 is a simplified example of such a functional flowchart. (For many projects, such charts may extend six feet or more and include more than one stream of information.) This simple chart explains how the consultant proposes to develop a set of maintenance procedures and appropriate documentation. In the actual case, such a project requires many more steps than those shown here.

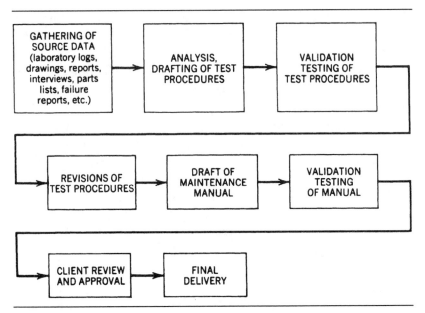

Figure 7 Simple functional flowchart of a proposed project.

There are two ways to graph this. One is to develop a fully detailed single chart that reveals all the steps in a single flow representation. The other is to offer a set of several functional flowcharts, one top-level chart showing only the main phases or functions, and the others each breaking out one of those main phases or functions in detail.

Figure 7 shows the flow as we normally read, from left to right, descending a step as we run out of space on the right, as we do in reading text. However, some individuals prefer to show the flow from top to bottom, as shown in Figure 8. This has some advantages, as well as disadvantages: It's easier to create, especially if you do not have a professional illustrator available and must create your own charts, and perhaps it is more efficient in its use of space. Too, this is somewhat cleaner—less cluttered and perhaps less confusing—than is the left-to-right presentation. On the other hand, since we all learn to read from left to right, it takes a little more adjustment to learn to read charts using this orientation.

The chart shown as Figures 7 and 8 is a functional flow in its simplest arrangement, as a purely linear and unambiguous process. In fact, few projects are that simple. Most processes entail iterations, options, and/or feedback loops, as in Figure 9, which is still relatively simple, but demonstrates that illustrating is a parallel or concurrent function, and editing creates a feedback loop for corrections and revisions.

A further refinement that makes the proposal easier to write, read, and understand is the addition of a milestone or schedule line to the functional flow, as in Figure 10.

Although these graphic representations are aids in both writing and reading the proposal, the initial goal of developing the overall functional flowchart is to aid you in at least four ways:

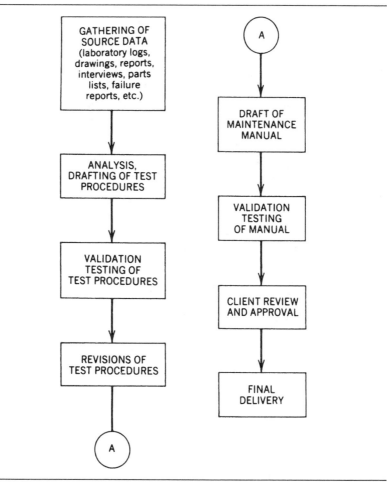

Figure 8   Alternative flowchart presentation.

- It is an analytical tool, helping you to understand the requirement.
- It is a design tool, helping you in designing the project to be proposed.
- It is a planning tool, helping you plan your presentation—the proposal itself.
- It is a presentation tool, greatly simplifying and easing the writing task.

Let's consider and explore each of these advantages briefly, after which we'll go on to discuss the alternative approaches to creating the overall functional flowchart.

The Flowchart As an Analytical Tool

Whether you develop the first draft of the overall functional flow of the project before, after, or concurrently with the development of your checklist, the act of compelling yourself to depict the flow process graphically enforces a discipline of thought—analytical thought—upon you. It is relatively easy to generalize in verbiage and even easier to deceive yourself about your understanding, but it is much more difficult to so deceive yourself when you try to portray the process graphically, in the logical order of "how" and "why" sequences. The result of that enforced study is to achieve a far deeper and clearer understanding of the requirement and what is needed to satisfy it.

The Flowchart As a Design Tool

The accurate analysis of a problem leads to the solution, to the design. Anomalies, inconsistencies, and non sequiturs so often

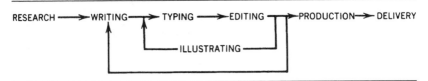

Figure 9   Functional flowchart with alternate flow paths.

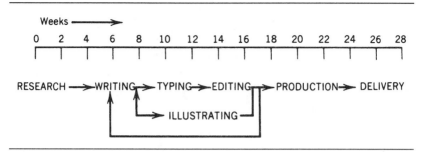

Figure 10 Functional flowchart combined with schedule chart.

found in proposal requests and their work statements are not always easily recognizable in text, especially in lengthy and complex statements. Perceiving these problems in text requires that you picture mentally the processes, as you read, and attempt to visualize all the phases and functions in relation to each other (flowchart the process mentally, that is!). This is difficult for any but the simplest situations and requirements, so it is not surprising that many logical absurdities elude us in reading proposal requests.

Once committed to presentation as a flowchart, those things show up quickly because the flowchart is a logic-based presentation. Redundancies, dead-end paths, and "you can't get there from here" anomalies fairly leap from the graphic presentation, guiding your hand in making the changes necessary to a successful and efficient design.

The Flowchart As a Planning Tool

In a sense we have already discussed the flowchart as a planning tool in considering its utility in planning the project design. But it is also a tool for planning the proposal itself, for it is the representation of the proposed project, and virtually everything in your proposal that pertains directly to the project is geared to that flowchart. The flowchart should be the unifying theme, and everything your words say should be entirely consistent with what the chart says graphically. You should therefore plan and outline your proposal with an eye on that chart so that your proposal *proves* your design and sells it to the client as most dependable, most efficient, lowest cost, or most whatever your chosen strategy dictates as sales arguments.

The Flowchart As a Presentation Tool

A well-designed flowchart is a good presentation tool, of course, as already noted. Properly designed, the flowchart (or any other graphic representation) will require little explanatory text. On the other hand, it should also serve as a reference for much of the related text, easing the burden of textual explanations. In fact, the really well-designed functional flowchart does far more than explain and support the basic design and schedule presentations. It also explains and supports arguments for the proposed design, for the features, for the costs, and for many other factors that must be explained and sold to the client.

Creating the Functional Flowchart

As in the case of text, a flowchart must go through at least one rough draft before being finalized, but there are alternative ways to create the first rough draft, depending on the quality and abundance of the beginning information available. In some cases, the client has furnished such detailed information and ideas about what is needed that a rough draft can be constructed by simply translating the words of the RFP directly into graphic form. In a great many other cases, this is not an option because the available information is insufficient or inadequate. Then, the draft flowchart must be constructed by more difficult and more time-consuming methods.

First Steps

The easiest case is that in which the requirement is conventional and uncomplicated, with established routine procedures and processes. For example, if the requirement is to develop a manual, conduct a survey, or write a computer program, the expert consultant who specializes in the appropriate field knows in advance what all the major steps and procedures must be. If you are faced with a requirement of this nature, you can begin your flowchart by first depicting the typical functions and phases of the work and then modifying your draft chart according to any special conditions, problems, or requirements of the client.

In another case, you may have little useful information beyond a definition of the required end result—a manual, report, computer program, installed system, training program, or other end product. In that case, you usually find the most practical approach to be one that starts at the terminus of the chart with a symbol or box depicting that end product. You then must work backward, using the "how" question to determine what must be the preceding step, and the "why" question to check and verify your chart. Figure 11 illustrates this. The requirement is for a survey to support a marketing campaign. The product required is a report of the survey, the details of which will be resolved later. But now a draft chart must be constructed.

The preceding steps are obvious ones, at least in general terms, although they will have to be adapted to fit the client's specific application and circumstances. But that will come later, in revising the chart. For now the need is to make a beginning, to take the first steps.

The steps leading to the development of the deliverable item are logical necessities. The survey report is created by analyzing the data; the data are analyzed by compiling them; the data are gathered and compiled by conducting the survey. And in the other direction, the survey is conducted to gather and compile the data; the data are compiled to be analyzed; and so on.

Asking these questions helps you construct the chart, and the answers help you examine the chart to be sure that all necessary steps are in there.

Working from Both Ends

In most cases, you know what must be at both ends of the chart because you must know what the required end result is to be, and you have knowledge of what you will have to start with. In the case hypothesized in Figure 11, the assumption was only that of a requirement to conduct a survey. Obviously, a client requesting proposals to conduct a survey must have given at least some basic information about the requirement, such as where the survey is to be conducted,

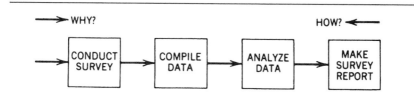

Figure 11   Beginning a functional flowchart: developing the chart from the end.

whether a survey instrument (e.g., questionnaire) is to be supplied or must be constructed by the consultant, and at least some other beginning information. Consequently, the actual case is likely to be more along the lines of Figure 12, where you can work from both ends to first define the requirement in at least broad functional terms, and then go on to refine the chart with all the details necessary to carry out a custom project. These charts are obviously so general that they can apply to virtually any or all such projects, and the typical consulting job is a custom project that is shaped and characterized by individual, often unique, needs and considerations.

Working with Open Ends

Despite this, the situation may arise wherein you do not have definite information as to a desired end product or even a specific starting point. This might be the case, for example, where you have met a prospective client, discussed a problem the client is experiencing, and been invited to or volunteered to submit a written proposal for solution of the problem. In such cases the client may simply say something to the effect that "I really don't know how to proceed, but I am willing to listen to any ideas you have."

This is a completely open-ended opportunity, and it is left almost entirely up to you to propose a project, based on your expert knowledge. You must decide where the project begins and where it ends, and you would presumably have asked the right questions to serve as guides in designing a project. This, however, does not change the basic situation: You still have the problem of making your prospective client understand what you offer and selling it effectively through a persuasive proposal. And you should still develop a functional flowchart to explain your plan and point out its merits.

The open-ended proposal is a double-edged sword. On the one hand, you have carte blanche to propose, and it may well be that you

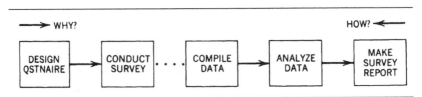

Figure 12   Developing the flowchart from both ends.

have no direct competitors for the work. However, you are still in competition, for you are even then competing with other possible expenditures of available dollars, and possibly with other departments and their needs. You must still convince the client that the project is of great enough importance to earn a priority for funding. If you go overboard in what you propose, you may price yourself out of the job. You may not necessarily lose it to a direct competitor, but the client may decide to postpone having the work done or forego it entirely. (However, it is also possible, if the client believes your proposed project too extensive and costly, that some of your direct competitors will then be invited to propose, despite the fact that the proposal opportunity resulted from your lead.)

If your work is such that you do essentially the same kind of work on each assignment or project, although tailored for each client, you may find it practicable to construct one or more standardized functional flowcharts that can be adapted to and customized for each individual project. Obviously, there is a great advantage to you if you can do this.

Which Comes First, Checklist or Flowchart?

There is an apparent anomaly here in that I have suggested both developing a checklist and developing a draft flowchart as a first step. The fact is that there is no flat rule possible for this because circumstances vary so much from one case to another, and circumstances often dictate what you must do first. If you have enough information to develop a substantial checklist of items, it is usually advisable to do that first and then utilize that checklist as an information source and guide in drafting the functional flowchart. However, if you have in hand a request and a work statement that are specific and detailed enough to lend themselves to direct translation into a functional flowchart, it may prove more fruitful to do that first. In the actual case, I find it possible quite often to do both concurrently, developing them as I study the request and correlating the two sets of results as they unfold. This latter course is probably the most effective, and I recommend it to you for all cases where you find it practicable. (The opportunity to correlate the two sets of results is especially helpful for finding potential problems as potential worry items and devising stratagems therefrom.)

A Common Dilemma

One question almost always arises at seminars during discussions of making and presenting such analyses as these: How much information can the consultant afford to offer in proposals? Won't unscrupulous clients steal the ideas and information from the consultant who is too generous with detailed information and use them in ways contrary to the consultant's own interests, such as doing the job themselves? Or, once the consultant has revealed how to go about it, won't unscrupulous clients pass such information on to competitors whom they favor?

Risks in Giving Free Samples of Expertise

This is a legitimate concern; such exploitation of consultants has happened, and this creates a dilemma: How much of your expert knowledge and analysis—the knowledge and skills that you normally sell—can you afford to reveal gratuitously without giving the store away, while still offering that minimum necessary to persuade the client to opt for your proposal?

It is worth noting here that a great many consultants worry about giving away any information free of charge, and some who write and lecture on the subject of consulting even offer specific advice on how to avoid giving away free consulting. Going to an extreme with this concern is the result of some sense of insecurity, the notion that your security lies in being secretive about your special work. (Some writers and lecturers who purport to teach consulting even offer lectures on how to make clients dependent on the consultant for all time to come!) These attitudes bear the seeds of their own defeat within them. If you are going to be effective in marketing your services, you cannot avoid giving away a few samples of your knowledge and consulting skills. Those samples are the very best evidence of your abilities, and it is difficult to convince any prospective client that you are the consultant to retain simply on the basis of broad claims to excellence as a consultant. You must get down to present-case specifics to be effective in selling yourself.

This is especially the case when it comes to submitting proposals. The typical client needs to compare you and what you propose with your competitors and what they propose. But that comparative evaluation goes far beyond a comparison of the universities you attended, the organizations that employed you, and the positions you held in the past. It is focused largely on what you have to say about the client's requirement and what you propose to do to satisfy that requirement. That is obviously the client's primary concern. If you avoid a technical discussion and projection of your approach to satisfying the requirement and ask the client to settle for a personal bio and set of claims to excellence, you might as well forego writing the proposal entirely and save your time and money. You cannot completely avoid the risk of having your brains picked unfairly. It's an occupational hazard, and you can only minimize it, at best.

This is rarely a serious problem when dealing with clients in the public sector—government agencies—but it can be a real hazard in marketing to the private sector, even with the largest companies. (I confess to having been so victimized twice, in dealings with large corporations in both cases.) In all fairness to such companies, however, it should be noted that when such things happen in dealings with large corporations, they are almost invariably the unscrupulous acts of individuals seeking personal advantages in their companies and are not sanctioned by management. Management, in fact, would be outraged by such actions and would probably make a serious internal investigation if charges of such depredations were made by any proposer. (Do note this for future reference, if you are or think you have been so victimized.)

Risk-Reduction Strategies

There is no absolute safeguard against this danger, but following are several measures you can take to reduce the danger of such unethical appropriation and misuse of your proposal. They are written here with formal multipage proposals in mind, but are equally valid for application to informal, letter proposals and can be easily adapted to use in those kinds of proposals.

LIMIT THE PROPRIETARY INFORMATION

Try to gauge and stay within that minimum amount of information necessary to demonstrate your competence and sell your approach and design. At least, try to hold back the most specialized and most proprietary information, information that is critical to success in the project.

COPYRIGHT YOUR PROPOSAL

Place a copyright notice on your proposal, and make it a prominent notice. The notice is not required, but it serves to alert readers to the fact of its existence. Near the bottom of an early page (usually the title page), type the words: "Copyright (date) by (your name)." The date used is usually the year or the month and year, although nothing prevents you from using a more specific date. You can use the abbreviation "Copr." or the symbol © instead of the full word "copyright," but the soundest practice is to spell out the word. One note: Many people follow this notice with other words, such as, "All rights reserved" and "Not to be duplicated without express permission." This adds no statutory protection but does advise readers what that copyright means and what your position is with regard to it. It won't protect you in a literal sense because copyright covers only a specific construction of words and not the ideas (you can't copyright the information), but it may discourage anyone tempted to misuse the information.

USE A NOTICE OF PROPRIETARY INFORMATION

Since the Freedom of Information Act has given anyone a legal right to demand and get a copy of a proposal submitted by someone else, the federal government has urged proposers to advise readers of any proprietary information contained in their proposals so that such proprietary and confidential information will be excised from any copy of a proposal made available to requesters under the act. It's a good idea to do this in the private sector, too. Here is what to do.

On the title page of your proposal, type a notice along the following general lines:

> The information contained in pages _____ and so noted is proprietary and is not to be revealed or utilized except for evaluation of this proposal and/or in performance of the services proposed herein. This, however, in no way inhibits the revelation and use of this information in behalf of the client in the event of award to this proposer.

Then you must indicate on each of those pages listed that material you claim as proprietary and so mark it "proprietary" and/or "proprietary and confidential."

Do not attempt to claim that the entire proposal is proprietary; that would weaken and possibly invalidate any later claim of rights to recourse, since there is always some material in your proposal that is obviously neither proprietary nor confidential. In this connection, however, it does not hurt to mark your entire proposal "confidential" and to make this marking a prominent one.

None of these are absolute guarantees against violation of what most of us believe to be an ethical code of behavior, but they do seriously lessen the danger in two ways: One, they advise those who might act innocently in revealing information they did not even suspect was confidential or proprietary; and, two, they serve notice on and should give at least some pause to those who might act wrongfully with full knowledge, but in the hope that their action will go unnoticed or that they might be able to plead ignorance, if detected.

Applied Planning for Letter Proposals

All of the foregoing pages of this chapter were written with formal proposals in mind. The informal proposal written as a letter of several pages is ordinarily written to propose a small project. Often it is written as a follow-up to an earlier contact, with no real assurance that the client will award a contract to anyone. These are necessary marketing activities and should be carried out as energetically and as often as possible, still recognizing that in such cases as these an elaborate study is not warranted and should not be undertaken.

On the other hand, you should not go to the other extreme and simply dash off a quick letter carelessly, for disaster can result from such a hasty action. Rather, you must judge the real prospect of winning some business and estimate the possible benefits, both immediate and long term, as in the probabilities of other, follow-on, business and/or other benefits. Therefore, do take advantage of all opportunities you encounter or can create by offering any prospect a proposal. Do prepare these proposals according to the same principles and philosophy followed in developing formal proposals for major contracts. But do scale the effort to the size and nature of the proposal, and do not make the mistake of one nationally known electronics/defense-industries engineering company that all but bankrupted itself by continually spending more to create the proposal than the total size of the possible contract that might result.

Let's go on now to talk about how to design a program.

Program Design

> Program design, a must of proposal writing, calls for clear, independent, and original thinking if the design is to be effective in creating a persuasive proposal.

Every Proposal Must Be Design Based

Understand, going in, that an RFP is a call for a consulting service. Clients do not request proposals when they want to buy proprietaries or standard services. They ask for proposals only when they need a custom service. Custom design is thus inherent in the concept of proposals. It is inevitable that a proposal must be based on and built around a specific program design. And it is usually the service that is the prime item proposed, although a product—for example, a computer program, manual, or report—is usually required to result from the service. Thus the design of the product, as well as the design of the proposed program to produce the product, is an essential element in the discussions. But even when R&D—research and development—is itself the principal service required, acceptable preliminary design goals and approaches must usually be proposed. Success in the competition thus depends on the client's reaction to your proposed design approaches.

Proposals Usually Describe Programs

Many proposals call for services in which products are incidental and of secondary importance. Still, there is a need for clear designs or, at least, clearly defined approaches to design of the program. Even proposing simple services, such as providing technical/professional temporary staff, must include a design for carrying out the obligation reliably. There are such concerns of the client as assurance of an adequate supply of qualified individuals and the ability to replace any without delay, if necessary. Sometimes the consultant organization must provide supervision and manage the individuals assigned, although they are working on the client's premises. It is also not unprecedented for the client to request evidence of the consultant's ability to recruit specialists or for additional specialists to be assigned to the project.

Program Designs Must Consider Possible Problems

You must think out all the possible problems, especially those that are likely to have been already perceived by the client, and provide for their solution in your design. Even when the client has not thought to ask for all the specific details, the more detailed your proposal and the more contingencies you cite and provide for, the more impressive and foolproof your design appears. The degree of detail offered is evidence of capability and careful planning, and is itself the foundation of a design or program strategy.

This means that the design or at least the factors surrounding it—approaches, design philosophy, and design logic—must be clearly apparent to the client. Mysticism and generalizations are not convincing or persuasive; they are not the evidence you need to sell your proposed program to the client. Only clearly stated details can prove the merit of what you propose.

Freshness and Originality

Comparing program design and program strategy to determine which is cause and which effect is a chicken-and-egg question: There is no firm answer. You may develop a brilliant design concept and derive a strategy from that. But you may do it the other way, too, evolving a strategy first and basing your design on that. The two are almost inseparable and evolve together in an iterative creative process, each influencing the other. But the question of creativity does enter into it, for it is possible to create pedestrian designs based solely on one's technical or professional discipline and classroom lessons, rather than on true creative inspiration. They are usually the conventional designs taught in training courses and often found in various texts and reference works, from which they may be borrowed.

Ready-made, standard designs exist in abundance, which is not a boon in proposal writing. Ready-made solutions arouse little enthusiasm on the part of clients, who have retained a consultant because they are convinced that they need custom services, calling for original thinking and creativity, a trait one expects in consultants. Such designs also bear little relationship to anything that might be called a strategy.

The Old versus the New

In proposal competitions, clinging to yesterday's solutions is likely to be effective in only those cases where no proposer has offered anything more imaginative than the tried-and-true design bromides. The client who was hoping to find something refreshingly new and different may sigh and select a proposal reluctantly. But there are many cases where a client, disappointed by all the proposals, simply rejects all and cancels or postpones the procurement. You cannot depend even on being selected as the best of a bad lot.

This is not to say that every proposal must be a display of creative genius or a bold departure. Quite the contrary, there are clients who prefer old, established approaches, regarding them as the lowest-risk, most reliable methods. Still, even they are attracted to fresh ideas, and it is possible to have it both ways—to be refreshingly original and yet not represent radical departures from convention. In fact, from a marketing viewpoint, it is far wiser to be evolutionary than revolutionary in your design: Being too different is likely to alarm any client, especially the conservative one.

Creativity

In 1899, Charles H. Duell, commissioner of the U.S. Patent Office under President McKinley, recommended closing down that office, saying that everything that could be invented had been. Ludicrous although that may seem today, there are those who still think that way, still showing that mental torpidity. Those lacking in imagination appear unable to understand creativity, even as exhibited by others. But that is not the only startling aspect of the subject. It also shows an almost inexplicable tendency by many to cling stubbornly to old, long-established biases, despite mountains of contrary evidence. So many "know" so many things that are not true. There is a great reluctance to give up long-held beliefs; many clients can be weaned from those beliefs only slowly and carefully.

Education versus Creativity

Studies of creativity turn up many surprises. One is that virtually all of us are far more creative as children than we are as adults because our educational systems and societal standards tend strongly to stifle our creative instincts and to actually wean us from them as we grow up. In fact, it has been shown that, in general, creative imagination is inversely proportional to levels of formal education. We tend to rely on what we were taught in all those years of inculcation in established doctrines and beliefs. We thus tend strongly to mistrust instincts and independent judgments, and to resist new ideas, no matter their origin. Probably a great majority of us operate on an unconscious conviction that having completed our formal education we have all or nearly all the learning we shall ever need. In fact, we are quite sure that most of the answers reside in those textbooks, reference books, professional papers, and other such documents.

Ironically, most such documentation is heavy with bibliographic notations and citations of many sources, so that it begins to reach the absurdity of an endless circle of scholarly authors quoting and citing each other's work, each to prove the soundness of his or her own work. This, presumably, enables an author to escape culpability (in the event of challenges) by assigning it to those presumably authoritative sources so painfully reported in the endless footnotes and other bibliographic annotations. And this only supports the tendency to resist new ideas, which for this purpose can be characterized as any ideas for which one cannot find suitable bibliographic citations to defend its use! Sadly, scholarliness is thus represented more often by knowledge of and research into others' writings than by independent and original thinking.

Conventional Wisdom

All of this is conventional wisdom with a vengeance, relying unquestioningly on consensus, rather than on independent reasoning. It is certainly the antithesis of innovation and originality. New ideas cannot survive in such an atmosphere. New ideas spring from a seedbed of questioning and seeking better ways, from a basic philosophy that there is always a better way. We need merely to seek it energetically enough, with open minds, and we shall find it, but comparatively few of us even make the quest.

Conventional wisdom bears within it its own negation, for in this fast-changing world—and the rate of change is itself increasing steadily—those ideas and methods that become conventional wisdom are already obsolete by the time they begin to assume that status. Thus anything that is recognized as conventional wisdom may be regarded with some skepticism.

Even the acknowledged thinkers of the world, our scientists, are susceptible to such human frailties. It was once a widely circulated idea that not more than six of the world's scientists understood the theories of Albert Einstein. That was something of a distortion. Most of the world's true scientists understood Einstein's equations, theories, and their subsequent implications well enough. What was probably true was that not more than a handful of the world's scientists believed Einstein's ideas and accepted the conclusions to be drawn therefrom. Those ideas were radical departures from old scientific beliefs. To accept Einsteinian physics meant giving up many treasured notions and a need to start over in some areas of scientific thought and speculation. For example, accepting the new physics meant abandoning a "natural law" that said that matter could neither be created nor destroyed. (The atomic bomb compelled changing that physical law to recognize that matter and energy are interchangeable.)

Even scientists, supposedly objective thinkers, have difficulty abandoning their conventional wisdom to embrace new ideas. Who wants to admit that he or she has been wrong for years, pursuing false gods?

Value Management (VM): Methodology for Creative Thinking

Value management is a discipline known also and perhaps more popularly by such other names as *value analysis* and *value engineering.* It sprang into existence in the engineering field as a result of serendipity, that mysterious art of finding what you didn't know you were looking for. (It is characteristic of creative minds that they tend to recognize opportunities in sudden and chance discoveries.) The problem with that name *value engineering* is that it tends to mask the fact that VM is applicable to virtually all human activity, that value can be managed in fields other than engineering.

The Origin of VM

During the Second World War, while utilizing substitute materials as a typical result of wartime shortages of strategic materials, a General Electric Company executive made the curious discovery that often the substitute material was better than the original material and often was less expensive in the bargain. He observed this to be a fact often enough so that he dismissed the idea of it being a freakish exception and thought it a phenomenon worthy of serious investigation. That serious investigation, carried out by General Electric engineer Lawrence Miles after the war, produced the original methodology, to which a number of enhancements and improvements have since been made.

The Essence of VM

In essence, VM is an organized method for creative improvement. Unfortunately, it is too often used only on existing products and systems in which so much investment has been made that it is often impractical to implement improvements. For example, in many manufacturing processes the initial investment in tooling (and sometimes in parts and raw materials inventory) is quite enormous. In such cases, a saving by design changes is often impossible because it would require retooling and scrapping inventoried materials. The write-off of these original costs would often nullify any saving. Thus, the benefits of value management have some built-in limitations when practiced in this after-the-fact manner. (VM can often tell you how it *should have been done originally,* but offers cold comfort now.)

Obviously, the better time for value studies is early in the design or predesign stages, long before front-end investments are made. This makes the method nearly ideal for application in the proposal process, where designs and design approaches are being penciled in as a matter of course. However, you need learn only a few of the principles and methods, for proposal purposes.

What Is Value?

The most difficult and least precise idea with which we must come to grips in making value studies is that of value itself—of what it is. Dictionary definitions require several column-inches of fine print, and yet they do not come firmly to grips with the definition and certainly do not produce an unambiguous definition.

Value is neither an absolute nor a constant. It is an abstraction, a notion, an idea. It changes frequently with changing circumstances. It is a noun that must be qualified by an adjective to have any substantial meaning at all. The value of the American dollar, for example, is quoted on financial exchanges every day because it is changing constantly as a *market value.*

Art works and many other objects have an *esteem* value, as well as a market value. Those values may be poles apart. You may, for example, have such esteem for the house you wish to sell that you place a far higher value on it than the market says it has. Or you may esteem and want something badly enough to knowingly pay "over the market" to get it.

A piece of jewelry may have an *intrinsic* value, which is the market value of the materials in it—gold, silver, and precious stones, for example—but it may also have an esteem value that is greater than its intrinsic value and equals its market value, as long as others esteem it equally.

So value is an elusive idea, and yet we do need to arrive at an agreement as to what we mean by the term if we are to agree on ways of managing value.

Fortunately, value management does not require that we agree on or even establish any absolute definition of value—intrinsic, market, esteem, or any other variety. In VM we can deal with value as a relative term only, without regard to its original idea, for the entire idea of VM is to increase or improve value, by whatever yardstick value is measured. VM can be used to improve esteem value, intrinsic value, market value, or any other value you wish to apply.

VM does this by making beneficial changes to one or more parameters of the item under study. The parameters of value are cost and utility. If we can make beneficial changes to either or both so that the result is greater utility at the same or lower cost, or lower cost at the same or greater utility, we have increased the value of the item. We might, that is, express value as a ratio of utility to cost. If we were to use a formula such as:

$$V = \frac{U}{C}$$

where V = value, U = utility, and C = cost, V becomes a figure of merit, directly proportional to the ratio Utility/Cost.

Neither of those two terms, *cost* and *utility*, is simple or absolute, however, as will become abundantly apparent in these discussions. There are many kinds of cost and utility, and an agreement on what these are is essential to an understanding of VM principles and methods. But before we attempt to come to grips with these terms and ideas, we must have a look at another fundamental of VM: the idea of *function*.

The Idea of Function

The heart of VM lies in the understanding and analysis of functions. It is on the basis of function analyses that VM studies begin, and it is on this basis that improvements in value are predicated. However, experience has demonstrated that a great many people with non-technical backgrounds have difficulty with the term *function analysis* and its significance. This may be due to the tendency of many technical professionals to speak in the jargon of their professions, rather than in lay English. Whatever the cause, it seems necessary to discuss this term and its meaning.

Like the term *value*, *function* is multifaceted in meaning. However, function is not as difficult to define as value is. It is fairly well defined by stating simply that *function* is what the item *does*. But that—what an item does—is itself at the heart of value and its management.

The first question VM asks of an item to be studied is: What is it? The answer to that question may be simply the proper or generic name of the item, so that it describes the primary purpose of the item. The purpose of the question is to identify the item and make its general purpose clear, in preparation for addressing the question of general function: What does it do?

How Many Functions or Kinds of Functions?

Only the simplest items have only one function. Most items do several things. A wristwatch, for example, indicates the time of day. But many watches also indicate the date, act as stopwatches, are miniature calculators, and are fine jewelry. So "what does it do?" is often not easy to answer unambiguously.

Identifying the Main Function

In value management, the question refers to the main (basic or primary) function. In the case of a watch, that is not difficult to see: There is not much question that the main function of a watch is to indicate the time of day. All those other things it does are secondary functions.

It is not always easy to decide what the main function is. Consider the typical accounting system used by businesses. Ask businesspeople what they think the main function of the system is and you will probably be advised that it is to "keep the books," "keep tax records," and other such ideas. The problem with these definitions is a common one: They strike all around the main function, but never come to grips with it because the analyst has failed to first answer the more basic question of why—why does the system exist at all? What is the basic *purpose* of the system? What *need* does it satisfy?

The fact is, in this case, that "keeping books" is how, not why, and keeping records for tax purposes is a secondary issue and has nothing to do with the main purpose of accounting. (The test is simple: Suppose there were no taxes to pay. Would you not still have an accounting system?) You do not keep a costly accounting system for the convenience or enrichment of government tax bureaus, but for the benefit of your own enterprise. Accounting is a management function and exists to aid management by providing information necessary to make sensible management decisions. Relevant information is a need of management. Even the fact of record keeping is not highly significant here, for that, too, is part of the means and not of the purpose, and the main or basic function always reflects the main or basic purpose.

Aids to Reaching Function Definitions

VM methodology includes measures that help in defining functions and expressing them properly so that they will be useful in the analytical process. Two important measures are these:

- *The Verb-Noun Rule.* Functions must be defined or identified by only a verb and a noun. (Occasional exceptions are allowed, when a verb or noun must be a compound word to be clear and definite.) The purpose is to enforce discipline and compel the analyst to make firm, unequivocal, and *objective* decisions. Otherwise, the definition of function is not at all useful.

- *Identification of the Purpose of the Item.* Ask yourself what is the true purpose of the item? Why does it exist? Why has someone gone to the expense of creating or acquiring the item? What is the need that must be satisfied by the item? This requires clear thinking and is at the heart of the discipline. Everything hinges on doing this properly, for everything that follows is based on this definition of main function.

Where the main function is not readily apparent, as in many but not all cases, the most useful first step is usually to identify that purpose by deciding what the desired end result of the item is to be. In the case of accounting systems, that is useful management information, information that enables managers to make wise and useful management decisions.

The second step is to find the verb and noun that express the definition most accurately and most usefully. And that may entail choosing either word first, depending on the individual circumstances of each case.

In this case, we have already decided on information, and it may be wise to use a compound noun, *management information,* since the unqualified word information is not likely to convey the full and proper meaning. In this case, it is also important to choose the verb carefully, for accounting is perceived by most people as a recording process, which is misleading for our purposes. Again, the recording and record keeping are part of the means, rather than the end, and it is important to take note of this. In fact, the most significant aspect of accounting's function vis-à-vis management information is that it is an active function and reports that information to the executives of the organization. Thus the definition ought to be "reports information" or perhaps "reports management information," or even "provides feedback," if that is more meaningful for you.

Secondary Functions

Secondary functions are of two kinds. Some are supporting functions, functions that are necessary to and support the accomplishment of the main function. Others are additional functions, not directly related to the main function.

In the example cited here, if the main function is to report information (to management), recording and record keeping are secondary functions, but they are also supporting functions. They are supporting functions because they are the means by which the information is accumulated and recorded steadily, day after day, so that it can be reported to managers periodically. (Monthly, quarterly, semiannual, and annual recapitulations and other derivative reports are made up for transmittal to the managers of most organizations.)

Other secondary functions, such as making up payroll checks, paying bills, invoicing sales, and calculating taxes, are not support functions because they make no direct contributions to the main function, although they are necessary functions and may make some indirect contributions to the main function. (The figures explaining and describing these activities are included in the reports, but the physical processing of the payments and other paper is not in support of the main function.) In all cases, you, as the analyst, must make a decision about which are the support functions and which are other secondary functions, not directly related to the main function.

The Significance of Distinguishing Secondary Functions

The purpose of the analysis is to prepare for the synthesis of a better way to satisfy the need. The front-end analysis is itself means and not end. Synthesis of improvement—a better system to propose to the client—is the end. It is thus critically important to identify the need that is to be satisfied, if you are to identify and define the main function accurately and accurately evaluate the contributions of secondary and support functions.

More specifically, once all of this is done, you can begin to make judgments as to how well the item performs its main function and satisfies the need. You can make judgments as to the usefulness or efficiency of supporting functions. And you can decide whether other secondary functions are necessary and make satisfactory contributions of some kind to the satisfaction of the need, for value improvement can result from a great number and a wide variety of changes. There are many deficiencies that you can find among existing systems and for which you would be wise to keep an eye open. Here are just a few of the more common ones:

Unnecessary frills. American designers especially appear to have a weakness for loading all their designs with bells and whistles—numerous secondary functions that have nothing whatsoever to do with the main function but only do the double damage of increasing cost and reducing reliability.

Reluctance to change. Even in this jet/space/cyberspace age, many virtual Stone Age designs are still appearing everywhere, reflecting the reluctance to change and, to a large extent, the reluctance of many to learn new things and keep up with their special fields.

The need to be clever. Unfortunately, many individuals design items as monuments to their own cleverness, rather than as the most effective and most efficient designs possible. The ego trip is understandable enough, but efficiency and effectiveness are the true goals.

The need to appear innovative. Many individuals build designs that are Potemkin villages in that they have the facade of smart modernity, but still reflect outdated thinking. The designers may recognize that times are changing, but they try to disguise old designs and old thinking with new paint.

Conversely, here are just a few of the ways to improve value in the synthesis of better methods and better designs (essentially, their message is *simplify*):

1. Eliminate unnecessary, trivial, unneeded, redundant, and/or noncontributing secondary functions.
2. Improve efficiency/effectiveness of main and support functions.
3. Reduce the number of steps required to carry out a function.
4. Reduce the human effort—labor—required to perform a function.
5. Automate functions and systems.

The Idea of Utility

The foregoing suggests clearly that value is represented by the ratio of cost to function of the item. Varying either, while holding the other constant, increases or decreases value. But there is more to consider than the main function alone, in most cases. There are such items as convenience or ease of use, efficiency, dependability, durability, and other factors that have to do with the quality of the item. Improving efficiency at a sacrifice in one or more of the other characteristics may actually represent a decrease in value. In fact, the term *function* is not entirely satisfactory as one of the terms necessary to define value. We really need another term, one that considers these other factors that refer to quality and efficiency, which cannot be ignored when trying to assess value, absolute or relative. The term I choose to use here is *utility,* and it is to include the main function, with necessary support functions, if any, and those other characteristics of quality and performance, referred to here.

That poses another kind of problem, however: How does one manage to somehow quantify these other factors? Without quantification of some sort, value management cannot have even the semblance of a science.

Cost Implications of Program Designs

It was this kind of need that prompted the Department of Defense some years ago to create the measure they called "cost-effectiveness" (which the press quickly referred to as a measure of how much "bang for a buck" a weapon delivered). One way in which value management copes with the need for quantification is *life-cycle* cost measurement, the estimated total cost of ownership over the entire life of the item, as distinct from the purchase cost. Life-cycle cost must include all the following costs:

- Acquisition or purchase cost
- Operating cost
- Maintenance cost

Operating cost may include labor, which is usually the highest cost factor in today's economic environment. It is always important in estimating cost consequences of a design to project the probable volume and level of labor required to implement the design operationally.

That does not necessarily mean that it is always possible to substitute equipment for human labor, even when it is technically possible to do so. Equipment entails its own acquisition costs, along with operating, maintenance, and depreciation or amortization costs. These need to be considered and evaluated versus labor costs.

Maintenance cost is not confined to machines and equipment. Even management systems and computer programs often require maintenance to correct bugs, to update the systems when conditions call for it, and often to adapt the systems to new developments and circumstances.

Another factor to consider where it is applicable is the end-of-life salvage value—what the remains of the used-up or obsolescent item are likely to bring in the marketplace—as an offset of those costs. Estimated with any accuracy, that total cost takes into account the other factors lumped earlier under the general category of "utility."

Impact on Proposal Strategies

The possibility of designing your program for lowest life-cycle costs without sacrifice of convenience, quality, or utility is an important point to consider in any proposal planning; it is a cost strategy that can be highly effective: Explain the idea of life-cycle costs, apply the concept to what you propose, and help the client assess the true costs of what you offer versus the costs proposed in competitive proposals. If you analyze and present your case well, you can demonstrate convincingly that the cost of acquisition is not the true cost of ownership. In this manner you can often overcome a competitor's advantage in offering a lower acquisition cost. Moreover, this concept of life-cycle costs is not confined to physical (hardware) items, but has validity also when applied to many computer programs, management systems, and other varieties of software.

To make the case effectively, you must do more than demonstrate the validity of the principle; you must apply it to the specific case you are proposing. You must somehow manage to quantify the various cost elements by identifying and unitizing each, and do so convincingly. Here, perhaps more than in any other place, you must present good evidence to prove your case, to show a logical and persuasive basis for your projections and claims.

Proposal Tactics

If designing for a low life-cycle cost is to be a strategy, tactics to sell the concept are necessary, of course, and they would normally proceed along the lines of any sales presentation: the promise of greatly to be desired end results, and then the evidence to validate the promise.

As a logical argument, a strong way to build the evidence, a first premise might easily be that of borrowing VM's basic idea that the item in question (whether it is a system, a service, a product, or anything else) is valuable only in what it *does* for the user, not in what it *is*. That's not a difficult premise to establish and sets the scene and tunes the client's awareness to the need to weigh results or utility in judging value.

The general evidence of an established idea and widely accepted truth is often a viable second premise. In this case, it might be the well-known principle of trade-off, sacrificing one thing to gain another. Here, it would be acquisition costs versus life-cycle cost.

There is a close parallel between this and the economics of developing a computer program. One can develop the program for either low acquisition costs (fastest, easiest way of writing the program) or for low operating costs (tightly written, hence economical of running time). One cannot have both, and if the computer program were to be run only once or twice, it would be sounder economic sense to write it as swiftly as possible for the lowest acquisition costs. But if it were to be run many times, as a more or less permanent element of the system, it would pay to spend more on its development so as to write a tight program and minimize the operating cost.

The mere fact of thinking it through and presenting this careful analysis and explanation is impressive to most clients, revealing as it is of the consultant's knowledge and the thought given to the client's need. But for maximum effectiveness, the presentation must go on to apply the principles to the case at hand, as noted earlier.

Suppose, for example, the requirement is for the development and presentation of a training program to be presented a dozen times. Here you have that same familiar problem. The program can be developed as an instructor-dependent course, one that requires presentation by highly qualified (but costly) instructors. That makes the course relatively inexpensive to develop (since it requires only a lecture guide, lesson plans, and a syllabus, usually, and depends on the instructor to provide the course content) but expensive to deliver.

The reverse is possible. You can develop a course that is dependent on autoinstructional programs, using videotape and other audiovisual materials, and bearing a light instructor load thereby. It requires relatively little live instruction and, in many cases, the instructor(s) need not be especially well qualified. The program so developed will be costly to develop and costly to produce but relatively inexpensive to present.

There is often a third possibility, one that is normally a compromise between these extremes: A "paper" autoinstructional course, as distinct from an audiovisual one, is thus relatively economical of both instructors and development/production costs, with a cost falling between those of the other two options.

Given such a case as this, your tactics would be to project and present the total estimated costs for each option and propose the one you think most economical, if achieving low cost is, indeed, your strategy. However, to be completely convincing, you must present your design factors and cost analyses in the greatest detail possible, even to the extent of validating your figures by citing the sources (e.g., quotations by vendors) and by offering specific physical evidence, such as catalog sheets and written quotations.

A typical cry comes up in the room when this strategy is offered to a group of seminar attendees: *What do I do when the RFP doesn't reveal how many times the course is to be presented?* (Actually, in many cases, the desired information is at least plainly implicit if not explicit.)

That is a typical problem, but it does not invalidate the tactic suggested here, and it does not call for asking the client to clarify the point. It's always risky to ask such questions, especially when proposing to a public-sector—government—organization, because the clarification is provided to everyone invited to propose, and you may be thus giving away to competitors much more than you get. There is a better way: Explain the options and the considerations important to the choice. Then you can pursue either of two courses: (1) Invite the client to choose one of the options, using the criteria you have provided to help guide the client in making the choice, or (2) if you think you can infer the information you need, explain the basic problem, make a recommendation of the option you recommend, but still offer the client the final decision or choice of options.

The opportunities to pursue this overall design and cost strategy are more numerous than you may imagine, for with a little imagination the idea can be adapted and applied to a great many custom developments.

This demonstrates a principle to bear in mind when developing a program design: Always consider the different possible approaches to the program, especially in terms of cost of each alternative, but consider all costs.

Giving the client a set of options and suggesting the need to make a choice often has another beneficial effect: It greatly increases the probability that you will be invited to visit the client for a discussion, possibly a presentation. My own experience has been that clients do not make independent choices easily. Once alerted to the options and alternatives, the typical client is usually motivated to want to know more—to discuss these with you, the proposer, to learn more, ostensibly—although I have always suspected that the client is really seeking guidance in making a final choice. In any case, your chances for success have suddenly increased many times!

Designing to Cost

Although VM has too often been used to close the barn door after the horse has gotten out, one of its spin-off developments has been the idea of designing to cost. That is, instead of permitting the design ideas to drive the cost, cost drives the design by basing the design studies on the question of how can the program be designed to achieve its goals for *x* dollars?

This poses another possible proposal strategy, suitable for certain circumstances. For example, when the client has specified or given clear clues to the available budget—and even government requests for proposals occasionally do that—design studies can be based on the question of what is the maximum program/benefits we can deliver for this figure?

Designing to cost utilizes VM in a special way, probably in the way it is used most effectively: VM considerations dictate the design by restricting it to the indispensable functions and the cost goals.

The Payoff Question in VM

Mechanical although it may appear when rationalized, the practice of VM is most definitely a creative exercise, and it is generally carried out by a team, working together in a brainstorming session that I prefer to refer to as "idea storming." One of the several benefits of such a collective effort to evolve ideas is the synergy—a result greater than the sum of its parts—that normally results from this free exchange of ideas, generated spontaneously and often triggering one another.

Having arrived at answers to such questions as "What is it?" and "What does it do?" (what is its main function?), there are other answers to be sought. But the most significant other questions, the ones that address the main objective of the exercise, are "What else would do that?" and "What would that cost?".

The answers to those questions point to the most effective and most efficient alternatives. However, remember that these questions are from the original value engineering/value management methodology, which was predicated on the assumption that the study was of an existing item, seeking to improve its value by reducing its production cost without losing any important function or characteristic—without, that is, losing utility or quality. But our case is different: We are projecting the use of VM-like methods to the development of original design. That requires a different approach. If we are to pose the question of what else—what to improve upon, that is—there must be some hypothesized design to improve upon or some alternative method for using VM principles in developing an original design.

Selling the VM-Analyzed Design

The idea of comparative VM analysis gives you a basis for sales arguments simply because it is much easier to sell against competition than to sell against prejudice. Merely offering something new and different and trying to prove its worth in an absolute sense is most difficult. You are flying directly in the face of that well-known resistance to change, especially that involving new and perhaps revolutionary ideas. Few clients want to be pioneers. It's much more effective to compare your own proposed design with less-desirable options to demonstrate superiority and sell your design. Obviously, you cannot demonstrate superiority without comparison. But here, where you are selling something unique—custom designs—you must create your own competitive item with which to compare your design. You must create what is sometimes called a straw man to be knocked down so as to validate your claim of superiority.

There are two ways to create or hypothesize the competitive model against which to sell your own ideas: One is to summon up some conventional design or method long used and make that the basis for your argument. The other is to estimate one or more approaches you expect your competitors to take.

That second course can be a bit dicey unless you have some substantial reason to believe that you know what your competitors will offer. (That is the case in many situations.) Unless you are reasonably sure of that, you will be well advised to follow the first course, a much safer avenue and usually a quite effective one. If your competitors are following the conservative convention and offering conventional designs, you are selling against their designs. But even if they offer innovative ideas, you are asking the client to compare theirs with yours and still selling against competition.

A For Instance

As an example of this strategy applied successfully, one consulting organization responded to an invitation from the U.S. Postal Service to develop on-the-job training for electronic and mechanical maintenance technicians in bulk-mail centers. (The students would have had training in basic electronic and mechanical technologies at Postal Service schools.)

The successful contender devised a training-development plan whose most attractive features were those that departed from conventional design and from the most disadvantageous methods of developing such training. Conventional maintenance training tends strongly to go overboard and provide far deeper and far more wide-ranging technical training than that required for maintenance. The successful proposal identified that as a typical weakness of maintenance training, pointing out the several disadvantages of doing that, and promised a design that would eliminate that problem. It proposed to train the technicians only in the precise needs of the equipment to be found in bulk-mail plants. But to make that promise convincing and persuasive, the proposal had to offer some credible method for doing what it proposed, for making good on the promise. It therefore offered a highly innovative idea, the application of a methodology it called "failure probability analysis" (invented spontaneously for the proposal), explaining what that was, the rationale for it, and how it would be used to identify and define precisely what training was required and how the training program should be weighted. And to sell that latter idea, the proposer developed another worry item for the client, a worry item that was itself the rationale for the proposed model of failure-probability analysis. That was necessary to convince the client that the innovative method was needed. It was based on the fact that much of the equipment in the bulk-mail center was hardly beyond the prototype stage and so had no operating history on which to base the maintenance-training design. The proposer stressed this problem and used it effectively to persuade the client to buy his solution. That points up another factor: You must do your homework—gather information on which to base your approach, as this proposer did in learning that most of the equipment in the bulk-mail center was of recent and untried design.

Offering such innovation has two potential hazards: (1) The client may be one of the conservative types who is apprehensive of change that appears revolutionary, or maybe for other reasons—perhaps there is a comfortably familiar existing system to be improved on or replaced but not changed seriously—the client is fond of conventional design and may be fearful of any but the slightest changes; (2) there is the hazard that the client may interpret what you say as an attack on or criticism of his or her existing system or of the method he or she believes in. Hence, you must be careful in your presentation that you do not unintentionally give offense by saying things that the client interprets as attack or criticism. (In general, avoid the appearance of criticizing, preaching, lecturing, pontificating, etc.) But you must also be careful to avoid appearing revolutionary. That threatens the client's sense of security, and you must never underestimate the prevalence of that insecurity. It lies buried not far beneath the surface in most of us and is quite easy to arouse, usually with disastrous results. In fact, you want to strive for the opposite effect—one of helping the client feel comfortable and secure in doing business with you.

There is something of an anomaly built into this. On the one hand, you want to be innovative and offer what someone else does not or cannot offer, selling your innovative design on the basis of advantages offered. And yet you want to avoid being too innovative or appearing to be revolutionary. But there is still another consideration, and that is how to gain the advantage of presenting your innovative design in a manner that commands attention and makes your proposal outstanding in that respect, as was done successfully in this proposal.

A Closer Look at the Creative Process

There are various theories of how the creative process works, and probably it works in more than one way. There are individuals, such as many prolific inventors, who can often come up spontaneously and consciously with useful new ideas on a regular basis. There are others who can do this only through laborious and lengthy processes. And there are those of us who develop new ideas occasionally and usually do not know how we did so or even think about it a great deal. (Unfortunately, on the other hand, many people develop great new ideas but never do anything about them, either through inertia or because of that common fear of having a new or different idea drawing sneers instead of approbation.)

Those who have studied creativity advise us that creativity is much more often a new combination of known ideas or components than it is a completely original idea or creation. Some even maintain that creativity is always a recombination of known factors or components into new patterns. There is a great deal of evidence for this notion. Certainly, examination of existing devices bears it out in a great many cases, because there are few inventions or other new developments for which the antecedents are not quite apparent. It was, for example, a long time before automobiles no longer resembled "horseless carriages" and that epithet was heard no more.

There is also much evidence that a major element in creativity is one's subconscious mind. In studies of creativity, three main stages appear to exist in most cases of creative breakthrough:

1. Concentration
2. Incubation
3. Inspiration

Again and again we learn from many of those with demonstrated creative powers that first they focus consciously on the problem until they have exhausted all possibilities that occur to them to be worth pursuing. Then they go on to other things and incubate the problem, which means that the subconscious mind takes over and works on it. And, finally, usually when they are relaxing at something with no particular heavy thinking going on, comes the inspiration or the solution flashing into their minds suddenly.

We are told that our subconscious never forgets anything. That appears to account for its great ability to work on problems. With greater recall, it has far more referents—relevant ideas—to consider than does the conscious mind. How often have you been frustrated by an inability to remember a name, title, address, telephone number, or other item that you ought to be able to recall easily, and then had it pop into your mind much later, when you are not thinking about anything related to it? That is an example of the unconscious mind at work, as is hypnotism and its effects.

There is no readily accessible direct link between the conscious and unconscious minds. Hypnosis is one way to establish linkage. Concentration—intense concentration—is another way. Hypnosis is based on maximum relaxation of the conscious mind. Evidently, it is that relaxation that opens the gate between the two and permits communication both ways. Ergo, the need to concentrate on the problem, incubate it, and wait for inspiration, such as waking up in the morning with the answer clear in your mind, a common and widely reported experience.

Other Analytical Tools

The checklists, the functional flowcharts, and the VM methods are all useful analytical tools, but they are not the only tools available to provoke introspective studies to analyze requirements and formulate strategies and approaches. Another used by some in proposal development is called the "why it can't be done" analysis. It can be utilized in virtually all cases, although it is more appropriate in cases where there is a complex or difficult problem to solve than when the requirement calls more for management and dependability than for problem solving.

"Why It Can't Be Done" Analysis

One major objective of this unusual analytical attack is the development of worry items through surfacing problems not readily discerned. (This, you may recall, is also one of the objectives of analytical tools and methods discussed earlier.) Addressing the requirement from this perspective calls for deliberately seeking out problems and looking for potential obstacles to the successful accomplishment of the mission, as you imagine the client or competitors might see them. This provides the seeds for technical and sales arguments (which are often the same, in proposals) by anticipating the objections and responding to them.

Personification

Some analysts find it useful to try to project themselves into the problem to gain greater insight into it. Charles Kettering (inventor of the automobile self-starter and the electric cash register, among other things), when he was working on improving the diesel engine and making it a more practical prime mover, imagined himself in the inner chambers of the engine, as he asked himself what he needed to work more efficiently as a diesel engine.

FAST Diagramming

Value management has developed its own special kind of functional diagramming, which it calls FAST diagrams, for *function analysis systems technique.* It consists of making the leftmost block represent the main function, following a "why" block, while supporting functions are represented in boxes proceeding to the right in order of priority. Other secondary functions, not essential to the main function, are placed above or below the line of flow in locations suggesting their roles in the item. Figure 13 illustrates this. Note that the main function must correlate with the purpose of the item. To further illustrate this, a simplified FAST diagram of the Postal Service proposal idea is offered as Figure 14. Note the how?/why? progression, including the why of the main function, answered by a block that describes the purpose of the item. The how/why questions verify the validity of the diagram, as they do in any other functional or logical diagram.

This is not all of it. There is more utility to the FAST diagram than appears here. Figure 15 illustrates this. A figure for whatever parameter is being addressed—money, time, materials, labor, or other—is measured or estimated for each function in the chain. This is done first for the original model or the one to which the proposed model is to be compared, and then to each alternative model. This enables the analyst to make comparisons and decide which is the best alternative.

Note that it is not necessarily greatest efficiency of cost in dollars that is the objective of the study. This kind of study may be undertaken to find the maximum design for the conservation of time, labor, materials, waste, or virtually any other parameter. You can use this to devise the shortest schedule, when that is what the client seeks, or any other parameter of effectiveness and efficiency. And to that end, there is a useful technique you may use to develop FAST or any other kind of diagrams with greatest convenience and efficiency. A case history will illustrate this, while it also illustrates the utility of VM to conserve schedule time.

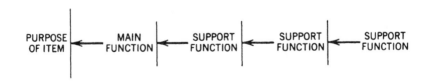

Figure 13 Principle of FAST (function analysis systems technique) diagramming.

Figure 14 FAST diagram of the Postal Service training proposal discussed in text.

An EPA Problem

The EPA, the Environmental Protection Agency of the federal government, was having trouble spending all the $10 billion it was authorized by Congress to give away in grants to communities whose water systems needed to be repaired, improved, and/or updated. There was a time limit on the program, but there were also requirements for qualifying each grantee and there were engineering/technical requirements. A Vermont engineering firm had been retained to help the communities make the engineering studies the program required with each grant application. Still, each grant application was taking far too long to get through the system, and it was almost a certainty that unless something was done soon the money would not be spent within the statutory time limit set for it by Congress.

Something had to be done to prevent the program from foundering. The Vermont firm was expert enough in the technical work that had to be done, but it did not have the kind of capability required to help the EPA speed up the program. The EPA decided that this was a case for VM, and assisted the Vermont firm by arranging for the services of three VM experts to help the firm streamline the grant process.

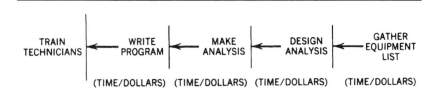

Figure 15 Further use of the FAST diagram.

After three days of work, the team—the firm's engineers and the VM specialists—reached the point where they had identified all the functions of the entire grant application process. At first they simply listed each function. Then they wrote each one out on a card. And finally they arranged the cards on a board, as a FAST diagram, in the order in which they occurred in the grant process, where all could study them.

That is a useful technique during the study phases of either or both existing designs and projected designs; it enables you to move the function cards around until you are sure they are in optimum order. That means that you need write up each function only once, instead of numerous times, using them as building blocks, while you design the FAST diagram.

In this case, once the cards were arranged in order on the board, the leader of the VM team began to question the engineers as to how long each step—function—of the process took, because the objective of this VM study was to reduce schedule time, not dollars. (Remember that the VM discipline can be applied to optimize any parameter.)

It was not long before it became apparent that the bottleneck and the chief problem lay in the many months it took the engineers in each community to write up the technical reports that were required by the grant regulations. In fact, they were taking from 90 to 180 days to write reports that should have been done easily within 30 days after the engineering work was completed, if they kept good logs and/or worked at their drafts while doing the engineering work, instead of wasting time later, gathering data that should have been easily at hand.

Once the problem was identified, the solution was apparent and not difficult to synthesize and implement. Obviously, something had to be done to aid the engineers in speeding up their report writing and to get the reports done with reasonable facility, but this was no longer difficult to perceive. And, once the specific problem—cause, that is—was identified, it was not too difficult to develop a solution.

Definition of the Problem

Note what happened in this case: Once the problem was properly identified and defined, possible solutions were suggested and, almost obvious, defined by the identification of the problem: Some measure to speed up the writing of the engineering reports was necessary. What remained was to identify and list the various options available to do this—there are several possible approaches to this—and then decide which was the best option to select and implement. These are the chief options available that are suggested by logical evaluation:

- Arrange for professional technical writers to work with the engineers and write the reports.
- Train the engineers in report writing.
- Design a standardized report form and require the engineers to begin completing the form earlier, as data accumulate.

The most practical and most easily implemented of these choices is the first one, although the idea of a standardized form for the reports is an excellent one and would probably facilitate their completion on schedule.

The Problem Is the Solution

The fact that the accurate definition of the problem contained the seeds of the solution was not a fluke. It is typical. In most cases, when the problem is truly identified or defined, it requires little additional analysis to identify the options available or to decide which of those options is the most practical and desirable one to select. Even in those cases where more than one solution appears to be completely viable and some further analysis is required to make the best choice, that is a relatively small task; the major task is done when the problem has been firmly identified.

The converse is that, until the solution or the direct approach to the solution is almost obvious, you may be assured that the problem has not yet been identified or defined properly. That should serve you as a guide in problem analysis, to help you to avoid confusing the symptoms or trivia with the true problem definition, so that you are guided to continue the analysis until you perceive the solution or the direct approach to it.

Confusing the symptoms with the problem is an easy thing to do, and we are frequently not conscious that we are doing so unless we have some distinct methodology to help us make the appropriate determination. Referring again to the EPA case cited here, to the federal agency officials the problem was that of getting all the grant money spent in time. That was the problem as they saw it and as they turned over to the Vermont engineering firm and the VM specialists assigned as consultants to the Vermont engineers.

On the other hand, that statement of the problem was not satisfactory for the VM consultants because it did not even hint at the cause of the delay in making the grant awards. (In the VM analysis, the first revelation was that the applications were taking too long to complete, which then led to the study of where the bottleneck was in the application process.) It was therefore not a statement of the problem at all, but it was the statement of a symptom, which demonstrated that there was a problem yet to be defined. Before the consultants could solve the problem, they had to know what the problem was, so problem definition was 99 percent of the task requirement. That also points up that a problem definition often depends on the orientation and the special interests of the individual offering the definition. Obviously, the problem viewed by those who address it by hiring someone to solve it is different from the problem viewed by those who must develop the specific solution. The interest of the EPA officials was to comply with the will of Congress and get the grant money allocated before the statutory deadline. That was all that really concerned them, so they cast their problem definition in those terms, in terms of their own need. The mission EPA set for itself was simply to find someone to solve the problem and turn over the search for a solution as a contracted project. A FAST diagram explaining that, from the EPA's viewpoint, would appear as in Figure 16. The main function was to provide engineering support to the grantees to help them accelerate the application and award processes, but the engineering firm required the VM support, so the EPA had to supply both, including the VM support as a secondary function that was in direct support of the main function.

This demonstrates that someone else's problem is likely to be only a symptom to you. The client is likely to cast the problem definition in terms of the desired result, as the EPA did (speed up the grant applications so we can get the program completed in time), but you must cast it in terms of a solution to the problem—what is required, specifically, to achieve that result.

This condition is not confined to clients who have problems that require technical analysis to develop solutions. It is equally relevant in those cases where there appears to be no question about the

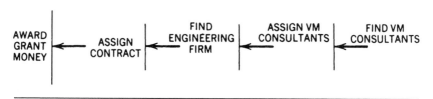

Figure 16   The EPA's FAST diagram.

solution—where, for example, the client wants a number of technical or professional temporaries to work on the client's premises and help develop a training program or a marketing presentation. Frequently, such clients need help in determining their true need; it is not always what it appears to the client to be, and you should never accept the client's view of the need or problem without examining it and giving it serious study. Part of your responsibility as a proposer is to analyze the requirement as stated and render an opinion on what the client needs.

There is always some element of risk in telling a client that he or she is wrong, of course, no matter how tactfully you say this, but you can gain a great deal of marketing leverage if you convince the client that you are about to save him or her from a disastrous mistake. It has been my personal conviction for some years, based on the experience of my own mistakes, that while you should be as diplomatic as possible, it is a great mistake to be less than honest with a client, especially about what you believe is in the client's best interests. It is almost always possible to do so without arousing hostility, if you handle the matter discreetly in your proposal.

CHAPTER
8

Writing, Communication, and Persuasion

> Writing is among our most ancient arts, the mark of civilization, in fact, and despite our best efforts, it has remained far more art than science.

The Role of Writing

The role of writing as a skill in proposal development has been deliberately downplayed in these pages until now. That was to bring sales and marketing skills to center stage, where they belong as the most important skills in proposal development. Writing skill must not eclipse or overshadow the role of marketing. Successful proposals are not merely written, but are developed as part of a lengthy sales/marketing process. Writing and its related functions are not the essence of proposalmanship, but they are the means. Now it is time to bring writing and other editorial skills on stage and accord them their due.

Sales and marketing know-how is necessary to the development of the all-important basic strategies and arguments of the presentation, but writing is the implementation of those strategies and arguments: Brilliant strategies and powerful sales arguments are seriously weakened by ineffective presentation, whereas even unimaginative strategies and pedestrian sales arguments can be made effective when presented well.

The Responsibility for Clear Communication

As a result of work by B. F. Skinner and other behavioral psychologists, modern educational theory and philosophy no longer place the total burden for learning on the learner, but impose a major part of the responsibility on the instructor or instructional system. The message is that it is the instructor or instructional system that is defective when the learner does not learn.

The same philosophy can be applied to writing. It is the responsibility of the writer to write clearly, unambiguously, and unequivocally, as perceived by the reader. Given a reader of at least average abilities to read and comprehend, and despite the frailties of language as a means for clear communication, it is at least as much the writer who fails when the reader gets a different message from the one the writer meant to send.

Recognize, therefore, that communication is a two-way process, involving both sending and receiving, and requiring success at both ends—success in forming and sending clear messages, and success in interpreting the messages as intended. It means also that it is not easy to write so that you cannot be misunderstood. It is difficult. It requires you to estimate the probable biases of your readers and to understand the connotations, as well as the denotations. It requires you to be sensitive to the emotional content of words, to understand, for example, the difference in connotation between *stubborn* and *determined*. Your choice of words affects your accuracy.

Persuasiveness in Writing

The purpose of all writing is to persuade. (An especially effective and successful sales manager of my acquaintance many years ago insisted that whenever an exchange between two people took place, a "sale" was made.) At the least, the writer wishes to persuade the reader to believe what he or she has written, and strives to be credible. However, that aside, it is obviously the objective of all sales presentations to persuade readers to believe and do whatever the sales presentation urges. We have, therefore, both persuasion and communication as primary goals of all writing, but especially of proposal writing.

There is a direct linkage between these two goals. Of course, it is necessary to communicate if you are to present those motivators and arguments that, you hope, will bring persuasion about. But there are other considerations that show the close linkage between these.

Belief versus Understanding

Disagreements are often dismissed as reflecting or due to "a lack of communication." The premise is that the parties did not understand each other. Of course, the opposite may be true: They may have understood each other all too well! Still, that cliché persists. The alleged lack of communication more often means that one party failed completely to convince the other—failed to make a persuasive enough argument, that is.

We have a common and probably mistaken notion about this too: We think that people tend to believe that which they have come to "understand." Therefore, the mistaken idea that a logical explanation will bring about understanding, and through that, belief and persuasion. Ergo, also, the "sincere" kinds of proposals that attempt to sell the proposer's services on the basis of pure, logical rationale.

Alas, the approach simply does not work because it has cause and effect reversed. People come to "understand" that which they have been persuaded to believe, and logic has nothing whatsoever to do with understanding unless the individual is prepared to first believe. Thus we have those who still stubbornly maintain that humans have not traveled to the moon or landed devices on Mars, but that the U.S. government has perpetrated a gigantic fraud for purposes of propaganda, and we still have those who refuse to believe that the earth is a globe. There are many who simply reject massive evidence that is contrary to their biases. They can never "understand" what most of us believe because they are unable or unwilling to believe. And, of course, all "understanding" is founded in belief somewhere in the chain of logic and reason, for we cannot verify everything personally. None of us has ever seen an atom, few of us have been to many of the more exotic places in the world, and even fewer of us have been to the moon. We accept these and many other things "on faith." That means that we find the individuals and/or organizations who report these things credible, and we believe their reports—or we don't.

Those who reject that which almost all of us accept and believe are among those characterized as part of what is termed "the lunatic fringe"—those individuals who are grossly and massively irrational by the logical standards most of us agree on and accept. To that extent they are extreme examples. But most of us are also irrational in many respects, albeit on a far less extreme scale. Most of us know very well the dictate of ordinary logic that belief arises from understanding. But emotional forces within us tend to demand that we "understand" that which we believe and to believe that which we prefer to believe because it satisfies some need within us. We thus have a rather profound ability to refuse to "understand" that which we prefer not to believe, as almost any argument on politics or religion will demonstrate rather quickly.

This is again testimony to the truth that we are far more creatures of our emotions than of our reason where our personal lives and desires are involved. This is the critical truth for sales and marketing. Every truly knowledgeable marketer knows that there is an easy way to persuade prospects to believe what you say: Simply tell them what they want to hear; they will always believe that, and they will require much less evidence to believe the promise they want to believe.

That is more than sardonic observation. It reflects, once again, the fundamental truth that the promise of great personal benefits is by far the one easiest to believe. The great motivators are emotional appeals. (Of course, there are exceptions: A relative handful of people are coldly logical, virtual human calculators, and all but immune to emotional appeals, but their numbers are so small that it is not worthwhile to worry about them as exceptions.) The most widely used motivators are promises of success, money, prestige, love, security, protection from life's harsh realities, and other "apple pie and motherhood" sweet dreams. There is some redundancy among these, in that all have some appeal to our common desire to feel secure. That is a basic need, and probably no one ever fails to feel a certain measure of insecurity in one sense or another. Perhaps the only difference is in what represents security to the individual prospect. Identify what represents security for your own set of prospects and you have the key to your own sales/marketing success.

Does This Apply to Proposals?

Many people find this easy to understand when applied to goods and services offered to the consumer for personal uses, but find it difficult to believe when applied to the business world. Are managers rational, impersonal, and unemotional when they buy for someone else—for an employer, that is? Are they psychologically and emotionally totally different as executives than they are as individuals? Or do they respond to the same motivators—motivated by consideration of their personal interests—when they are making purchase decisions for their employers?

The answer to that latter question is yes, of course. Most people in positions of authority and responsibility perceive their personal interests as very much involved in any decisions or actions they take in connection with their positions. In fact, executives are frequently far more emotion-driven when acting for their employers because they perceive their prestige and security to be even more immediately at stake than when they are acting as consumers. In that latter case, perhaps no one else will know of any fiasco resulting from a mistaken judgment. But in the case of acting for an employer, a mistake may have direct and potentially severe consequences to one's career. That concern can be a most powerful motivator.

Of course, there is the other side of this coin, too: An executive is an individual motivated by the desire for gain, as well as by the fear of consequence. Therefore, the possible career benefits of doing well and becoming a local "hero" in a wise and highly satisfactory procurement are necessarily possibilities to be considered most seriously.

The proposal writer should consider these, bearing in mind that all organizations, whether small businesses, huge corporations, or government agencies, are made up of people and that those people are motivated in their decision making by the same fears and desires as are others.

Generalizations are always hazardous, of course, and there is no single motivation that is equally effective in or appropriate to all situations and all individuals. To devise successful strategies and make effective appeals, especially those that hinge on judging the best personal motivators of those making the final judgments and decisions regarding your proposal, it is absolutely essential to know something about those individuals personally, as well as about the circumstances surrounding the requirement in general. The motivator that is effective with a conservative client—for example, fear of failure if an innovative approach is proposed—may fall flat with a risk taker who wants to draw attention from the corporate hierarchy by buying an innovative approach and launching a dramatic initiative in the company.

Credibility

Important though it is, the promise of a great benefit or avoidance of a great danger is not enough to bring results. The client wants to believe the promise, but needs some basis for believing it. It is a matter of credibility.

There are two aspects to credibility. One, there is the proof or evidence, discussed earlier. We are emotional creatures and far less rational than we prefer to believe, but we are not entirely irrational. No matter how much we want to believe the promise of some much to be desired benefit, we still demand at least a modicum of evidence to give us a basis for accepting the promise. So proof—evidence—is one necessary element of credibility, but there is at least one other: the presentation technique itself. Just as powerful strategies are weakened by ineffectual writing and uninspired strategies are strengthened by skillful writing, so the impact and credibility of any evidence offered is dependent on the skill with which it is presented. The language has its own profound psychological effect on the reader. And there are many traps for the unwary in this area of concern alone, including hyperbole and generalization as hazards to be avoided.

HYPERBOLE

There are perhaps uses in which hyperbole is an aid to the purposes of the writer. This is rarely the case in proposals. Here the claim of "many thousands," when it is obvious that the actual number must be only hundreds, is a disastrous faux pas. Here the use of Hollywood-style superlatives—*magnificent, enormous, sensational,* and others of that stripe—are deadly for your purposes. Such obvious exaggeration for effect is understood by moviegoers and tolerated, often even with amusement, because it does not affect the individual greatly and because there is little at stake except the price of a ticket and an hour or two of one's time. On the other hand, the aura of insincerity or frivolity is the diametrical opposite of the effect to be sought in a proposal and is not easily tolerated by executives to whom a proposal and the consulting project are serious business matters. It is therefore wise to avoid hyperbole and be as precise as possible—totally businesslike—in offering evidence of any kind in your proposals.

GENERALIZATION

Almost as deadly as hyperbole in its effect is the all too popular practice of generalization. This can stem from either of two possible weaknesses in the proposal effort and in writing technique generally. Often it is simply a technique of laziness and evasion. Rather than undertake the labor of searching out the details, the writer resorts to generalization as a convenient expedient. But sometimes it is an act of desperation. The writer has no real facts or reliable details and does not know where or how to seek them out, or what to do as an alternative to generalization. That is the result of a lack of imagination in writing—in writing research, to be more accurate.

NOUNS AND VERBS

Both hyperbole and generalizations may result from the too enthusiastic use of superlatives—adjectives and adverbs. Restricting function descriptions to nouns and verbs enforces a discipline and compels the value analyst to make a firm commitment to a precise definition. In writing generally and in proposals particularly, a similar practice of rigid economy in the use of adjectives and adverbs forces a discipline of thinking on you as a writer. That, together with a careful avoidance of generalizations and philosophical ruminations, invigorates your writing style and, more important, lends your writing an air of authenticity and authority lacking in writing that violates these principles. The result is a greatly enhanced quality of believability.

Don't Reinvent the Wheel

It is not always necessary to go to great pains to find and present detailed information. Quite the contrary, there are many ways to minimize the effort without sacrificing results. Following are several examples to illustrate what you can do with a bit of resourcefulness and enough energy, for which the moral may well be: *Don't reinvent the wheel.*

Written Procedures and Policies

In some cases, where the project requires that the consultant make many purchases as the agent of the client, the proposal request will require that the consultant include a description of his or her purchasing procedures and policies. The independent consultant or small consulting organization may very well not have a formal purchasing manual or written procedures, and thus some consultants are inspired to meet this proposal requirement with vague generalizations or even by ignoring it. (Surprisingly enough, even some rather large organizations do not have formalized procedures and written policies for these functions, other than a typed memorandum or two.)

In other cases, the proposal request may demand a copy of personnel procedures and policies, quality control directives, and/or other such formal documents. Again, the unwary proposal writer often responds, if at all, unsatisfactorily, with evasive pontificators that tend more to reveal than to conceal the lack of such formalized policies and procedures.

The sensible approach to meeting this requirement in such circumstances is to create the requested document spontaneously for the proposal. That document need not be a slick, bound manual, as it would be in a large corporation. It is perfectly acceptable for it to be a typed document bound with a staple or a standard report binder. Nor is it even always necessary to create such a document from scratch. You can often pick up another organization's manual or procedural/policy document to adapt it to your own situation and needs. It is wise to be alert for opportunities to acquire such resource documents for your own proposal library, where the document will be available when needed. There are also publishers who sell generic purchasing manuals, employee policy manuals, and other such publications as staples that you can easily adapt to your own needs. Your own stationer may carry such items; call and inquire.

Quantified Data

Sometimes a client will want some quantified data by which to assess your experience or other qualifications. In one case, a client seeking a technical writing consultant asked for an account of qualifications on a quantitative basis of technical documents produced—numbers of documents of each type, numbers of pages, and other such figures—rather than of years of experience. The consultant who wrote the winning proposal in this case did not have project histories recording those figures, but he did have a good recall of specific projects. He made a series of estimates, using a procedure that he believed produced results that were reasonably accurate, and reported the resulting figures. He was also careful to report the exact figures produced by the estimating method and did not round them off—a wise precaution. (Neatly rounded off numbers tend to be suspect—e.g., "97,850 pages" is far more credible, hence far more persuasive, than "100,000 pages.")

Resources

In proposing a large training project, for which the details of proposed curricula and supporting materials was a requirement, the consultant who wrote the successful proposal sent for the catalogs of textbook publishers, bought a copy of a government publication listing several thousand training films and other audiovisual training materials, and borrowed a dozen reference books from the nearby public library. Careful scanning and a large cut-and-paste operation based on the ideas gained from these sources soon produced a meticulously detailed program that left virtually nothing to be desired and cost very little to create.

The client was more than impressed with the magnitude of the documentation that appeared in the proposal, which was far more voluminous and detailed than the client had expected or than competitors produced: He admitted to being "overwhelmed" and even awed by the enormous effort the consultant had apparently expended on the proposal. Ironically, because the consultant had been so resourceful, the required effort was really not very great as compared with the impression of effort it created, and it was that very factor that permitted the consultant to include such a great volume of painstaking detail. That would simply not have been possible had he chosen to pursue all the details by the direct means of chasing down each item individually.

Again, this illustrates the principle that there is always an easier or better way to get something done if you allow your imagination some freedom from conventional thinking and if you remember that injunction to avoid reinventing the wheel. Even if the idea or information you need is not precisely what you want, it is almost always far easier to modify that and adapt it to your needs than to start from scratch to create a copy of something already in existence.

Today, with the wealth of information available so readily in cyberspace, it is almost criminal to neglect this rich source of information that should be consulted first, using the available search engines, before going to unnecessary trouble and expense.

What Is "Bad" Writing?

Writing "well" has more than one meaning, depending on application and kind of writing. Certainly it means something different when applied to the novelist than it does when applied to the scientist or philosopher writing in their respective fields. And it means something else again when applied to the writing of proposals. Therefore, while some of what is said here might have some application to writing in general, that is pure coincidence. We are concerned here only with what is "good writing" in proposals and related materials.

Mechanics

We will not dwell on the mechanics of using language—grammar, spelling, punctuation, and so on. The assumption here is that you can use the English language with reasonable fluency, that you know the basics of sentence structure and other basics of using our language, and that you will turn to reference sources and software programs for guidance in that area should you need it. However, there is at least one observation that should be made on the subject of usage.

What is acceptable usage in "creative" writing is not always acceptable in proposals. For example, the novelist may use sentence fragments—phrases lacking the essential sentence elements of subject and predicate, or even single words—as sentences, as well as perhaps many other violations of the "rules." Creative writers do these things to achieve special effects, and readers understand that. But in the formal business atmosphere of proposal writing, such uses are not normally acceptable. Proposals should be straightforward narrative expositions, conforming with normal rules of usage.

This is not to say that there is no need to achieve special effects, such as dramatizing certain points, in proposals. But there are ways to do this without violating accepted usage. "Bad" writing, as discussed here, has nothing to do with the mechanics of usage; it has to do with failures to communicate, failures to persuade, and failures to make an effective presentation generally.

Content and Organization (Not Grammar and Punctuation)

The chief proposal-writing fault that can be characterized as "bad" writing is not linked to usage, but to something far more serious. Even if your use of the language turns out to be a little shaky, a competent editor can fix that, but this other problem is not so easily repaired. It is the matter of essential content and organization. Editing cannot repair serious faults of content and organization, and even rewriting often cannot repair it, for the problem stems too often from such common faults as the following.

LACK OF SUBSTANCE

That "lack of substance" can mean any or many of a great variety of faults and conveys to the client such impressions, regardless of their validity, as the following:

1. Your proposal shows little understanding of the problem, as though you wrote it without having done a proper analysis or reaching a true understanding of what the client wants.

2. You have done only a superficial research job in gathering data and organizing a plan to be proposed. It lacks the necessary detail to permit a proper evaluation.

3. You really do not know what you are talking about because you appear to be insufficiently expert in what is needed or in the relevant field of technical/professional specialization.

4. Your proposal ignores what the client has requested and offers a plan that is inappropriate and perhaps is even an off-the-shelf plan offered to every client, no matter what the client has requested.

5. Your plan has good elements but is not well organized, perhaps not even wholly coherent, and is thus all but impossible to understand, much less to evaluate.

6. Your proposal is spotty and inconsistent in coverage, having some excellent parts, but then having some sketchy and vague areas too, often in important matters. The impression this creates is that you are expert in only some of the relevant areas and lacking badly in others.

This adds up to a serious deficiency of content. It says to the client that you are not responsive, for one reason or another—that you do not understand the problem, are not qualified to solve the problem, did not make a serious study of the requirement to develop a plan, are incapable of developing a plan, are reluctant to commit to a serious proposal effort, cannot think well, or suffer other deficiencies.

LACK OF COMMITMENT

Unless the client happens to be acquainted with you from some past relationship, you will be judged primarily on the impression your proposal makes. If your proposal conveys an impression of one of the aforementioned deficiencies, it is unlikely that you will ever be favorably regarded by that client. Moral: If you cannot or will not make a serious commitment to the proposal and all it requires, you are much better off to "no-bid" the request and wait for a more favorable occasion to respond.

A Simple Definition of Bad Writing

Note that the postulate of a client's opinion or reaction is based entirely on the client's perception of truth. In fact, for our discussion here, bad writing is simply writing that fails in its purpose. Even if your proposal contains an excellent plan—perhaps even a brilliant one—it is the impression your proposal makes on the client that will influence him or her. Poor writing of itself, in the sense of awkward usage and dull rhetoric, may have a bad effect and cast you in an unfavorable light in general terms of your professional image: The client tends to believe that as a competent professional, you ought to be capable of expressing yourself clearly, if not eloquently, and the failure to do so creates a seriously adverse impression. But entirely aside from that, there is the potential disaster of failing to bring the client to complete comprehension of everything your proposal offers. Obviously, even the most brilliant plan and most impeccable credentials will avail you nothing if the client does not understand and perceive them. Ergo, the importance of logical and coherent organization and the other essentials of clear writing. And that includes the use of every legitimate communication device you can muster in behalf of delivering your messages with absolute precision, such as an abundance and free use of well-conceived and well-executed graphics, tables and matrices, explanatory titles, headlines, captions, and any other aid to understanding that you can conceive. Once again: Make it easy for the reader.

Writing Is More than Words

It is important to perceive in this that "writing" does not refer to the use of words alone. That touches on one of the common faults exhibited by some writers. They seem to use tables and matrices only when the data to be presented appear to be those that are usually offered in tabular or matrix presentations—when tabular and matrix representations fairly force themselves upon the writer—and they often turn to graphics only as an afterthought, tacking them onto the manuscript in an obvious outboard design.

To use the various communication aids effectively, they must be integral to the proposal, conceived as part of the basic vehicle of communication. Specific examples that appear in these pages may be borrowed to use as models.

Organization

There are a number of classic patterns in which to organize information, including these basic ones:

1. From the general to the particular, usually in a growing pattern of focus on specific detail until the final point is made, in a kind of deductive-reasoning process, establishing the principles and then applying them to a specific case

2. Particular to the general, in a kind of inductive-reasoning process, discussing the specific data and inferring the principles or main message from that

3. Chronological, from beginning to end (present) or from end to beginning, tracing the course and process

4. Order of importance or priority, lesser to greater or vice versa

It is even possible to mix these methods, although inadvisable if it can be avoided because it is simpler to be coherent and easier on the reader if you pursue a consistent pattern of organization. Mixing them successfully—without causing confusion—calls for expert writing skills and careful control of the reader's orientation. This is probably a task for the experienced professional writer and a dangerous adventure for anyone else.

Each of the methods has its pros and cons, according to the circumstances and objectives of the application. Explaining how you've arrived at a given approach is often best accomplished by a chronological presentation that describes how you evolved the ideas for your approach over some series of experiences or earlier achievements. On the other hand, sometimes it is best to trace the history of your approach by describing it and presenting the chronology in reverse, from the present to its origin. You must judge for yourself which is the more effective method.

Similar considerations apply to all other methods. You, as the writer, must be the judge of the best method of organizing discussions. But note this: Each discussion (sometimes that means each section or chapter of a proposal, but it may mean a discussion within a section) must be organized along some logical path. You need not use the same method for each discussion (and probably will not wish to do so) as long as you make clear to your reader what the pattern of presentation is to be. You must be careful never to leave your reader behind as you move on with your material. That means that you must observe a few absolute basics of what is taught in formal classes as composition.

Composition Basics

You must create and maintain a unity of thought in each element—sentence, paragraph, subsection, or other. A sentence deals with one main idea, and another sentence is required to present or discuss another, different idea. Similarly, paragraphs and other elements are each about some single subject or thought.

You must keep the reader posted on what is to be the subject of the paragraph, subsection, or other element. The paragraph opens with a topic sentence that telegraphs the meaning. (Study any of these paragraphs as examples.) For a larger element, you probably require an introductory paragraph, although in some circumstances that may be a single sentence. A book, on the other hand, generally has an introductory chapter, as does a formal proposal of any size.

When you are through with the subject and ready to go on to another one, you must begin another paragraph (or larger element), with its own topic sentence (or introductory element). But you must provide a transition or *bridge*. That is a device that indicates the logical connection between the elements to maintain the continuity of thought. Otherwise, the reader is almost sure to become confused— disoriented, in fact—and find it difficult, if not impossible, to follow your argument. Study these paragraphs as examples and note that there is more than one way to create those bridges. Probably the best way is to prepare the reader in advance for each transition by ending each element with an introduction to the new subject to come, using some linking word or term (one that the reader will immediately recognize in the next paragraph) to make the connection. But you can also do this in reverse, beginning a new paragraph with a reference in your topic sentence to the preceding one. Headlines, titles, and captions can be used to help with this also, and we will discuss those, too.

Headlines and Captions

It is often painful for me to observe the missed opportunities resulting from the failure to use headlines, titles, and captions freely enough, and especially from their unimaginative use, so that they do rather little to help the writer even communicate, much less persuade. Headlines and captions, such as titles of figures and tables, offer you many special opportunities to communicate and to persuade, as well as to help the reader follow the transitions of discussions from one subject to the next. Titles and captions should be used to help create that logical transition, but not as the main or sole vehicle of transition. The headlines, titles, and captions can be employed to do a great deal more to help you create a proposal presentation of great impact and powerful persuasion.

Briefly, a headline is used to introduce each major new subject; titles are used to characterize and introduce new chapters or sections; and captions are used to introduce figures, tables, matrices, and other such special presentation devices. (At least, that is how we shall define those terms here.) They aid the reader in following the continuity of thought and perceiving the main topics. And, at least in theory, they also help the reader find his or her way back to specific portions of the presentation that they wish to read and review again. (In fact, the array of chapter titles, headlines, and captions in the table of contents ought to offer an approximate outline of the proposal.)

Unfortunately, too often writers are satisfied to ask nothing more than that of their titles, headlines, and captions, which results in such unimaginative headlines as "INTRODUCTION" and "GENERAL," and captions such as "Table of Characteristics." And aside from the failure to exploit the titles, headlines, and captions in some positive way, such unimaginative uses often fail even in their most basic purpose of serving as guideposts for the reader simply because the words are so trite that they do not register with the reader.

At the minimum, strive to use fresher words for your titles, headlines, and captions, to help gain the reader's attention and make the reader aware of them and what they say. Find fresher words to say "introduction" and "general background." Find something more imaginative than "schedule" to introduce a milestone chart or table. Find words that not only explain and telegraph major topics and presentation aids, but also sell them by stressing the positive aspects— the benefits they promise the customer and the evidence that validates the promises.

Tables and Matrices

Tables and matrices are basically devices for listing items that have some coherent interrelationship, making their presentation in a listing or cross-listing more efficient and more useful than a mere narrative description. *Matrix* refers to a tabular presentation in which items are so related that some correlation among them exists, whereas a *table* may be a simple listing, as illustrated in Figures 17 and 18.

Something more than mere identification of the table should be reflected in the table captions (called *legends*). Remember the nature of a proposal: It is a sales presentation, and every opportunity to sell should be exploited. (This is explained by specific examples in a later chapter.)

Graphic Aids

Illustrations are a must for most proposals, making things as easy as possible for the prospect. Bear in mind that the client is probably faced with a number of proposals to review—perhaps as many as 30 or 40, in fact. While there may be some psychological leverage in

EVALUATION ITEMS	POINT VALUES
Understanding of requirement	10
Approach:	
Analysis	5
Viability	5
Success probability	5
Qualifications:	
Staff	20
Organization	10
Management:	
Project organization	15
Methods and procedures	20
Costs	10
Total:	100

Figure 17 Simple table. Criteria for evaluating proposal.

what appears to be a substantial proposal (one of many pages), the client does not look forward with any great pleasure to studying a great many words to evaluate what you are offering. Most clients are appreciative of anything that relieves the necessity to read a great deal, and that is precisely what a good illustration must do.

The purpose of an illustration is to convey meaning, and an illustration should be used wherever words alone are not really ade-

PROCUREMENT METHOD	NUMBER OF ACTIONS	TOTAL $(000)	% TOTAL
Fixed price	345	7,653	11.6
Cost plus	123	12,565	19.7
Two-step	12	1,645	3.6
Sole source	4	983	1.8
Set-aside	3	765	1.3

Figure 18 Matrix-type table. Analysis of procurement methods.

quate—that is, where an illustration can convey meaning more accurately or more efficiently than can words alone. In writing a proposal you must often present both concrete ideas and abstractions, which means that you must present both images and concepts. Words rarely convey an image as well as an illustration can because words are merely symbols that must be interpreted by the reader. They cannot deliver as accurate an image as a single drawing or photograph can. When an accurate and precise image of the object must be conveyed, words simply won't do; an illustration is required. On the other hand, words will suffice to convey an *idea* or *concept.*

Abstractions present a more difficult problem in communications. The idea of a vector, for example, which is the result of two or more forces acting in different directions on an object, is almost impossible to explain properly to a layperson without an illustration, and the vector in electrical applications is more difficult to explain than is the vector in mechanical applications. (In fact, it is generally introduced first via mechanical theory for that very reason.) For abstract ideas, analogies that employ illustrations are often the only practical solution. They convey the meaning much more effectively than does text and require far less text to do it.

Analogies, Metaphors, and Other Imagery

Illustrations are not necessarily drawings or photographs. There are verbal illustrations, illustrations by referents, or illustrations by textual analogies that the reader can easily visualize. In describing the earth as shaped somewhat like an orange, round but flattened slightly at the poles, the writer takes advantage of the fact that the word *orange* is a familiar referent: Everyone or almost everyone in the western world knows what an orange is and how it looks, so it is safe to assume that a drawing of an orange is not required to explain the concept. Nor is it necessary then to offer a drawing of the earth, if explaining its oblate shape is all that is desired.

The use of imagery reaches its peaks in fiction and in popular nonfiction, but ought to be limited rather strictly in proposal writing to that which is absolutely necessary to present concepts. It is far too easy, when employing imagery, to become fanciful and be carried away into that very hyperbole and other exaggeration cautioned against earlier.

Focus on Word Choice

Purple prose—use of words found only in unabridged dictionaries (and even then, often archaic terms no longer in popular usage), banalities, pompous verbal posing, and the deliberate use of relatively unknown words when simpler words are readily available—is bad writing. A study of such prose, including some of the kinds of prose that have become known as bureaucratese, often reveals an interesting fact when it is translated into simple English: Such prose often says absolutely nothing, and only the fact that it is in such convoluted form conceals this truth from the casual reader. Ironically, the deception is not even deliberate, usually. Some writers appear able to conceal even from themselves the fact that they have nothing to say and offer a storm of obscure words and pontifical prose that, they manage to convince themselves, has some significance.

The causes of this are usually any of several, at least these:

- The failure to truly think out what you want to say, the main point or objective of the writing, or what the presentation strategy is to be.
- The failure to plan ahead by outlining, preparing notes, gathering the data, and, as noted above, truly thinking about the subject before attacking the keyboard.
- The failure to do adequate research, an absolute must. You cannot write a really good 5,000-word proposal by researching and gathering 5,000 words of information. You must usually have gathered many times 5,000 words of source data, from which you garner the 5,000 words you need.
- The notion that glib writing can substitute for substance.
- The fear of making clear and unequivocal statements, dreading the possibility of being challenged and, even worse, proved to be wrong. (If the writing is sufficiently ambiguous and tortuous, especially if it is such that what it actually says is by no means clear, there is less possibility of being challenged successfully. Ergo, consciously or unconsciously, the writer who lacks confidence in his or her information tends to write badly.)

The federal government, because it is a huge bureaucracy and bureaucrats are what they are, is a frequent offender. To do something about the thousands of pages of paper on federal procurement, Congress created the Office of Federal Procurement Policy within the Office of Management and Budget. A team of people spent over five years combining, reorganizing, and rewriting some 60,000 pages of regulations, bulletins, and memoranda, creating a single, unified, and allegedly simplified set of procurement regulations, the Federal Acquisition Regulations (FAR). A team of people were employed in this effort, each member required to undergo a week's special training course in writing, in the interest of producing documents in clear, lay English. One resulting regulation, typical of the entire result of all that enlightened labor, repeats an earlier one that says that a contractor may not charge the government twice for the same thing, but it takes a full page of small print to say it, which is an almost verbatim repeat of the regulation that was to have been simplified. Unfortunately, that typifies the results of an expensive effort. (There seems to be no cure for bad writing in bureaucracy.)

The late Bertrand Russell, a British theoretical physicist, mathematician, and philosopher, was one of the world's great thinkers; he was also a prolific writer, and often a sardonic one, reporting his observations with obviously great amusement. He observed in one of his philosophical writings that it was his great good fortune that everyone knew him to be an educated man so that he had no need to impress anyone and could afford to write in the simplest of English. His many writings are a model of clear and simple English, written solely to inform the reader, with no thought of self-importance. He had, as noted, risen above that need.

That is the lesson to be learned about writing simply and clearly: Keep in mind your reader and your reader's needs only. Give no thought to yourself and your image. You can't get a better image than that of being a clear communicator.

The Matter of Readability

Readability is a matter closely associated with our notions of what is good and bad writing. But it is a subject with a surprise or two. One of those surprises is that most of us, even those fortunate enough to have graduate degrees, are most comfortable reading at about an 8th-grade level! (That is approximately *Reader's Digest* level, often used as a standard.) In fact, while almost all of us are high school

(12th grade) graduates and many of us also college graduates, a great many of us do not read at all well beyond that 8th-grade level.

It is more than a surprise: It is a shock that Americans generally, even the most educated among us, are poor readers. (It was once my sad duty to advise an experienced lawyer—most reluctantly, I should add—on what a certain clause in a contract meant.) But it is a fact, and we know that the 8th-grade level is the most appropriate one for even formal documents.

Early systems for measuring readability and adjusting it were crude and unwieldy. The computer has come to the rescue here again, with suitable software to aid that process.

The Special Problem of Letter Proposals

The letter proposal is a special problem in several ways. It is appropriate when the project is small or the possibility of an award is unknown: You write an informal letter proposal as follow-up marketing, perhaps to qualify the prospect. This does not justify the investment of a great deal of time and money. Yet, if the proposal is to be received seriously, it is necessary to make all the major points and present all the sales arguments here as though it were a large, formal proposal. The scale of the presentation does not change that; no presentation should be made without a serious effort to make a sale.

To complicate the problem, it is more difficult to be concise while still delivering all the necessary messages and making all the important points effectively. The medium imposes its own restriction. Don't be misled about this: It may appear to you that the letter proposal is easier to write because it is much shorter, but it is difficult to be brief and yet effective.

Do not, therefore, impose unnecessary restrictions on yourself in writing a letter proposal. I have suggested two to four pages as a typical size for a letter proposal. That is by no means a standard or a rule—a letter proposal needs to be as long as necessary to do the job; you may make it any length, and you may include appendixes, exhibits, or other enclosures to supplement it. Moreover, you certainly may use headlines, captions, and illustrations of any kind, as in a formal proposal.

Of course, that two- to four-page letter proposal may require that you write eight, ten, or more pages first and then boil out the excesses to arrive at a four-page proposal. The best writing results from relentless editing.

On the other hand, you find that the simple, little letter proposal you started out to write proliferated quickly into something more formidable, not truly a formal proposal, yet a bit oversize for a letter proposal. In such case, you may find it helpful to simply add a few refinements such as a title page and table of contents, treating the presentation as a semiformal or miniproposal.

What you call it is not important. What is important is simply that you make all efforts to create as effective a presentation as possible. The only "rule" is that you do what is necessary to win.

CHAPTER 9

Special Presentation Guides and Strategies

> The objective of a proposal is not truth but persuasion.

Sales (Main) Strategy versus Presentation Strategy

Successful presentations do not happen by chance. They are the result of successful presentation strategies implemented effectively. The proposal is itself a presentation, a sales presentation. Sales strategy—also referred to as win strategy, main strategy, and capture strategy—however, should not be confused with presentation strategy. They are not the same. The presentation strategy is conceived and employed in direct support of the sales strategy, but it is essential to distinguish between the two.

The sales strategy is based on that critical consideration that you hope and expect will motivate the client to accept your proposal and award you the contract. The presentation strategy or strategies—you may use more than one—is designed to give your proposal maximum impact in several respects. Your cost or technical (program) strategy also may be your sales strategy, but it is unlikely that even the most clever presentation strategy would of itself win the contract. Rather, you should expect a successful presentation strategy to help make your entire proposal, but especially your sales strategy, an effective one by achieving all of the following objectives:

- Dramatize and focus attention on your main sales strategy.
- Capture the reader's (client's) attention.
- Generate and sustain the client's interest.
- Make it easy for the client to read and understand everything your proposal has to say.
- Inspire respect for your professionalism.
- Make your promises and proofs totally believable.
- Make your appeals persuasive.

Focusing Attention on the Main Sales Strategy

This is the most important point, since it is the basis of your entire effort. It must therefore drive the presentation strategy. If you plan to capture the contract by virtue of a superior technical plan, for example, it is that claim you must focus on. But you must focus on something more specific than the claimed superiority of your plan: You must pin down the specific benefit of the plan, that which makes it superior. Will it save the client money? Reduce costs? Boost sales? Be a beneficial new breakthrough? Solve some distressing problem? Decide what the benefit is and explain just how your plan will accomplish this result and deliver the benefit. Make absolutely sure that the client knows precisely what you promise and your rationale for promising it. And, of course, be sure it is some important benefit. But there are other objectives, as discussed next.

Capture Interest

You cannot focus your client's attention effectively if you do not have the client's full attention. Otherwise, the client may very well go through the motions of reading your proposal, out of an obligation to do so, but with considerably less than full awareness of what you say in those pages. More significant, the client may read your proposal without paying special attention to those things to which you need to direct the client's special attention. Your strategy may fall flat simply because it does not impact on the client's consciousness—that is, it does not strike a nerve.

TV commercials offer many object lessons in using opening "hooks" to grab the prospect's attention. Movies and TV plays, for example, open with some exciting or curiosity-arousing scenes to capture the viewer's attention and only then switch to the commercials, titles, and other less fascinating material, hoping they have now made the viewer captive.

There are a great many ways to capture a reader's attention, but you would not want to resort to some of the more bizarre devices that might capture a client's attention, for you must command the client's respect for you as a professional, while your representations must also be credible. Therefore, while you must find ways to command attention, you must do so in ways that are entirely in keeping with your profession and the serious image you must maintain. For example, while it is perfectly acceptable to use simple line drawings to help present a message and/or gain attention, there is some potential hazard in using cartoons for the purpose, and you would probably be wise to refrain from doing so. But there are many other factors of importance to consider in connection with getting attention.

Sustain Interest

Getting the client's attention is only a first step in getting your message across and supporting your sales strategy; you must do whatever is necessary to *hold* that attention by appeals to the client's direct interests. It is futile to get attention without arousing genuine interest.

You can see such common mistakes made frequently in commercial advertising and sales presentations, even those emanating from large and successful organizations. Here are just a few examples.

IRRELEVANT, TRIVIAL, AND EVEN CRYPTIC ATTENTION GETTERS

Frequently some clever device is used to get attention, but too often the attention getter is something that has no direct relationship to the main subject matter (or, even worse, to the prospect's interests) and so the prospect's attention is gained only momentarily and interest is not even genuinely aroused, much less sustained. One advertisement, for example, that is supposed to appeal to meeting planners and persuade them to book their business meetings into the advertised conference center uses a modest-sized headline that urges the reader to set the highest standards for his or her conference, and then identifies the hotel and conference center by name, with a woodcut type of drawing, saying very little else. Actually, it is stretching things to even class this as an attention getter, for it is not that at all. It doesn't do anything to command attention and does even less to arouse the reader's interest with its almost meaningless hints of quality and prestige.

Even worse, perhaps, is the advertisement of a well-known super-corporation that tells you that your computer "should look you straight in the eye." Only with careful reading of the body copy do you discover that this refers to the dubious benefit of having the monitor mounted on a swivel, so that you can change its angle for your comfort. This is a useful feature, but hardly a major one and certainly not one important enough to be the focus of the sales strategy, as this advertisement attempts to make it.

REVERSE ORIENTATIONS AND EMPTY CLAIMS

An even more serious and more common mistake is the offering of items intended to command attention that do not do so because they offer the prospect no inducement to pay even slight attention to the message. Instead of being oriented (appealing) to the interest of the prospect, they are oriented to the interests of the advertiser. Typical of these are those appeals that stress how great the advertiser is as the reason to favor that advertiser with patronage.

In a specific case, a speaker advertises his services by headlining the claim that no other speaker has his credentials; he features his picture prominently but fails to give the reader even a hint of what he speaks about, much less what his speaking does for the client or even what those vaunted credentials are.

Another firm offers what it claims are "high-quality, low-cost data switches," going on to pile a few more unsupported claims on top of that, but offering not a shred of evidence to support the claim of high quality, although it does offer what appears to be a rather reasonable price for the unit.

THE DEADLY SIN OF CLEVERNESS

The irresistible urge to be clever and to parade one's cleverness is the force underlying many of these disastrous approaches to presentation strategy. Puns appear to be the most tempting Loreleis that attract copywriters. For example, one presentation that is aimed at selling a sophisticated laser printer promises that "with the right tools you can nail the competition" and then supplies a photo of an assortment of worn hammers and other hand tools, along with an assortment of nails, to complete the pun. Still not satisfied, the writer goes on to beat the pun over the head a bit more by showing readers how to "hit the nail on the head," and so on. Finally, if readers can find the patience to plod on and endure more of this heavy-handed and irrelevant humor, they may finally discover what the advertiser is selling and learn of some promised benefits, but they seem rather anticlimactic by now.

All of these are guilty of the most common sin of sales presentations: They are so busy being clever, boastful, and self-congratulatory that they neglect their real job—selling the product or service. They forget to think in terms of the client's interests—what the client wants and what they can do for the client. That is all the client is or should be interested in—not in how clever you are, in being entertained, or in any of the many elaborate, but unsupported, claims you might make.

The evidence of capability, dependability, honesty, and other attributes necessary to make the sale are of interest, but only if and after you have presented the one thing the client really wants to know about: what you are going to *do* for him or her. If the client is not interested in gaining a benefit you promise, what difference do all your other representations make? None, of course. Those claims are part of the proof, at best, but what are they proving, if there has been no promise?

One fallacy responsible for this disaster of presentation writing is the mistaken notion that claims alone are sales arguments and will be perceived by the client as promised benefits. In fact, some writers of sales copy appear to believe that the more extreme and "louder" the claims of excellence are, the more powerful and persuasive those claims will be. Of course, the opposite effect usually results: The more extravagant the claim, the more unquestioning credulity, even naïveté, it demands of the client. Even if the client were to be swayed by your excellence rather than by some specific promises of benefits, you would have to prove that your claims of excellence were justified before they could help you. Obviously, the louder the claim or the more extreme a promised benefit, the greater the proof required.

Make It Readable and Clear

Anything the client finds difficult, troublesome, or inconvenient in any way discourages the sale. It is for this reason that so many sales appeals include preaddressed, postage-free response envelopes and order cards, many of which require only the recording of a credit card number, along with a name and address, to place the order. My own mail-order office-supplies vendor asked only for the name of my bank and my account number to open my charge account, for example, and we have done business together for more than a dozen years since. But I have not opened an account with a local supplier who invited me to do so, because he would require me to fill out a long and complicated form to establish an account.

Many examples used here to illustrate the principles of sales presentations were drawn from conventional advertising because they are convenient and obvious examples, but everything illustrated has equal application to proposals. However, probably nowhere is the application to proposals more significant than in the case of making the presentation easy to read and understand. A prospect might fight through a few hundred words of less-than-crystal-clear prose if the interest aroused were great enough, but asking the client to struggle through several dozen pages of stilted and difficult copy is another matter. Many clients faced with that prospect will give it up with a sigh and turn to the next proposal in the stack.

But even that is only one consideration with regard to readability and clarity. There is the matter of communication per se. Your text can be quite accurate and thorough, although difficult to read, but prose can also be easy to read, while failing to be clear. For the client to either be puzzled by your meanings or misinterpret them is just as deadly to your purpose as discouraging the client's reading entirely. You can't sell something to the client when the client does not understand what you are selling or your arguments.

Therefore, we are actually talking about two separate matters regarding writing per se, and they are not directly related to each other. Keep your organization of material, usage of the language, and chosen vocabulary as simple as possible, for ease of reading. Do not, however, permit this to interfere with providing comprehensive and accurate coverage, including all necessary detail and getting the facts straight.

Most of us have several personal vocabularies: We speak with one, we read with another, we write with still another, and we think with yet another. The size of individual vocabularies varies widely, from as few as 5,000 to 10,000 words to as many as 40,000 to 50,000 words. If you are one who is blessed with a large vocabulary, don't permit that blessing to become a curse by trying to utilize all of it in your writing. The real blessing of a large vocabulary is that it is an enormous asset to your reasoning powers: People with large vocabularies tend to be superior thinkers. Reserve most of that large reserve of words to help you think, and try to keep your writing vocabulary between that 10,000- and 20,000-word range. You won't be writing down to anyone in so doing, but you will be helping yourself develop a brisk and highly readable style.

Promote and Maintain Your Professional Image

Professionalism has probably as many meanings as *consulting* does, varying according to the individual's bias. Some individuals believe that only physicians and lawyers are true professionals, but we also make reference to "professional plumbers" and other tradespeople as professionals at whatever they do. However, because consultants provide custom services, are often entrusted with the client's proprietary and confidential information, and are often given almost carte blanche freedom on the client's premises, the relationship must be based on great respect for and trust in the consultant.

That requires a highly professional image. For our purposes here, the term will refer to an image that goes beyond mere competence. It must be one that reflects an aura of authority in your special field, but it must reflect also dignity, integrity, dedication to your profession and to your clients, and trustworthiness in general.

Should your handling of the proposal undermine that image, it will be a direct threat to your prospects for success. To protect your image, and even to enhance it, you must use the language well and, at minimum, avoid such faux pas as misspellings, ungrammatical constructions, and humorous misuses of language. The latter types of error convey a strong image of a semieducated individual, which is hardly what you would wish. But even when you know better, you can make such gaffes unconsciously in writing.

Such mistakes in usage can result in deadly unintended humor detected in proposals, as in the case of a writer attempting to explain that the proposed design for a piece of equipment that would serve a critical function would have a "backup" set of duplicate components. Although he meant to describe circuit redundancy, he spoke of the "duplicity" of the design. Another writer, explaining the system by which identifying numbers would be assigned to a large array of terminals, introduced the subject with a headline that announced the subject to be discussed next as the "assignation" of the terminals.

It's a good idea to have someone edit or review your copy to detect errors and do something about them. But it's even more important to avoid trying to sound impressive through the use of language. The way to be impressive in your writing is by offering clear and accurate expositions with ample details. Unlike generalization and philosophizing, which come across as opinion, of course, carefully detailed exposition reflects knowledge and competence.

Make Your Presentation Believable

The offering of comprehensive and accurate detail is itself a powerful influence in making your arguments credible, but there are other elements that contribute to credibility. One is the avoidance of hyperbole and superlatives generally, as discussed earlier. The subdued tone of description that consists of nouns and verbs and shuns all hyperbole is a tone of quiet confidence, and clients find that reassuring.

Frankness, such as ready admission that problems may be encountered (as compared with the soothing syrup of bland but unsupported promises that some proposal writers offer), is equally reassuring because it, too, reflects self-confidence.

Still another reassuring sign is to either avoid making your promises appear too extravagant or, if you believe that you can deliver truly remarkable results and wish to promise them, be sure that your proofs do justice to the promises and are in proportion to them. But, again, no verbal "shouting," if you want to be taken seriously.

Many writers have great difficulty in disciplining their writing this way; sometimes their enthusiasm is a bar to this. However, it is always a good idea to have a competent editor go over all your copy and excise all the extravagant prose that is not substantiated factually. Your editors should be instructed to do just this.

Make Your Appeals Persuasive

Persuasiveness of your appeals has been an underlying theme throughout this chapter so far and is a general objective in all those other discussions. However, it is useful to single this out and establish it as a special objective to remind yourself that all sales presentations have persuasion as their ultimate objective and that everything in the presentation must contribute to that ultimate goal.

A Few Tips on Writing Style

Part of the image you should be trying to develop and nourish should be that of being thoroughly businesslike, which means alert, efficient, and direct. And to encourage that image in your writing you should develop a crisp and vigorous writing style. Here are a few tips to help you do that:

- Write in active voice, rather than passive voice. That sentence is itself an example of active voice. "Proposals should be written in active voice," would express this idea in passive voice.

- Use frequent stops in long sentences—colons, semicolons, and dashes—especially for interjections. Long sentences with stops are the same as a series of short sentences and are as easy to read.

- Get to the point. Ideally, telegraph the point when you introduce the subject. Or, at the least, march directly to the point without detours.

- Make positive statements as often as possible, and avoid over-qualification of statements. Even when you are not certain of the point or cannot state something as an absolute fact, you can present it without sounding evasive and indecisive. Whether you are actually indecisive is not the point; it is whether you are *perceived* as being indecisive that is the point. For example, instead of the multiple and redundant qualifications and evasions often found in research papers—"The indicators tend to suggest the possibility that . . ."—say something such as, "The possibility is that . . . ," which commits you no more than the first version does, but sounds far more authoritative and positive.

There is no doubt that, to the sensitive and perceptive reader (and you must assume that the client is that kind of reader), your mental set manages to come through between the lines of what you write. Unless your writing reflects confidence in what you say and propose, it is unlikely that the client will have that confidence. Confidence, or the lack of it, is something you share with your reader, whether by intent or otherwise.

The need is for balance: confidence, promises of desirable results, clear expression, easy readability, and positive statements, balanced by reasonableness, accurate detail, and substantial evidence to support all promises and claims.

Applying the Ideas

Now let's look more closely at how you can apply these ideas to the specific proposal elements. The suggested general proposal format, with brief notes explaining the main section titles and subheads, is presented in Figure 19. This is a generalized format and must be adapted to each specific situation, for some situations may require large, formal proposals offering entire teams of specialists and their services, whereas others will be one-person projects. Still, whether you offer only your own resume or those of a dozen associates or employees, the principles are the same: The client wishes to know how well you understand the requirement in its essence, how you propose to satisfy it, what your management philosophy and procedures are to be, what your technical/professional qualifications are, what your specific experience is, whom to call to verify your experience and competence, and other such matters.

The Matter of Headlines

The format shown in Figure 19 uses generic titles and headlines, rather than those that should be used in actual applications. A presentation strategy must be developed for each individual case, according to the merits and circumstances of each individual case, but there are some principles that should be followed for all cases. One of these is that to maximize the effectiveness of the presentation strategy everything, including titles, headlines, figure captions, and table captions, should be conceived and composed for maximum contribution to the selling process.

The first section or chapter of a proposal is normally introductory, introducing both the consultant and the consultant's understanding

SECTION I: INTRODUCTION

ABOUT THE OFFEROR	A brief introduction, with your basic qualifications; scene setting; explain that details come later
UNDERSTANDING OF THE REQUIREMENT	The requirement in essence, with obscuring trivia stripped away for a clear view of the central need or problem; sets stage for next section

SECTION II: DISCUSSION

THE REQUIREMENT	Elaboration of the understanding, bringing in related considerations, establishing basis for analysis
ANALYSIS	Exploration of all possibilities, surfacing of probable problems (potential "worry items"), pro and con discussions of alternatives
APPROACH	Logical conclusion of analysis, pointing to synthesis of design, identifying approach opted for and justifying decision; scene setting for next section

SECTION III: PROPOSED PROJECT

PROJECT ORGANIZATION	Description of team and/or task organization to implement approach opted for; logic of organization explained
MANAGEMENT	Principles, quality control, cost control, other controls and administration
PLANS AND PROCEDURES	Procedures, forms, standards, criteria, liaison with client
STAFF	General description of self, associates, and/or others
DELIVERABLE ITEMS	Qualitative and quantitative specifications in detail
SCHEDULES	Chart, tabular, or milestone presentations
RESUME(S)	Employees/associates who will provide services

SECTION IV: QUALIFICATIONS AND EXPERIENCE

RELEVANT CURRENT AND RECENT PROJECTS	Tabular data, brief descriptions, names, phone numbers of clients
RESOURCES	Facilities, equipment, personnel, other relevant resources
REFERENCES, TESTIMONIALS	Supplement to project histories, including certificates, letters of appreciation, other such evidence of merit

MISCELLANEOUS

FRONT MATTER	Title page, table of contents, response matrix, executive summary
APPENDIXES	If/as needed

Figure 19 Brief definition of each proposal section and subsection.

and preliminary appraisal of the requirement. Almost everyone therefore titles it "Introduction," "General," or other such generic title, thereby missing an early opportunity to make an important point. To get the maximum benefit, compose a title that reflects some important benefit, theme, or virtue of what you are offering. Work at making this an attention getter, while it still relates directly to your offer. And if you can tie this in to somehow support your main strategy, so much the better.

Here are a few examples, some hypothetical, some drawn from real-life case histories:

"A New Broom" (The proposer was bidding for an ongoing contract and had gotten word that the client was dissatisfied with the incumbent and wanted to make a change.)

"A Different Kind of Service" (You have something new and different to offer, especially when that is central to your strategy.)

"A Fresh Viewpoint" (The proposer believed that he could offer an entirely new and far better approach to solving the client's problems.)

"Solutions Designed to Match Your Problems" (A proposer stressed custom-designed services.)

The subheads, listed generically for the first section as "About the Offeror" and "Understanding of the Requirement," should likewise be tailored to the situation. "About the Offeror" might become "Scientific Programming Specialists—We're Small Enough to Make You Our MIC (Most Important Client)" or whatever suits your situation and your strategy. The idea expressed by that latter example of a subhead is a reminder that large consulting firms often tend to treat small contracts, especially from small clients, rather casually. It is thus a powerful strategy to do more than overcome the possible liability of being a small consulting firm and convert that into an asset. But if you are a large organization, you might stress that with something such as "We're Large Enough to Have All the Resources to Satisfy Your Need."

"Understanding of the Requirement" should likewise be changed to something more pungent, such as "The True Problem" or "The Essence of the Requirement." However, although those are improvements over the generic subhead, even those can be further improved by composing a subhead that is more directly relevant to the individual proposal. If the proposal were in response to that hypothetical client with a problem of unreliable reports coming from the computer, the subhead might dramatize the requirement in its essence along the lines of "Finding the Cause of Unreliable Computer-Generated Reports Is the True Requirement." That, of course, is almost ideal for laying the groundwork to discuss the requirement in the second section of your proposal, which might then get a title following up that idea, such as "Seven Possible Causes for Unreliable Computer-Generated Reports" or "The Most Efficient Way to Track Down the Trouble" and even a subtitle, such as "A Discussion of Analytical Techniques and Trouble-shooting Methods." The various headlines in your discussion section would then guide the reader through the main points and main logic of the approach and the methodology you propose there.

Of course, if you happen to have a special technique or special resources, such as a proprietary program, to help you do this job more efficiently or more effectively than anyone else can do it, by all means strengthen those by working direct references to and indications of those into your headlines and titles.

When to Write the Headlines

The kinds of headlines just listed are actually abstracts or summaries of sales arguments. There are two ways to develop them. One way is after the body copy is written, which is probably the way most headlines are written. The other way is to prepare a highly detailed outline and convert major outline topics into headlines.

The latter is an excellent approach, if you devote the time and effort to developing a detailed outline. In this, the outlining or "idea processing" software offered today with modern word processors can be a great help.

How Long Should a Headline Be?

Some of those headlines and titles can become fairly long, even two or more lines, as some of the examples used here demonstrate. That should not be an obstacle. First of all, there is nothing wrong with lengthy titles and headlines, despite popular belief to the contrary. Book titles, which themselves serve as headlines when well conceived, furnish many examples of lengthy titles that did not hamper the sale of the books and probably contributed to their success. Here are titles of several highly successful books, best-sellers and hardy perennials:

- *The Entrepreneur & Small Business Problem Solver*
- *How to Form Your Own Corporation without a Lawyer for under $75.00*
- *How to Succeed as an Independent Consultant*
- *How to Write, Publish and Market Your Book*
- *How I Turn Ordinary Complaints into Thousands of Dollars*

The supposed rule about keeping titles and headlines short is not even conventional wisdom; it is pure mythology, perpetrated and perpetuated by individuals expressing misguided ideas. The almost unlimited number of successful exceptions reveals that. The simple fact is that if your headline or title captures the attention of clients by appealing to their own interests—that is, if clients *perceive* it to be in their interest to read what you have to say—wild horses will not stop them from reading your headline and as much body copy addressing that interest as you care to offer. For that and for no other reason, those books and advertisements cited here as examples were successful, some of them continuing to run in successive editions for many years. Only when and if readers stop seeing their own interests in what you say will they stop reading. It's that simple—and that complex. Study these and other examples you encounter of lengthy titles and headlines and see if they do not appeal directly to the self-interests of many potential readers.

How to Develop Titles and Headlines

There is only one really sensible rule for judging how long titles, headlines, and copy generally must be: The titles, headlines, and copy must be exactly long enough to do the job, and not one comma longer. Of course, that leaves us with the problem of determining just what *is* "long enough"?

For headlines and titles, that is long enough to make the promise clear. For copy in general, the answer is clearly implied in one of the many observations about the editing process: Editing is typically a function of reducing the bulk of a writer's copy, eliminating, probably, about one third of the original manuscript.

Like most generalizations, this one has many exceptions, but it does reflect (1) the common problem of excessive verbosity on the part of a great many writers and (2) the fundamental truth that even the most skilled writers usually overwrite (sometimes deliberately) in their first drafts and then tighten their manuscripts in revision through boiling out a great deal of nonessential material and/or finding more efficient ways to express their ideas. (It gives rise to the platitude that all good writing is *re*writing.)

This latter idea is especially appropriate to writing advertising and sales materials, such as proposals, including titles and headlines. The best practice, for most of us, is to write a first draft that says everything you can think of that is relevant, using as many words as you need to set it all down. In that draft you concern yourself primarily with including everything that contributes to the client's understanding of what you propose and to persuasive arguments for what you propose, drawn from your own knowledge and whatever research and data gathering you have done. It is more urgent, in this draft stage, to see to it that you have not left out anything important than it is to be eloquent and efficient in your language.

Once you have satisfied yourself that you have included all the relevant information available, you can begin the self-editing process to edit out extraneous material, tighten expressions, polish your language, and seek the hard-hitting headlines and captions.

With titles and headlines the process often has to be varied somewhat because quite often the headline or title you select initially proves to be inappropriate to what you have written. Therefore, maintain an open mind about titles and headlines and be prepared to edit and revise them ruthlessly, or even to scrap them entirely and make a fresh beginning at coining effective combinations of words.

Once you formulate the headlines and subheads for each discussion, you may want to work on titles for sections and captions or titles for illustrations and tables, working these over until you have polished them for maximum effect: words that you hope will strike a nerve.

Three Basic Kinds of Presentation Strategy

The strategic objective we have been discussing here is that of getting attention, and we have been examining one general strategy that is always available to you in pursuit of this objective: devising titles and headlines that command attention through appealing to the client's self-interest and dramatic presentation. But there are other ways to get attention and capture interest. However, before exploring the several other ways, let's study at least three basic approaches to this, each of which represents a different kind of presentation strategy:

- The copy itself: what your proposal says and how it says it
- Cosmetic effects and special elements of the proposal
- Special devices related to or in support of your presentation overall

Your copy—the words you use, their organization, supporting graphics, headlines, and other such elements—is the most important element of presentation effectiveness, but there are cosmetic effects also to be considered, such as the design of your graphics and special effects. A helpful pictorial on the cover of your proposal and supporting running heads and feet on the pages between the covers also help. Then, too, there are the special devices, such as separate charts, computer disks, and audio- or videotapes offered to supplement your proposal. All contribute to a total presentation that strikes a nerve and makes an impression. But of all, the one of these elements that is indispensable is the copy.

Dramatic, Striking Proposal Copy

More about Titles and Headlines

Titles and headlines can be major elements of presentation strategy. To maximize benefits from their use, give a great deal of thought to composing them and use them freely. They dramatize and stress important points in your presentation and sales arguments. Used freely, they can do even more than enhance your presentation strategy: They can reinforce your sales strategy and guide the client through your proposal to lighten the burden of reading by serving as guideposts. The main messages then come through, even if the client does not read every word carefully. An advertising rule is that you must sell what you advertise in the headline. If you fail with the headline, the best body copy will not rescue your copy.

To implement this idea, create a title, headline, subhead, or caption for every important point in your proposal. Titles and major headlines should draw attention to all major points you wish to make, but they can also summarize lesser points. All key points should be covered in headings, so that even if the client were to read only the titles and headlines he or she would have gotten most of the main messages and understood the main thrust of your proposal. (That consideration alone justifies the titles, headlines, and the effort to develop them.)

Test the entire array of your titles and headlines (they should be in your table of contents) by scanning them to verify that they accomplish three things:

1. They provide a reasonably detailed outline/abstract of your proposal.
2. They present and point out every important point in your proposal.
3. They offer a valid sales argument for your proposal by providing promises and proofs.

Section I: The Introduction

OBJECTIVE OF SECTION I

The introduction is brief but important. If you are responding to an RFP, you may expect the client to read your proposal. But if you want a busy client to read an unsolicited proposal, you must do something up front, in the introduction, to capture that interest. Capturing the client's attention and interest should be your main objective here.

ABOUT THE OFFEROR (FIRST SUBSECTION)

One way to hook the reader is to introduce the most attractive, novel, and/or dramatic element of your proposal immediately. Ordinarily, you use that "About the Offeror" opening discussion to furnish your business name, a few words to qualify and explain your interest and qualifications, summarize your credentials briefly, and advise the client that all of these will be offered in detail later. That much is routine. But we are looking for nonroutine matter here.

These summary explanations should be dramatized here for their greatest effect. If you happen to have something impressive or novel to say about any of these things, by all means do so here. More important, search out the most impressive, novel, dramatic, or appealing promise, evidence, or fact in your proposal and introduce it here on page 1, even before introducing yourself.

Obviously you can't do this until you have written your proposal and decided precisely what to offer and how you would do the job. Therefore, the introduction is written last—when you know exactly what it is that you are introducing. If you are the type of writer who needs to work with a lead, as many writers do, you will probably need to draft a working introduction, which you expect to scrap later, when you write the final introduction and introduce that interest-capturing jewel you have extracted, preferably that item which is at the heart of your program strategy. Here are a few examples of such items:

- A promise of extraordinary results, with only a hint of why and how you can offer this and the promise of details to follow shortly
- Ditto the above for remarkably low costs or speedy results
- Hints or even brief identification of a serious problem (worry item) and the promise of a soon-to-come explanation of how it will be solved
- Some extraordinary resource available or searched out especially for the project, such as a well-known authority persuaded to serve on the project or the pledged assistance of some prestigious organization

The strategy underlying such tactics as the above is fairly obvious. Most are teasers, arousing the client's curiosity, as well as interest, through promising that full revelation will be made in later pages, but all bear some direct suggestion that the client will benefit directly from the proposed program.

It is usually possible and certainly desirable to work that hook or some broad hint of it into the section title and/or subsection headline that precedes the initial text of this first section.

UNDERSTANDING OF THE REQUIREMENT (SECOND SUBSECTION)

This, too, should be brief, but it is an outstanding opportunity to capture client interest early. Always remember that the client may not be expert in the work required and presumably is not, since he or she is seeking help. Therefore, the client may very well be not only intensely interested in your view of the problem but greatly influenced by it. Most clients are likely to read your feedback analysis of the requirement as a first indicator of your capability. The "understanding" portion of you proposal's first section is therefore an opportunity to (1) help the client gain a better understanding of the true problem and (2) score points as you get down to cases (down to the true *essence* of the requirement).

Keep this discussion short, since it should identify and focus on the core issue of the requirement. (Otherwise, you may blur the focus and obscure the client's view of your main point.) Show here that you are not distracted by peripheral issues, but are keeping your eye firmly on the ball.

This subsection should also introduce something to help hook the client—build interest—even more firmly. First, make it abundantly clear that you are focusing here on only the essential or core problem and will analyze and discuss the requirement overall more discursively in pages to come. If at all possible, raise a worry item here (or expand on one raised in the first subsection) and promise to have a great deal more to say about it soon. Or, as an alternative, suggest some technical boon or special asset you will provide, again with the promise of fuller discussion soon.

The purpose is, of course, to build suspense and desire to learn more about these questions you raise. Accordingly, for maximum impact you must link these to something important to the client, and the most important thing at this point is the overall success or failure of the entire project. Therefore, don't waste time and energy on items that affect relatively trivial matters, but seek out those that bear directly on and seriously affect overall success and failure.

Section II: Discussion

OBJECTIVE OF SECTION II

Section II is a major element in the entire sales effort. Here is where you must do the bulk of your selling, for, while it is ostensibly the technical discussion that explains your understanding and approach to satisfying the requirement, it is also your principal sales argument. If you fail to convince the client here that yours is the most desirable plan or set of services, it is unlikely that you will be able to do so elsewhere in the proposal or by other means than the proposal, no matter how well you reinforce your arguments with other proposal sections and/or related sales activity.

Your "understanding" summary in the first section bridges directly into this section, where you unfold your program strategy, after first elaborating on your understanding to explore the requirement more fully. Here you must continue and expand the discussion, especially those elements about which you have raised questions or made promises. Here you present your analysis in detail, with your rationales ("thinking out loud") so that the client can fully understand the logic of the process and develop a belief in the worry items you project, your technical approach, and the results you promise.

ANALYSIS

It is in this section that you employ a competitive strategy by (1) demonstrating greater insight into the problems and needs of the client, (2) revealing greater wisdom in responding to those needs and problems, and (3) unveiling your special methods for being less costly, faster, more reliable, or better than others in some way. Here, too, is where you try to persuade the client to make specific comparisons of your offer with that of others. The ways already suggested for doing this are relatively subtle, however, and depend on the chance that the client will make specific, point-by-point comparisons, in addition to the inevitable general comparison.

Subtlety is totally out of place in most sales presentations; you need to be direct without being crude. One way to do this in a proposal is to make an actual statement of the qualifications you believe necessary for success in satisfying the client's requirement. This, if it is persuasive, virtually compels the client to make that point-by-point comparison that is usually an effective competitive strategy when handled well.

MAXIMIZING IMPACT

To introduce this idea of listing specific qualifications required to handle the assignment successfully, you must somehow demonstrate the logic (prove the validity) of your analysis. This is best done in some striking manner that focuses sharply on that logical progression of ideas that build to a climax presented as your approach to the project.

APPROACH

The approach you propose is a key element because many clients study this as an indicator of the practicability of your proposal. (It is often listed in RFPs as a weighting factor in evaluating proposals.) It is thus essential that you define your approach quite clearly and justify it as the logical outcome of your analysis. It helps, also, to dramatize this so that the reader cannot miss it.

An excellent way to dramatize this and draw attention to it is by giving it special treatment, such as by making it a figure, with suitable introduction, rather than including it in the main text. Figure 20 suggests a format for doing this, using as an example that requirement of the U.S. Postal Service calling for materials for on-the-job training of maintenance technicians for bulk-mail plants.

Note the head data and, especially, the "Most Critical Task" item. In this case, as in many others, there is a task that is not only critical to the success of the project, but is not well recognized. In this case, it was not readily apparent that it would be necessary for the contractor to identify the maintenance requirements and design the maintenance programs (electrical/electronic and mechanical) before designing the training programs themselves. The client had furnished no information on course content, evidently overlooking the need for this or assuming that the contractor would design the maintenance program. This changed the nature of the qualifications required. The request had been issued apparently with the thought that consultants specializing in training design and development would be the chief respondents.

This consideration raised a question as to consultant qualifications necessary, as Figure 20 shows. It argues and presents evidence supporting the position that competence in training-system development is not enough and that the consultant must have technical/professional qualifications in understanding electrical/electronic and mechanical technology and systems, and in the design and development of maintenance programs for such equipment and systems. (It is difficult enough to write a training program in a highly

Basic Requirement: Develop on-the-job materials for bulk-mail maintenance technicians to be trained for work in 21 bulk-mail centers.

Most Critical Task: Design and develop maintenance data and maintenance program for each option.

Most Important Secondary Problem: High turnover (attrition) rate of technicians leaving Postal Service and going on to other employment after heavy Postal Service investment in individual's training.

Special Problem: Much of the equipment is new, virtually prototype, with no maintenance history on which to base development of curriculum and weighting of course content.

Important Design Objectives and Approaches to Them:
1. Design maintenance program especially for bulk-mail equipment: Research, compile list of and technical data on all bulk-mail equipment; analyze and project estimated maintenance needs.
2. (Devise and perform failure-probability analyses.)
3. Structure training to minimize turnover of trained technicians: Avoid overtraining, to minimize turnover of technicians. (Confine course content to Postal Service equipment and provide technical coverage only to depth/extent required for Postal Service maintenance.)

General Qualifications Required:
1. Technical knowledge/experience in electrical/electronic and mechanical equipment and typical maintenance needs and practices.
2. Experience in design/development of sophisticated maintenance systems for electrical/electronic and mechanical equipment.
3. Capability for gaining access to and using technical data on Postal Service bulk-mail equipment.
4. Capability for development of maintenance-needs projections on quantitative as well as qualitative basis, drawn from research.
5. Capability to translate the data into a comprehensive and suitably weighted training specification.
6. Knowledge/experience in training-systems design generally, including the development of all documentation necessary, and in OJT systems especially.

Figure 20   Major strategies implemented in a single presentation.

technical subject when the writers are not personally expert in the subject. In this case, the writers had to also design the maintenance program in which the learners were to be trained. That requirement could easily be inferred but was not plainly apparent in the request. It was reasonable to assume that the client had not really considered the requirement in this light.)

To design this for maximum impact you must have some idea of (1) who you are competing against, (2) your competitors' strengths, (3) the client's perception of truth, and (4) what you must assume that the client knows. However, remember also that you are really only dealing with those strengths, weaknesses, and qualifications about each proposer that the *client* knows about, generally based on what each proposal says. Therefore, if your competitors fail to grasp all these points and thus fail to describe and list all those special qualifications (a common shortcoming in many, many proposals), they might as well not have them at all, for the client will assume then that they do not have such capabilities. And even if they are able to say, "Me, too," in later follow-up presentations, they are in seriously weakened positions—to your own advantage.

This kind of presentation is in itself a major competitive strategy when you believe that the client has overlooked some important point of which you can make capital, as in this case and in many others. (Remember the point made much earlier that it is often possible to persuade the client to accept arguments that are actually your own modification of the requirement?)

Figure 20, then, turns out to be a summary of the most important points of the client's request, the proposed approach, and the main strategies, all presented in a small package. It is a presentation, although it can be used on a much wider basis, as a result of its scope.

This tabular figure is such a powerful tool that it can be used effectively in many and possibly even more important ways than in support of your Section II discussions. You might even do well to introduce this figure quite early in your proposal and use it as an attention getter and interest-arousing hook on its own. It is quite suitable as a basis for frequent references throughout the proposal and can thus become a major tool for exploiting all your strategies. It can even be the chief basis for your entire presentation, along with the functional flowchart, as an effective means for aiding the client in following your arguments and understanding the logic of your approach to satisfying the requirement. An effective way to use such graphic summaries and overviews is to expand them into large charts suitable for viewing in a meeting room (e.g., 3 × 4 feet) and using those charts in either (or both) of two ways:

1. Supply the charts to the client by including them with your proposal, calling them "exhibits" or "enclosures." (This has been highly effective in getting special attention and impressing clients favorably.)
2. Use them as the basis for verbal presentations ("dog and pony shows"), following up the proposal submittal.

Section III: Proposed Project

OBJECTIVE OF SECTION III

In some respects this is the true essence of your response—the proposal per se—for this is where you commit yourself to specific actions and end items to be delivered. The main objective here is to deliver the true proof of your offer: what you propose to *do,* in absolutely specific terms. Previous sections of your proposal have theorized, philosophized, explained, and argued. Now you present a detailed specification of what you pledge yourself to do and commit yourself to deliver. This is the essence of the contract you offer. There is some flexibility in what it ought to include, but I recommend that it include all the following items: (1) management specifications, (2) resumes, and (3) graphic elements.

MANAGEMENT DISCUSSION

Management is often a prime concern with clients, who tend to recognize that technical capability and competence are not enough when a project is not capably managed. A great deal is written and lectured about management every day, much of it vague and philosophical. But clients about to entrust important work to an outside contractor want to know specifically what management will be provided. Specificity and detail are the key elements, and that applies to all elements of management, including organization, controls, deliverable items, and schedules—especially two elements that many proposal writers neglect: quality control and specific procedures that will be used to ensure proper control of all operations.

Here again you can gain an advantage over competitors by the mere fact of being entirely specific, where many proposal writers are defensive and do whatever they can to avoid specific commitment, especially in the matter of thinking out and planning details of management plans.

Resumes may be offered here or in the next section, but wherever they are offered, the almost inevitable question of format arises.

RESUME FORMATS

In the question of resume formats, many proposal writers have the deplorable tendency to confuse the resume requirements of a proposal with those of a job-seeking resume and to make at least two basic mistakes in the presentation of resumes in the proposal. One is to structure the resume as one would for a job application, and the other is to use a boilerplated or standard resume for all proposals, without regard to the specific needs of each requirement and the proposal responding to it. If you invest the time and money in a proposal—usually a significant investment—it is foolish to try to save an insignificant part of your investment by using a standardized resume. The resumes should be customized to each proposal, using a format along the lines of Figure 21.

Name

Normal position
(e.g., President, Systems Analyst)

Proposed position
(e.g., Project Director)

Summary introduction: General qualifications in narrative format— most relevant achievements, experience, education, special training, including current employment, in order of importance/relevance to project, without regard to chronology. (Keep brief for maximum focus and impact.)

Experience details: Chronology of positions/functions/assignments in current and previous employment. (Precise dates not required; approximate time periods satisfactory.)

Education, other details.

Figure 21   Suggested format for resumes in proposals.

The format suggested there is such that it is possible to revise resumes rather easily for each new proposal, especially if you are using a word processor. The logic of the format is rather obvious, of course, tailored to the individual proposal and the requirement to which it responds.

Priority in presenting information in a resume should always be given to accomplishments first (patents, awards, outstanding achievements of any kind, as long as they are somehow relevant to the requirement), to experience second (previous positions, most relevant and important ones first), and then to education and educational achievements (degrees, honors, and awards).

The customization of the resume to each proposal is thus primarily in the position proposed and the introductory paragraph. The remaining data, which is entirely amplifying detail, can usually be kept unchanged. This makes it fairly easy to customize resumes for each new proposal, with even the most basic word processor.

GRAPHIC ELEMENTS

Graphics are as helpful here as they are elsewhere. If the requirement is such that it requires a staff of several people, you must have an organization chart of some kind, as in Figure 22. Schedule commitments may be made by a tabular schedule, as in Figure 23, but are often more useful if presented as part of a milestone chart, as in Figure 24, since this kind of schedule presentation aids the client in visualizing the interdependence of the various events. And resumes may be offered here or in the next section,

Another presentation that belongs in this section of many proposals is a tabulated estimate of tasks, assignments, and hours. This

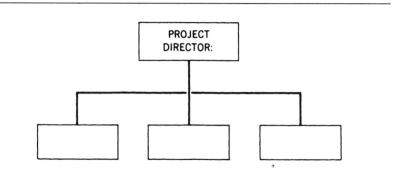

Figure 22 Typical organization chart.

ITEM	WORKING DAYS AFTER AWARD
Preliminary meeting	1
Report of initial analysis	10
Client review, comments	20
Submission of revised plan	30
Work begins	35
Draft of final report	90
Client review, comments	120
Revision, submission of revised report	150
Client signoff	180

Figure 23 Tabular schedule of events.

type of presentation is illustrated by Figure 25. There are several reasons for including such a chart or table in this section:

1. It reduces the risk in proposing because it compels you to plan
    in detail, rather than in broad terms, and thus makes you cal-
    culate effort and costs realistically. It's too easy, otherwise, to
    take the easy way out of "ballparking" your estimates, with

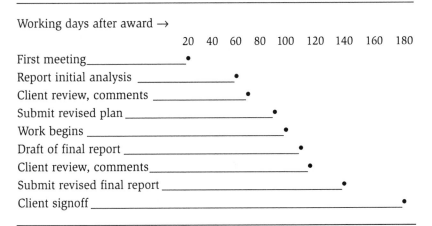

Figure 24 Milestone chart as schedule.

TASKS, ASSIGNMENTS, AND EFFORT REQUIRED

Tasks	Staffing		Totals
	Project Manager	**Second Investigator**	
Totals			

Figure 25   Suggested format for presentation of task/labor estimates.

the hazard of under- or overestimating the effort required and the cost of the project. Force yourself to do the detailed planning. This gives you confidence in your estimates.

2. It is excellent evidence of your mastery of the requirement and what is needed to satisfy it, on the basis that this represents planning detail, which is itself evidence of capability for designing and managing the work. It thus gives the client the same confidence in your estimates that you feel. In general, moreover, an abundance of detail in a proposal is almost always highly impressive and favorably so.

3. It supports cost estimates, demonstrating their validity.

4. It contributes to your competitor strategy as a silent but eloquent commentary on the proposal of any competitor who is less frank and less thorough.

It is wise to be equally thorough in all other areas of this section. Try to present as much detail in your qualitative and quantitative descriptions or estimates of deliverable items, for example. If you are going to develop a manual or report of some kind as the end product of the service you render, describe it in some detail: Provide estimated numbers of pages, illustrations, and tables; a detailed outline of content; number of copies to be provided; and other relevant data. If there are to be interim products, formal presentations, seminars, or other items developed, do the same for these.

Section IV: Qualifications and Experience

MAIN OBJECTIVE OF SECTION IV

The main goal of this section is to demonstrate your competence and dependability as a consulting service entity. Even if you are an independent consultant, functioning alone—"Peter Smith & Associates," for example—you must manage to discriminate between this presentation and your personal resume, thinking of yourself as an organization, rather than as an individual practitioner.

For one thing, the client wants the reassurance of knowing that your services have been and are acceptable to others, that you are capable of carrying out the proposed program in both technical/professional knowledge and abilities and in the practical sense of having the resources to do so, having relevant experience and accomplishments, physical facilities, staffing resources, and anything else required.

Some clients become concerned that the consultant may be straining his or her resources to cope with the requirement and that even a relatively small problem or small miscalculation could cause the program to abort. So one objective in writing this section is to point out that you have adequate resources for the program and for backup, if needed.

In previous sections you worked at selling the client on and building client confidence in your plans and personal credentials. Now you must sell the client on and build confidence in the capabilities and reliability of the professional entity you represent, whether alone as an independent practitioner or as a larger business entity. Provide such information as the following.

RELEVANT CURRENT/RECENT PROJECTS

Regardless of whether the client requests it, a presentation of current and recent relevant projects and clients is a useful item. Of course, many projects are confidential, and many make you privy to confidential and proprietary information. Many clients may not wish to have even the mere fact of some of their projects revealed without their permission. It is therefore wise to request that permission before identifying clients or revealing information about current and recent projects.

Within whatever constraints that may impose—that is, to the extent that those constraints permit you to—this is the kind of information a subsection on relevant projects ought to include:

- Name, size, type of project
- Relevant details
- Client
- Brief contract history: degree of success, adherence to schedule and budget, other indicators of success
- Contact person (individual who can verify data), with telephone number

The project descriptors should be presented in order of importance and relevance to the proposal. Therefore, like the resumes, this table should not be completely boilerplated, although many of the individual project descriptors may be, so that the table can be easily modified for each new use. The descriptors are probably most efficiently presented in a tabular format, but a new table should be organized to suit each proposal. Again, if the descriptors are written up as elements of one or more computer/word processor files, reorganizing them into a new table for each proposal is relatively simple.

PROPOSING ORGANIZATION

Clients are usually interested in the specific organizational unit offering the proposal. If you are a department or group within your company, explain this and show it with some kind of organization chart. Show, also, where and how it reports in the organization, especially to reflect the degree of control the proposed project directory is likely to enjoy in the organization. Show the client that the project is important enough to you to give it some priority in staffing by assigning a senior person to head it and direct the work. (See also paragraph to follow titled "Corporate Organization.")

FACILITIES AND RESOURCES

There are various kinds of facilities and resources in most organizations. Following are some kinds of descriptions that are appropriate to demonstrate your total capability to carry out the work proposed:

Physical facilities: Office space, office equipment, computers, laboratory resources, warehouse space, or other. This can be a simple tabular listing, but it can be supported with drawings and/or photographs.

Software resources: Library, files, computer programs, or other such facilities.

Additional staff: Other staff persons who could be made available to support the project, if needed.

It is also appropriate to list and explain access to additional facilities and resources beyond those that are integral parts of your own organization, so that you can provide additional insurance against the program becoming crippled in any way. Those might include resumes of associates available to you, of laboratory facilities you have made preliminary arrangements with, or of other organizations that have agreed to back you up, if necessary.

REFERENCES AND TESTIMONIALS

The names of current and recent clients appearing in your table of relevant current and recent projects, if you have been able to list a few, are references, of course. But it is always useful to present a list of references generally (again, with permission of those listed) and especially useful to include such testimonials as laudatory letters of appreciation and complimentary remarks in forms rating your seminar and other presentations.

It is usually not difficult to get such letters after you have been in business for a time, but clients rarely think to send them on their own initiative. On the other hand, many clients will cheerfully furnish such letters if you request them, and you can gather an impressive set of such testimonials in a short while.

CORPORATE ORGANIZATION

If you are an organization of more than a single subdivision within a corporate entity, it is appropriate to explain this, illustrate it with a corporate organization chart, and show where the proposing entity fits into the overall structure. Again, remember that no client wants to see his or her project treated casually, but the client wants to see it treated as an important responsibility.

MISCELLANEOUS

There are several other areas in the typical proposal, all of which should be at least introduced here, although they will be discussed in more detail later and are miscellaneous matters at this point. Some of these fall into the general classification called *front matter,* which means that they customarily appear before the first page of text; others are appended or loosely attached to the proposal.

Response Matrix   A most important and useful element of front matter in a proposal that is a response to a formal request for proposals is a tabular presentation I refer to as a *response matrix.*

I pointed out earlier that clients usually do not have an easy time evaluating proposals on a comparative or even on an absolute basis because each proposer employs a different format and different philosophy of presentation and response to the request. The response matrix helps the client evaluate proposals by offering a guide in the proposal to each item the client wishes to see covered. It is, in fact, a virtual map to the proposal, in that sense.

The response matrix is developed along the general lines of Figure 26, which presents a suggested format and a few sample entries. This guides the client's review so that you get credit for responding to all requirements, including some that may not have been explicit, but that you deduced from your own study of the client's needs, as stated and as you inferred them from your analyses.

This matrix is useful for all proposals, but is especially valuable when proposing to government agencies, for they make actual numerical evaluations of your proposal's technical merit. This type of presentation almost invariably maximizes the technical scores achieved by the proposals in which it is used.

The items are rather easy to gather, if you have made up the checklists at the beginning, as suggested, for they contain the items that go into this matrix. That, in fact, is one of the several reasons for the checklists.

Be sure, in making up your matrix, that you direct the client's attention to your various graphics devices, as well as to textual passages: The matrix helps you bring more impact to your presentations in this way by directing the client's attention to the specific places in your proposal where you make your best and clearest arguments.

The blank right-hand column is for the client's convenience to verify and check off your responses and make notations, as well.

REQUEST FOR PROPOSAL ITEM	PROPOSAL RESPONSE	CLIENT COMMENTS
pp. 3, 4: Understanding of the requirement	pp. 1–3	
p. 12: Current/recent experience	pp. 1, 5, 15–18	
p. 14: Facilities and resources	pp. 19–22	

Figure 26 Format for response matrix.

Executive Summary Years ago, when I wrote proposals at what was then the Communications and Weapons division of the electronics firm Philco in Philadelphia, a standard section of our proposals bore the title "Why Philco Should Be Awarded This Contract." This plainly stated the objective of this section: It was a section in which we summed up the principal selling points of the proposal and asked the client to focus sharply on our main arguments. Today that practice and intent is reflected in most formal proposals in a portion of the front matter titled "Executive Summary." A subsection of or prominent paragraph following the executive summary might well be titled "Why This Contract Should Be Awarded to (your name)."

Nominally, that element is intended as an abstract of the proposal, and yet it is not so titled. It is titled so as to suggest that this is intended for those busy top-level executives who would not normally read the entire proposal and have no need to pore over details that are usually of interest to only the technical/professional staff specialists and technical managers. (Of course, despite this, everyone reads the executive summary.)

The executive summary should summarize the proposal, of course, but it must focus primarily on the benefits and proofs—the reasons for favoring the proposer with the contract. This is its purpose in life, and it should appear in each proposal, regardless of whether the client has requested such a summary.

Appendixes and Exhibits

An appendix is a place to present information that you expect to be of interest to some but not all readers of your proposal. It's the way to avoid burdening readers with details they do not wish to wade through, without denying that information to those who will find it useful and do want to see it. That includes such things as additional resumes (although some proposal writers put all resumes in an appendix), drawings, papers from technical journals, reprints of articles, and other such matter.

In some cases, particularly when it is impractical to provide more than one copy of the item (and many proposal requests require multiple copies of the proposal), the term *exhibit* is employed, and the item is not an integral part of the proposal but is an exhibit of the proposal. (Some writers use the label "exhibit" to identify such items as illustrations in the proposal.)

Another Device: Storyboarding

There are a number of other devices and ways to strengthen your presentation. These are, in fact, not truly new or novel as editorial and publications devices, but they are not used as often as they should be in proposals because proposal writers are usually not familiar with them. In fact, some organizations use what they call a storyboard approach to proposal writing, which makes use of some of these devices.

Storyboards

The term *storyboard* springs from the audiovisual and movie industries, where it is used as a planning and presentation tool. In its simplest form it consists of a series of simple sketches and accompanying text, somewhat like a cartoon strip. These are organized into logical sequences.

Adapted to proposal writing, the storyboard becomes a bold headline or title at the head of a page, followed by a "blurb" or "gloss," followed by amplifying text. The goal is to present a new topic, in this format, on every page. But even if it is not always possible to start a new topic on every page, as it often is not, it is possible to start every new topic on a new page, along with its headline and blurb.

Blurbs and Glosses

The gloss is a rather time-honored device, found even today in many formal textbooks, where it appears as a marginal note in small print, summarizing the text alongside which it appears.

A blurb is just a bit different. It is a brief statement, such as the summary of an article or some intriguing element of an article, which appears under the title of the article in a periodical. (Significantly, the term is also applied to brief advertising messages.)

Technique

In the storyboard technique, the blurb appears under that bold headline at the top of the page, and the blurb has as its purpose summing up the important substance of the page, almost as an explanatory subtitle or abstract of the page. However, its purpose is to sell, and it is used to make the greatest contribution possible to that function, so it is generally used to stress or dramatize a selling point that should dominate that page or topic.

Used together to exploit them fully, all these many devices, tactics, and techniques can double your chances for success. And even if you have a truly outstanding offer to make, you need to do these things to get a fair reading and fair consideration of your offer.

CHAPTER 10

Graphics

Why Graphics Are a Must Item in Proposal Writing

The Three Basic Sales Problems/Objectives

Graphic aids—illustrations—are more than a convenience; they are a necessity, and the consultant who tries to write a viable proposal without using adequate graphic aids is working under a self-imposed handicap that is likely to prove crippling, if not fatal.

A great many proposal writers tend to use too many words and too few graphics. The purpose of a proposal is persuasion, of course; it is a sales presentation. That means inducing someone—a client—to decide that he or she is wanting something that you sell. But the sales problem is not always a simple one, nor is it always the same problem. It may be any of three basic sales situations and problems, as summarized here:

1. In many cases, particularly where you are submitting an informal and/or unsolicited proposal (which usually means a non-competitive one), you are probably simply trying to persuade the client to want the kind of service you offer, since you are the only one offering it to this client.

2. On the other hand, if the client has already decided to buy the kind of service you offer, your marketing problem and the

main objective of your proposal is to induce the client to buy that service from you, rather than from someone else.

3. In some cases, you may have the double task of persuading the client not only to buy the service, but to buy it from you. (Some sales presentations succeed in accomplishing only the first of these tasks, and so create a sale for a competitor!)

Understanding Must Precede Persuasion

Whichever the sales mission you are embarked on, you must somehow help the client to understand your arguments easily, particularly the promise(s) you make and the evidence you provide to validate the promises. And you must see to it that you do not place a burden on the client to study your proposal, understand your program, and grasp all your important points. In short, accept the necessity to do the selling without expecting any effort by the client. That means, keeping your entire proposition simple and straightforward.

Words versus Graphics in Communication

Words are the principal and most used means for communicating among ourselves as a matter of pure necessity. Over the centuries, we have developed ever more sophisticated and efficient means to transmit words to each other, in terms of mass communications and communications over long distances. Still, there is evidence that the earliest communications, other than vocal sounds, was via graphics. Throughout the world we find artifacts attesting to this, from crude prehistoric drawings on the walls of ancient caves to sundry forms of art (paintings and sculptures of every kind) created by every civilization and society we know of since Homo sapiens emerged from the caves and began to build shelters.

It is significant also that movies, and subsequently TV, were immediate successes and that worldwide TV transmission and reception were among the earliest and most popular applications of satellite communications systems. Moreover, the use of computers for generating graphics also proliferated rapidly, with the translation of spreadsheet data into graphic representations (e.g., charts and graphs) the primary goal of many software programs.

Why Graphics?

Illustrations of all kinds, but especially graphic illustrations, facilitate and improve communications for more than one reason:

Pure efficiency: In a great many cases a good illustration is simply more efficient and more effective than words are in getting a message across: A simple drawing, properly conceived and executed, gets an idea across to a reader almost at a glance and usually requires less physical space than equivalent text.

Less effort required: It requires less effort to absorb a concept or image presented graphically than when the reader must read and translate words. The illustration presents the desired image directly. With words, the reader must translate the language into mental images or concepts.

Greater accuracy: Even with the greatest effort, readers are rarely able to translate or interpret words to create the precise image you want. Words are merely symbols and require the reader to search for a referent, so that the ways in which readers translate language are dependent on their own vocabularies and personal referents. We all introduce our personal memories and biases into our interpretations of what we read. Ergo, it is not surprising that each reader's interpretation of the meaning of any given textual passage is somewhat different from anyone else's interpretation. A drawing or photograph of an object, on the other hand, tends to be seen the same way by every reader.

Various Degrees of Complexity

All of the foregoing is true for even the simplest communication needs, such as helping the reader visualize the appearance of an object. But it is even more true for more complex cases of communication, such as those cases where it is necessary to assist the reader in perceiving and understanding an abstraction or a complex relationship, such as a flow process. You cannot expect the reader to find it easy to grasp the concept of phase relationships in an electrical or electronic circuit or the theorem of Pythagoras, for example, unless you offer some graphic devices to facilitate understanding. But it is not only in technological subjects that the problems of conveying abstractions and complex relationships arise. The problems are the same in many presentations that are not technological in any sense. Presenting and explaining business problems, societal relationships, professional functions, political processes, and many other subjects can be equally complex and challenging to present in easily understood explanations. Moreover, it is often necessary to create explanations that are easily understood by laypeople.

It is not always a case of using graphic devices simply to aid the writer in making the presentation and the reader in following the explanations. In some cases it is simply not possible to make a sensible presentation by words alone, so that graphic aids become an absolute necessity, rather than merely a convenience. So we must consider all these cases and the many ways to cope successfully with the presentation problems of each case.

A Few Underlying Principles about Graphics

The Sales/Marketing Consideration

What has been and will be said here about the logic and practices of using graphics properly is true for all applications of writing and publications work. However, remember also that these ideas become even more important when they are applied to the preparation of proposals. That is because the proposal is a sales presentation, and while the reader of a book or report might struggle through difficult text passages that could and should have been made easier through graphic aids, the client reading a proposal is under no compulsion to do so and is likely to discard the difficult-to-follow proposal. Therefore, in addition to every other guideline, principle, rule, and/or caution offered to help you judge where, when, why, and how to opt for a graphic aid, always consider also the possible contribution an effective graphic aid may make to sales persuasion—to winning the contract, that is.

Relative Costs

Graphics used in proposals—drawings and photographs, normally— are relatively expensive. It is possible today to create many, if not all, your own drawings at professional or near-professional quality by turning to the many desktop publishing programs. There is even the possibility of generating some thoroughly acceptable drawings with your own personal computer and most basic graphics software. And even without special software, with a little imagination you can use your word processor to generate many useful drawings. (Some examples will be shown.) But even when you generate the drawings yourself, creating a drawing can be costly in time, if not in dollars. And where special art departments are used to generate highly professional finished drawings, there is a definite dollar expense involved.

Consequently, it is understandable that the complaint is sometimes raised in publications groups that graphic illustrations, especially detailed drawings that are generated for one-time use, are too expensive to be used in any case where the use is not an absolute necessity. The argument is that a page of illustration costs several times more than a page of straight text.

This reflects a lack of understanding about the economics of using graphics—using them properly, that is. It is one of the deterrents to the use of graphics, leading to the impoverishment of product quality (of the quality of your proposal, that is). What the originators of such objections do not take into account is that the comparison is faulty: The cost of a page of illustration should not be compared with the cost of a single page of straight text, but with the cost of several, perhaps many, pages of text. A good illustration eliminates and makes unnecessary at least several pages of text; if it does not, the illustration is a poor one. It fails in its mission and should not have been created.

Why Many Graphics Fail

There are three common reasons for the failure of a graphic illustration, with only one a reflection on the illustration per se: That is the case in which the illustration is poorly conceived and simply does not do the job it ought to do. The other two cases are one in which the illustration is either unnecessary and is used where no illustration would be helpful or another where the writer fails to take advantage of the illustration and insists upon using a great deal of unnecessary language to explain what the illustration already makes quite clear. This, in fact, defeats the basic objective in using the illustration. The unnecessary text is a needless expense and a needless added burden to both the writer and the reader.

The point, then, is that the graphic illustration is as much a basic form of communication as is the text and should be so regarded and handled. If it needs lengthy explanation, it is not a good illustration.

Relevant Rules and Principles Inferred

All these types of failure point to more than one basic rule or principle, the first and most general of which is that a graphic illustration is not or should not be a supplement to textual presentation but is itself as primary and independent a means of communication as are the words. Each has some dependence on the other, of course, but the interdependence is incidental, and each medium must stand on its own. And to do that, each must be used where it is the right medium to meet the need.

That means that as a writer of proposals you must think and plan in terms of what you wish to communicate before you consider how you will do so. First of all, bear in mind that everything you must communicate is either concrete or abstract information. More basic, perhaps, is the consideration of whether you are trying to communicate an image or an idea. We think in both images and words, and even when we are trying to understand and digest abstract ideas or concepts we tend to conjure up images in analogizing the concepts. Obviously, when the reference is to some common object or idea that is familiar to everyone, it is rarely necessary or profitable to employ a graphic illustration; the reader will furnish that mentally. The judgment of need for an illustration should be based entirely on judgment of what is to be communicated and how that is most effectively and/or efficiently accomplished.

Remember in this connection that efficiency has a somewhat different meaning here than it might in another application. That is because here we are talking about sales presentations, and efficiency refers here to more than efficiency in communicating information; it refers to effectiveness in persuading the client to your arguments. In many cases a graphic aid will be more persuasive than words, even when it might not communicate information any better than words would, and so it adds efficiency in achieving the primary objective of the proposal. So we must also consider the impact of graphics in terms of persuasiveness, as compared with the persuasiveness of words alone.

General Types of Graphics

There are many types of graphics, and they vary widely in costs, time required for their execution, the skill required to create them, applications for which they are most suitable, and other parameters by which they may be compared with each other. A first broad discrimination might be made between photographs and drawings.

Photographs

Photographs have rather limited use in proposals, generally, although there are exceptions. In the case of a project that required the proposer to offer a warehouse site with ready access to a seaport and all facilities necessary to dockside operations at such a port, at least one proposer offered photographs, including an overall aerial photo of the proposed site, with appropriate *callouts* (arrows and labels surprinted on the photos) indicating the various facilities.

One great advantage in using photographs rather than simple drawings in such a case as this, is the much greater credibility of photographs. In fact, in such a case as this, where the question of suitable facilities bears on the client's final decision, drawings purporting to show the facilities are claims, whereas photographs are evidence. Even elaborate and costly "artist's conception" types of drawings (often developed by architects to depict the final building planned) are a reflection of what the proposer promises, while photographs invite the client to view with his or her own eyes a far more persuasive alternative, obviously.

There are, of course, special cases, such as this, in which a photograph is certainly the most effective and probably the least costly way to get the information across to the client. In general, however, photographs may be used to show clients your own facilities and equipment, where that is relevant—offices, library, data processing system, and/or whatever else is evidence of your ability to serve the client's needs well.

Photographs are usually less costly for this application if you have them prepared in printed form in sufficient quantity to simply bind them into all your proposals or, as a practical alternative, to include them in a standard capabilities brochure that you use as part of the qualifications section of your custom proposals.

General Types of Drawings

For proposal purposes, drawings to be considered are almost always of the general type known as line drawings. That general category encompasses all types of graphs, charts, and pictorials that do not include subtle shadings, as do photographs and renderings in oils, watercolors, charcoal, and other such artistic interpretations. (Although some shadings are achieved even in line drawings, they are achieved via mechanical means or special ready-made materials that anyone can use.)

It is, in fact, rather difficult to draw up a complete list of types of line drawings, for there are a great many classes and subclasses, according to both the characteristics of the drawings and the applications to which they are put. Even the following list does not convey a complete profile of all the possible types of line drawings, but does serve to establish that there is a broad range of types from which to choose the most suitable type for a given application:

Pictorials	Bar charts	Flowcharts
Pie charts	Networks	Plots
Milestone charts	Logic trees	Organization charts
Matrixes	Block diagrams	Cartoons
Clip art	Tables	Graphs

Even within these types there are many broad subdivisions possible. Note, also, that this list includes matrixes and tables, which are not really drawings but are functionally in the same class as line drawings. Again, this will be borne out in the following discussions, some of which will include examples of types of line drawings.

PICTORIALS AND DIAGRAMS

A simple pictorial is shown in Figure 27, which depicts a simple local area network in a ring configuration. This network is also presented and explained in the simple pictorial of Figure 28.

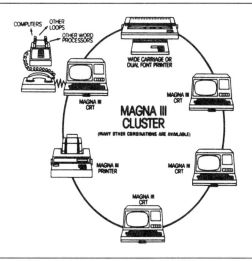

Figure 27 Pictorial representation of the local area network in a ring. *(Courtesy of A. B. Dick Corporation.)*

These illustrate quite clearly the difference between the two methods of graphic presentation. Both offer the same information, but obviously the pictorial drawing is somewhat more effective in demonstrating the system suggested. And it is more effective in more than one respect. First of all, the pictorial is far more effective than the block diagram in reflecting the general idea of the system. It requires hardly more than a glance to understand the system, at least in general terms, whereas it takes at least a little study of the block diagram to grasp the overall idea, even with the various labels and identifiers. That is the key to the principal difference: A reader can recognize instantly such familiar items as desktop computers and telephones, even before reading the labels. The labels are almost entirely merely supportive. On the other hand, the labels in the block diagram are the only means of communicating most of the information, requiring the reader to make the translation from words to images.

The need to translate the labels isn't the only difference. The pictorial conveys the idea of a ring configuration much more efficiently than does the block diagram and would do so even if the block diagram was arranged in a circular or oval pattern. That is an important part of the concept here because there are several other possible configurations for local area networks. In addition to that, however,

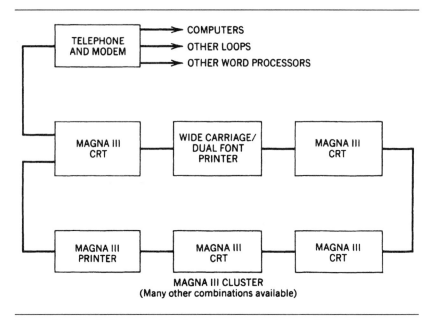

Figure 28   Block diagram of the local network in ring configuration.

since the reader is not required to translate the words of the block diagram into the images of the equipment but is shown a good representation of the equipment as it actually appears, the writer is in far better control of the communication.

That is perhaps the most cogent argument for the use of pictorials whenever and wherever practicable: It does offer you far greater control of what the reader sees and "hears" in reading your proposal.

Unfortunately, pictorial drawings tend to be more expensive than many other illustrations because they usually require the services of professional illustrators. (There are exceptions to this, which we will explore later.) They also tend to require more lead time to prepare. For both reasons, it is usually impracticable to use them indiscriminately, and so their use should probably be confined to the most important messages you wish to deliver to the client and perhaps to broad and general overviews of complex projects. They often prove especially useful in this application, for they are often the key to brushing aside the trivia and the distracters and focusing, at least for the moment, on the real essence of the problem.

On the other hand, even disregarding cost entirely, pictorials are not always the most effective graphic illustrations to use. For some applications, other graphic representations, such as networks, are more effective in helping the client grasp the concept easily.

NETWORKS

(These are also known in their various manifestations as CPM, for critical path method, and PERT, for programmed evaluation and review technique.) Networks are especially useful for showing serial and parallel relationships, interdependencies, alternate paths, and numerous other absolute and relative characteristics of the assorted elements. An illustration such as that of Figure 29, for example, can demonstrate that there are several paths to the ultimate goal or objective of the project and facilitates demonstrating to the client the validity of premises underlying a discussion of viable alternatives.

In Figure 29, item 1 represents the starting point of the project, and item 16 is the objective. The ideal path from the start to the objective is the shortest one, a straight line from 1 to 16. However, since it is rare that any project goes that smoothly, you have anticipated possible forced detours of the project or, better yet, planned the various alternatives that you will have ready, in the event that problems materialize.

Thus, this figure helps you explain what is necessarily a rather sophisticated and fairly complex project plan, while it also demonstrates the high caliber and thoroughness of your planning and preparation.

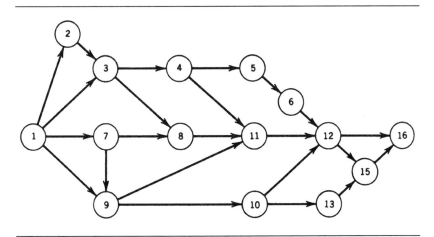

Figure 29 Simple network.

In such drawings as this, you can label each of the numbered elements or you can simply prepare a set of notes—a legend, in fact—explaining each numbered element.

FLOWCHARTS

In a simpler presentation, an illustration such as that of Figure 30 may be used. The boxes in which the various steps and functions are explained can be any shape—rectangular, circular, or other. Several different shapes are shown in Figure 30 to illustrate this, and many people use an assortment of shapes in such illustrations, as a matter of trying to make the illustration interesting and pleasing in general appearance, as well as informative. In some applications, such as computer program flowcharts and logic diagrams, the shapes of the boxes have individual and distinct meanings—specific shapes are used for specific applications, as illustrated in Figure 31.

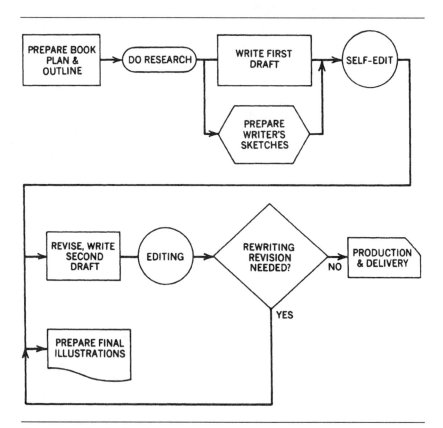

Figure 30   Simple flowchart.

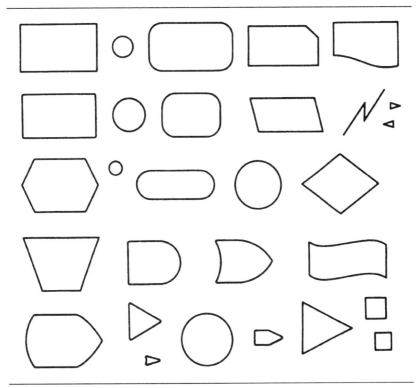

Figure 31   Standard drawing templates.

DRAWING AIDS

These and similar drawings were created originally with standard drawing templates, which are readily available in art supply shops and at many well-stocked stationers. Templates have been designed for a quite enormous variety of applications in all kinds of professions—all the engineering fields, architecture, mathematics fields, and many others. You can have a choice of literally dozens of different kinds, many of them in a number of sizes, too. Templates are only one kind of drawing aid; but there are many other drawing aids available, including boxes, arrows, borders, symbols, and other such devices in pastedown (self-adhesive) and transfer (decal) forms. And again, the variety is broad and applicable to many fields. Today, however, although these aids to drawing still exist and are still offered in supply establishments, most of this work can be done much more easily with modern computers and software.

CLIP ART

There is also *clip art,* which is material available especially for use as illustrations and which can be purchased in sheets and/or in booklets at supply stores. Again, however, today you can copy clip art from files in your computer, using graphics programs. A small sample of such material is shown as Figure 32.

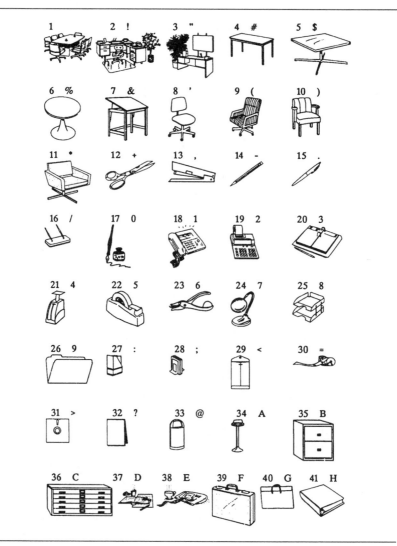

Figure 32 Sample of computer-generated clip art. *(Courtesy of Prosoft®.)*

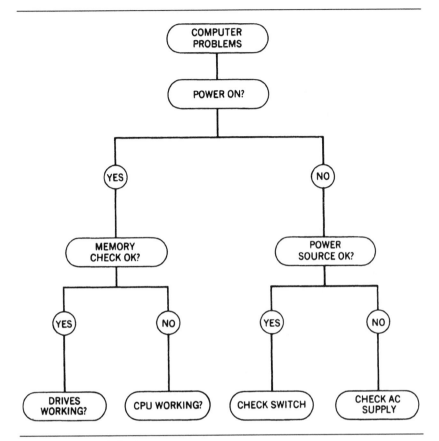

Figure 33 Simple logic tree.

LOGIC TREES

Logic trees are another useful idea to illustrate a kind of binary or Aristotelian logic: the progression of yes-no, high-low, go-stop, or other mutually exclusive states to reach a conclusion. A simple example of this is shown in Figure 33.

11

The Executive Summary (and Other Front Matter)

Front Matter

Used properly, the executive summary often proves to be the most important element in the proposal. At the least, it would be a serious error to underestimate its importance and so fail to utilize it effectively. But there are other elements of front matter, too.

In any formal publication, certain elements appear before page 1—before the presentation begins, that is. There are, usually, a title page and a table of contents, as the minimum. But there are often other elements as well: prefaces, forewords, abstracts, and notices of various kinds.

Formal proposals are not an exception to this, although they generally include in their front matter elements not normally found in most other formal publications. The title page and table of contents are de rigueur, found in just about every formal publication of every kind, including formal proposals. Other elements normally found in formal proposals include an abstract, executive summary, foreword or preface, and in some cases other special elements, such as a very useful one I refer to as a *response matrix.* That and the executive summary are probably the most important elements of front matter in proposals.

What Is an Executive Summary?

Many things are not quite what they appear to be, and to some extent that may be said for the executive summary. The term itself suggests that an executive summary is a kind of abstract of the entire proposal, offered to help executives absorb the main thrust and major points of a proposal with a brief reading. That is true in a most general sense. But there is more to the matter than that. An executive summary is far more than an abstract—or it certainly ought to be—in the hands of an astute marketer. It is probably the most important element of the front matter and an important element of the proposal overall.

The executive summary is, in principle, particularly appropriate in proposals that are highly technical and/or include a great deal of almost painful detail. In fact, it was the growing complexity of technical detail presented in major proposals, along with the massive and unwieldy size of many proposals (literally thousands of pages and several volumes, for many large contracts) that inspired the idea of the executive summary and all but mandates its continued use.

The rationale underlying the idea is simply that in a great many cases it is impractical and unnecessary for executives on the client's staff to read entire proposals. They will not normally read the main text of the proposal for more than one reason: The executives may not be in a position to appreciate and appraise the technical detail, but even if they are, it is an inappropriate and inefficient use of their time to read the entire proposal. The typical executive needs only to get a general overview and thus a broad appreciation of each proposal. There are usually specialists on staff whose duties include studying proposals in depth, including the technical detail, and making their evaluations and recommendations to management.

From this you may conclude that only management executives read an executive summary, since it is to management that the executive summary is addressed. Experience shows, however, that, almost invariably, everyone who reads the proposal reads the executive summary, and reads it first. It serves the useful purpose, from any reader's viewpoint, of providing an advance orientation and thus a road map to help the reader grasp the proposal overall. (From the proposer's viewpoint, it offers other benefits, the main subject of this chapter.)

The executive summary is therefore an element that everyone reads, and that fact should suggest some uses to make of the executive summary.

The Uses of an Executive Summary

In Chapter 9, I referred to the executive summary as a proposal element, mentioning Philco, an electronics firm and defense contractor (later acquired by Ford Motor Company). It was the practice there to include in each proposal a final section titled "Why Philco Should Be Awarded This Contract." This section of Philco's proposals recapitulated and summed up all the major sales appeals and arguments that had appeared in the earlier pages of the proposal.

This organization was not the least bit coy about its desire for the contract and its conviction that it was by far the best-qualified proposer for the job. Philco was at pains to assure the client that it did, indeed, sincerely wish to win the contract and did believe that it was in the client's best interests to make the award to Philco. (Marketing is no place for subtlety or modesty, and no place for shrinking violets!)

It is still perfectly proper to include in your proposal some element that makes that desire and conviction plainly apparent to the client by stressing it and drawing special attention to it. (Remember that the proposal is a sales presentation.) Today, however, the convenient and popular mechanism for doing so is almost always that executive summary. The inclusion of such an element in proposals has become virtually a de facto standard. But it appears in the front matter of the proposal, rather than as a final section, and it is probably more effective there.

The executive summary thus becomes a major sales tool, perhaps the most important one in your proposal. It becomes the opening argument of that sales presentation you offer a client as a proposal, and in so doing, it provides certain distinct strengths that can prove decisive:

1. You get an unusually good opportunity to get attention and arouse interest immediately—even before the client comes to page 1.

2. You gain the benefit of being able to establish that important first impression favorably.

3. You can condition the mind of the client—position yourself and your offer advantageously.

4. You can focus the client's attention on the key points and, in so doing, greatly increase the impact of those key points when the client reads and recognizes them again in the main text.

For these reasons it is important that you do not underestimate the importance of the executive summary, but expend enough effort on it to use it to your greatest advantage.

What to Call an Executive Summary

For discussion purposes, I use the generic and descriptive term *executive summary* here. On the one hand, you want to persuade the client to read this section as a time-saver that will offer a quick appreciation of the entire proposal. On the other hand, you do want to take advantage of all opportunities to persuade the client to your cause, to sell.

There is therefore considerable advantage in employing the principle enunciated earlier of making all the titles, headlines, and captions work for you in selling by stressing the benefits and proofs you offer. On the one hand, the title "Executive Summary" is important because many clients expect (and some even demand) such a section of your proposal to be offered, and they will look for it by that name. The client may well be dismayed if he or she cannot find a portion of text so named; that is, the client may fail to recognize an executive summary if not identified clearly as such. On the other hand, you want a title for this element that helps sell your proposal, while also persuading the client to read this curtain-raiser of your proposal. One way to have your cake and eat it too is to use a subtitle, such as the following:

Executive Summary:
Advantages Offered by (your name)

The subtitle should follow that philosophy of making titles work in behalf of the sales effort. Following are some suggestions for such subtitles, offered here as idea starters. (Still, they are generic in nature, and probably you can come up with better ones.)

Summary of Leading Features

Summary of Benefits

Why (your name) Should Be Awarded This Contract

What (your name) Proposes to Do for You

The Benefits of (your name's) Proposed Program

A Few Relevant Principles

Since the client will expect the executive summary to provide an overview and virtual abstract of the proposal, it is important that you do provide that in writing your executive summary. However, your goal is to accomplish that while still achieving your marketing goal of making the executive summary an important principal selling tool. Therefore, every item listed in the executive summary must be couched in positive terms, as a sales argument. In fact, it is helpful to think of the executive summary as being a miniproposal in and of itself, with the following objectives:

1. Introduce yourself briefly, but in highly positive words—words that demonstrate the advantages you offer.
2. Focus on the most critical or important aspect(s) of the requirement (your main strategy) and demonstrate that you have the necessary 20/20 insight.
3. Sum up, in clearly focused and to-the-point delivery, the benefits and proofs—the sales appeals and arguments.

A Case History as an Example

Nothing makes all of this quite as clear as an actual example from a case history. The successful proposal of North Atlantic Industries, Inc., for a large and important Navy procurement of a digital item of equipment owed at least part of its success to an excellent executive summary. A description of the firm's executive summary, along with an outline that includes the actual headlines used, is presented here to help illustrate these principles and practices:

THE PROPOSER: SUPPLIER OF THE AN/USH-26(V)
North Atlantic Industries (NAI) pointed out another Navy program that it was carrying out successfully, mentioned some outstanding achievements in that program, and demonstrated the relevance of that experience and accomplishment to the proposed program. NAI pointed out, for example, the excellent performance and demonstrated reliability of the cited equipment and a Navy award for excellence in quality.

SUPPLIER'S COMMITMENT
NAI stressed the importance of the procurement, pointing out key elements, compared favorably and point-by-point the needs of the program with what NAI had to offer, and pledged NAI's total commitment to the goals of the program. The firm observed that the program had an importance larger than might be suggested by its relatively modest size, also pointing out that the program would be relatively small to a large corporation, but was large and important to NAI, as a small company. *(This was to stress the advantages of using a smaller company as the contractor, of course.)*

BASIC PREMISES
Here NAI drew four points, analyzing the requirement and pointing out the four critical considerations it perceived as what ought to be the areas of concern in developing a design, with due regard to the present state of the art and what could be reasonably anticipated as probable future developments, given recent experience in the fields of interest.

A LOGICAL CONCLUSION
From the above, NAI presented, as a logical conclusion, the indicated prime requirements of any practical design, specifying that these were carefully considered in drawing up the NAI design.

A LOGICAL SOLUTION
Here NAI set forth its specific design objectives, derived from and chosen as the logical outcome of the preceding technical arguments. This was to prove the integrity and authenticity of the technical analyses.

AN ADVANCED DESIGN
NAI provided here some additional data on the proposed design, pointing out that it was truly an advanced design, as promised and suitable to the requirement, and responsive to the capabilities of current technology.

TOTAL COMPLIANCE
NAI affirmed here that it was in total compliance with the RFP in its response, as it will be in its performance.

EXCEEDING REQUIREMENTS
Here NAI listed nine individual and specific items in which it pledged that it would not only meet all requirements, but would actually exceed them—deliver more than is required, providing the client many special and additional benefits.

SPECIAL FEATURE
This promised feature overcomes to a large extent one of the drawbacks—relatively slow access—inherent in using tape for storage purposes.

SOME EXAMPLES OF ENHANCEMENTS
NAI described possible enhancements to the design—options the client could elect to include—and listed nine specific items under this headline.

TECHNICAL SUPPORT SERVICES
Here NAI summarized the required support services and how its organization could and would respond to these.

GEOGRAPHICAL ADVANTAGE
NAI perceived an advantage in its locale (Long Island, New York), which is a center of relevant industries and resources, and pointed this out.

UPGRADABILITY
This paragraph showed how both the system and the individual units proposed could be upgraded, and done so quite easily, in the field.

MANAGEMENT
Here the proposer summarized its several levels of management—technical/project, general/administrative, and corporate—as they would relate to the program.

WHY NORTH ATLANTIC INDUSTRIES SHOULD BE AWARDED THE CONTRACT
This headline should have a familiar ring. You may remember that it was once the title used for an entire proposal section. As used here, it introduced several paragraphs that reinforced briefly all the arguments that had gone before, but then presented the final argument that NAI should be awarded the contract because what was proposed was what the client needed—i.e., that the design was exactly right for the requirement.

How Long Should an Executive Summary Be?

An executive summary, by its nature (i.e., as a summary), should be short. In the case history offered here, the summary met this criterion: Despite the length of this explanation and the use of 14 headlines, this entire presentation was not more than about 2,500 words, nine double-spaced pages. In a proposal of nearly 250 pages, that is less than 4 percent.

There are, of course, no specific rules governing the ideal length of an executive summary. However, aside from the fact that its very name dictates that it must be short with relation to what it summarizes, a lengthy executive summary defeats its own purpose. It cannot, for example, succeed in focusing the client's attention on key issues and critical points if it rambles on about many other matters or fails to get directly to the point for each item covered. It is therefore largely a matter of individual judgment, but here is some guidance to help you form judgments in developing effective executive summaries:

1. The executive summary cited here as a case history represented approximately 3.6 percent of the total proposal. That is a reasonable percentage, although it is desirable to make it even more concise, if possible. Two to three pages of executive summary for every hundred pages of main proposal is a good rule of thumb for sizable proposals.

2. Do not misinterpret this as an absolute yardstick by which to measure all executive summaries; it is not that. A commonsense rule for length is this: Make the executive summary long enough to present all those points you believe to be decisive, but no longer than that. That is, do not shortchange your presentation because of any perceived hard-and-fast rule of maximum allowable size. Far better for it to be a bit longer than it ought logically to be and present everything important than to be brief and fail to present important items. Never lose sight of the purpose of the executive summary: It is designed ostensibly to present a brief overview of your proposal, but the chief objective is to make a sharply focused and hard-hitting sales presentation by summing up your most cogent arguments. It therefore needs brevity, but it also needs completeness, to get that job done.

How to Write "Tight" Executive Summaries

Rewriting Is Far More Important than Writing

Concise and effective executive summaries are never written; they are rewritten. That is a rule for all writing, in fact: The experienced writer does not expect to get his or her best work down on paper (or on a floppy disk) in the first draft. The first draft is (should be) written in complete freedom, getting thoughts on paper or computer disk. In subsequent drafts—and even the best writers often find it necessary to revise through several subsequent drafts—the writer works a steady improvement in a number of ways:

- Cut excess verbiage.
- Organize effectively.
- Use a dynamic style, even telegraphic, in some cases.

Rewriting (and Editing) Means Cutting Copy Down

Almost invariably, the essence of editing, and certainly the first task of editing, is to boil down the copy, which is almost always overwritten. Many, perhaps most, writers are too verbose, and the editor can often delete as much as one third of the copy without losing anything important. Recognizing this, many professional writers simply do not worry about verbosity when they are writing a first draft. In fact, they make a concerted effort to get all the ideas down on disk or paper, with the full expectation that they will then review what they have, choose the best and most relevant material, and eliminate the extraneous material and excess verbiage themselves, even before the editor sees the copy.

This is especially true and probably the best approach for writing an executive summary. First go through the proposal and transcribe all the "goodies"—promises, benefits, proofs, credentials, and whatever else appears to help. Then go through this and begin to sort, determining which are the most important items and which are merely clutter and should be dropped.

This process requires self-discipline. There is an almost instinctive tendency to be "polypharmacal"—to put everything into the prescription in the hope that the larger the number of ingredients, the greater the possibility that one of them will work. But it is a self-defeating idea because too many items will dilute the overall effect and weaken the presentation. Force yourself to discriminate between important and unimportant items, and scrap the latter. Unless yours is an exceptionally large proposal, try to restrict the number of items to not more than ten. Then start organizing the items into a logical sequence and work especially at selecting the most powerful ones for the first three in the list.

Organizing the Executive Summary

The logical sequence for your executive summary is not necessarily the same as that used in the case history cited here. You will have to decide what sequence is best for you—best for the implementation of your strategy, that is. Logically, you should lead with whatever is your main strength. In the case of North Atlantic Industries, one of the firm's major strengths was the record of performance it had already established with the client on a previous contract, and NAI decided to lead with that. Your own case should be decided on its own merits. For example, your main strength might be one of these (or one of many other things, of course):

- Special capabilities and/or experience/accomplishments
- Special resources
- Features of your plan
- Technical advantages offered
- Insights into the requirement
- Cost-reduction ideas

Whatever your decision, build your approach around that major item, use it as your lead, and build your case on it.

The Next Stage: Achieving a Dynamic Style

That first stage addressed reducing the number of items to those of greatest importance. It was necessary to gather up all the items first, of course, and then make judgments about which to keep and which to discard as not being important enough for the executive summary. With that done, it is time to address the second stage of condensing the summary. That is an editorial kind of stage: Items will not be eliminated—presumably, you have by now dropped all items that were not truly essential—but the presentation will be tightened up and made more vigorous by dropping unnecessary words and simplifying expression generally. It is usually acceptable to use special space- and time-saving devices, too, such as telegraphic style (eliminate articles, such as "the" and "a," use briefest verb forms, such as "run" for "running," use bullets for listings, and otherwise get meanings across with greatest possible economies of presentation).

The purpose of all this effort to keep the executive summary as short as possible is not only to conserve the reader's time, but also to achieve a much more dynamic style. These measures add a great deal of vigor to the style, increasing the impact of the words. For example, compare the following two items, portions of an executive summary. The first was written in simple but conventional style and represents the final stage of drafting and polishing the copy before reducing it to the telegraphic, punchy style of the final version.

[Original Version]

Medical Management, Inc. (MMI), offers to provide a detailed medical management plan that includes a complete set of step-by-step procedures; a complete (eight-hour) training seminar for as many of your staff as you wish us to train; complete documentation in the form of procedural, policy, and training manuals; and special consultation services at no charge for 90 days following installation of the MMI system.

MMI offers extra options, at nominal additional costs: (1) MMI will make this a turnkey program—will ourselves install the system: operate it for 90 days and debug it; train your staff; and then turn over the trouble-free and smooth-running system to your own staff. (2) MMI will remain on call for one year, as needed to help solve problems, deal effectively with new and unanticipated problems, and/or answer questions and provide additional training for your staff. (3) MMI will operate your system for a full year, while providing training and customizing all procedures, policies, and documentation for your own organization.

[Revised, Final Version]

Medical Management, Inc. (MMI) proposes a detailed and specific program:

- Complete step-by-step procedures
- 8-hour training seminar for all staff
- Policy, procedural, and training manuals
- 90 days free consultation

Also, for nominal additional costs, these options:

- Turnkey program: We operate, debug, train, and turn over after 90 days.
- MMI on call, for full year, as consultant, troubleshooter.
- MMI operates system for full year.

Note that the final version is far less verbose without missing any of the important points, but is far more vigorous, making each point sharply and guiding the reader's attention to focus on the benefit and not become distracted by irrelevant adjectives and adverbs. The client has no difficulty in grasping immediately the specifics of your offer—and your proposal is an offer, not a pleading.

Executive Summary in a Letter Proposal

A small program usually calls for a letter proposal, rather than a formal one. A letter proposal is rarely more than two to four pages, even with a program outline. Obviously, such a brief and informal proposal will not include a formal executive summary, such as that discussed and shown here. Nevertheless, the letter is still a proposal, and it is, as such, also a sales presentation.

For that reason, the philosophy of the executive summary still applies, although it may appear as a simple narrative paragraph or two. On the other hand, it is perfectly proper to make a laundry list type of presentation, as in the examples just used, when there are a number of items to be featured. Whichever the case, the summary should be as close to the opening of the letter as possible or should even be presented as the opening itself, as in the following examples of each style.

Because Marketing Consultants, Inc. (MCI), has stored in our computer and other files over 200,000 of our proprietary marketing materials, we are able to assemble a custom-designed system for you almost literally overnight and at unprecedented low cost. And while we will make recommendations, you have the opportunity to review these materials and make choices of your own.

On the other hand, it is possible to adapt the listed-item and telegraphic style where there are numerous points you wish to stress:

Marketing Consultants, Inc. (MCI), offers clients a unique service:

- Widest choice of materials & styles in industry—GUARANTEED.
- System completely custom designed for you—GUARANTEED.
- Turnaround (delivery) in less than one week—GUARANTEED.
- Lowest cost anywhere—GUARANTEED.

MCI can do this for you because our library has over 200,000 proprietary designs and marketing materials in our computer and other files. We make recommendations, but you have the right to make choices.

Other Front Matter

Sequence of Front Matter

The following sequence is recommended for the front matter:

1. Copy of letter of transmittal (inside cover)
2. Title page
3. Executive summary
4. Preface or foreword, if used
5. Note introducing response matrix
6. Response matrix
7. Table of contents

TITLE PAGE

Unless you are preparing a truly large formal proposal and are going to the considerable expense often associated with the preparation of such large proposals, your letterhead is likely to serve well as the basis for the title page of your proposal. Figure 34 is an example of such a title page.

The example includes reference to an RFP—request for proposals. Where such a formal request does not exist, for whatever reason, reference is simply not made—that is, the two lines beginning "in response to" are simply deleted.

The notice of proprietary information is likewise not always appropriate. Where it is, however, such a notice should be printed on the title page, and the actual material cited should be identified as confidential and/or proprietary on those pages by suitable notations there.

HRH COMMUNICATIONS, INC.

P.O. Box 1731   Wheaton, MD 20902
Fax: (301) 649-5745   Voice: (301) 649-2499

PROPOSAL
Offered to Hardesty & Hardesty, Inc.
in response to RFP HH-86-001
dated June 22, 1998

NOTICE:
Information contained in pages 33–37, 45, 49,
and 76–82 is confidential and proprietary to
HRH Communications, Inc., and should not be
disclosed to anyone not a recipient or reviewer
of this proposal. However, in the event of
award, this information may be disclosed to
and will be used in behalf of and according to
the interests of Hardesty & Hardesty, Inc.

July 15, 1998

Copyright June 1998 by HRH Communications, Inc.

Figure 34 Typical title page of a formal proposal.

If you are submitting a formal proposal to a government agency, the RFP will normally suggest the wording for this proprietary notice, but it will be along the general lines shown in Figure 34.

The copyright notice is a good idea for all cases, as further protection for your confidential and proprietary information, as well as for your proposal itself. A great many people are imitative, especially when they observe a success (as in every industry), and there will be those who are likely to plagiarize your exact wording if and when they manage to get copies of your successful proposals, which happens frequently these days. You are entitled to copyright your proposal, and you need to do nothing more than what is shown to secure to yourself a common-law copyright. (It is only necessary to have that copyright registered with the Copyright Office of the U.S. Library of Congress if and when you get involved in litigation concerning your copyright, and you can register it at that time, if it ever becomes necessary.)

TABLE OF CONTENTS

The table of contents of a publication lists, as a minimum, the titles of chapters or sections and the page numbers. Some writers choose to list for each chapter all the major headlines, thus offering almost an abstract of each chapter, probably an exceptionally good idea for a proposal presentation. (See the table of contents for this book as a general example.)

Among other refinements possible for the table of contents, although not universally practiced, is the inclusion of additional sections in the table of contents headed by such titles as "List of Figures" (or "Illustrations"), "List of Tables," and "Foreword" or "Preface."

Unlike books, proposals do not often carry prefaces or forewords, although there is no good reason why they should not do so, except that the executive summary serves at least part of the purpose generally served by a preface or foreword. However, there are other purposes that can be served by such introductory remarks. For one thing, in the large consulting organization the CEO (chief executive officer) may utilize this to address the client with assurances of his or her personal concern and pledge of conscientious effort. (This is otherwise conveyed in the letter of transmittal, but is almost certainly more effective in a foreword or preface.) But it may be used to carry any special message of preliminary remarks deemed suitable and helpful.

RESPONSE MATRIX

The item I choose to call a response matrix is an especially important and useful element of the front matter. It's a device to help ensure that you do respond to all matters of concern, but even more important, it helps the client verify that you have done so—that your proposal is completely responsive.

It is derived from the request for proposal and, more specifically, from those checklists you made earlier in analyzing the requirement and what the client wished you to respond to. It may be several pages long and usually is, for any proposal of size. Figure 35 is part of a single sheet from one such matrix. Note the column titles: "Specification" refers to the RFP and what it specifically calls for. "Compliance?" calls for a "yes" or "no." "Exceeds?" also calls for "yes" or "no." "Proposal Reference" refers to the proposal, listing the page and paragraph numbers (where paragraphs are numbered, as they were in this case), and leaving a rightmost column blank for the use of the client in checking off the compliance with all specifications.

Of course, this form should be modified and adapted to your own needs, which are likely to be less formalized than this one was. For example, you may not have numbered paragraphs, and you may even not have a formal specification to refer to, and so you may wish to substitute other column titles, such as "Need" for "Specification."

This is an important element and should be developed carefully and introduced with a brief explanation that it is provided to assist the reader in locating specific responses to required information, as well as to ensure that the author of the proposal has made all necessary responses.

Letter of Transmittal

Informal or letter proposals are complete in and of themselves usually. Formal proposals usually have three elements:

1. Technical proposal (may be more than one volume)
2. Cost proposal (often required to be a separate document)
3. Letter of transmittal

MATRIX TABLE SHOWING COMPLIANCE WITH ELEX-T-551

| Specification | | Compliance? | Exceeds? | Proposal Reference | | Title/ Remarks |
| | | | | Par./ Graphic | Page No. | |
Par.	Title/Subj.					
3.5.8	Printer copy	YES	—	2.3,1, 2.3,2	2–14, 2–46	
3.5.9	TEMPEST	YES	—	3.1	3–1	
3.5.10	ELEC. DESIGN	YES	YES	2.3, 4	2–14	
3.5.11	THERMAL DESIGN	YES	—	2.5, 6, 8, 9	2–16, 2–17	
3.5.12	TEST MEASURE.	YES	—	2.13	2–18	
3.5.13	TEST PROVISIONS	YES	YES	2.15	2–20	
3.5.14	CLASS A TEST	YES	—	2.15	2–21	
3.5.17	CLASS B TEST	YES	YES	2.16	2–22	

Figure 35 Sample response matrix.

The letter of transmittal is a courtesy, but it is more than that, too. Many consultants believe that the letter of transmittal is of great importance, although others think it is mere formality and of little significance in making an award. The truth falls between those extremes, of course, as truth usually does. But the importance of a letter of transmittal—or the lack of importance—is at least partly the consequence of its treatment. Obviously, if you treat it as a pure formality, that is all it will be. However, you can compel it to assume greater importance if you design it to be more important.

The matters that a letter of transmittal ought to cover are these, as a minimum:

1. Confirm that the proposal is a response to some specific RFP (hereby identified), an informal request, submitted as agreed to earlier, or citing whatever circumstances led to the proposal.

2. Make brief mention of the requirement to which it responds and the chief characteristics or features of the proposal (but especially of any major feature).

3. Confirm that you are authorized to make the offer and that it is a firm offer.

4. State the period of time for which the offer made in your proposal is firm.

5. Make an offer to provide any additional information desired in any form desired, including in writing and in face-to-face discussions, with or without formal presentations.

The letter of transmittal is addressed to the client or to whomever issued the request for proposals, such as the client's purchasing agent. (In the case of proposals to the government, it is normally addressed to the contracting officer.)

It is a common practice of many consultants to bind a copy of the letter of transmittal inside the cover of each copy of the proposal, so that every reader of the proposal can read the letter also.

The Cost Proposal

Everything discussed in this chapter has, so far, been front matter. The remaining two items to be discussed here are not front matter, but require only brief discussion and can be fitted here as well as anywhere else. One of these items is the cost proposal, where a separate cost proposal is required.

The reason for making the cost proposal a separate item is to withhold from evaluators all knowledge of costs. This is done to encourage evaluators to make their evaluations of technical proposals uninfluenced by cost considerations. Therefore, if you plan to bind a copy of your letter of transmittal into a technical proposal submitted to a government agency, you must exercise care to see that no cost information is included in that copy of the letter.

Governments almost invariably require separate cost proposals and usually provide forms upon which to list costs and explain how the proposer has arrived at the bottom-line figure. Usually, the cost proposal is only a few pages, at most, although there can be exceptions to this also.

Appendixes

The remaining item to be considered is the appendix. This is a simple item also and is a place where you include material that will be of interest to some readers, but not to all. That might include additional resumes, drawings, professional papers cited in the body of the proposal, sample materials, or other items qualifying to be appended, but not included in the main text.

CHAPTER 12

Common Problems and Ideas for Solutions

> "When someone hands you a lemon, make lemonade." Despite the triteness of this often repeated expression, the idea is valid, and you can make it a reality in almost all cases, a reality that will place you in front of the pack.

Questions for and about Small, New, Inexperienced Proposal Writers

The problems you encounter in writing proposals are probably much more common than you think. Following are a few typical ones to illustrate this. In fact, these examples report on questions I have gotten again and again from many readers of my earlier book, *How to Succeed as an Independent Consultant* (John Wiley & Sons, 1983, 1988, and 1993) and other writings on the subject, especially those on the Internet.

> *I am a very small business, and I can't list a half dozen qualified specialists as staff employees for those projects that need a half dozen or more professionals. How can I handle that?*

There are several variants of that question. Some of the inquirers are independent consultants, having no employees. Some are partnerships without other employees. Some are even part-time consultants. But all address the same question: Will it be disastrous to admit that they do not now have all the staff necessary or will it be disastrous to propose that they will hire employees or use associates to perform on the contract?

There are a number of analogous problems, all related to a common problem of being small or new and therefore perceiving great difficulty in putting up a show of strength in the matters of resources, experience, and other qualifications. Here are some other questions that reflect those kinds of concerns:

I am just starting out, and I really have no experience to describe or other clients to list. How do I answer a requirement to list current and recent projects?

I have only a little experience [or] I have a little experience, but sometimes it is not the right kind for the project, although I know that I can do the job.

I work at home. Do I need a downtown office in a building so that I look as though I am a real professional? Is having my office at home unprofessional? What do I do if the client wants to see my facilities for handling the job? I can arrange to use a friend's office address as a kind of front. Would that be a good idea or a bad one?

How do I avoid using long and difficult words, as you advise, when I am in a field that communicates in such jargon? Won't clients think I am unqualified or inexperienced if I don't use the right jargon or buzzwords?

Should I be incorporated to make myself look more important in my proposals? Doesn't being a corporation add prestige?

Does it help to have an important-sounding name, such as "International Marketing Associates, Inc.," instead of "John Smith, Consultant," or "John Smith and Associates"?

There are other questions that reflect the questioner's inexperience with proposals and often with some of the practical problems of producing multipage bound documents. Here are some other questions that reflect inexperience, fears, and uncertainties:

Should I have my proposals typeset and printed, with printed covers and professional artwork?

What about that statement in some government requests that warns readers against submitting elaborate proposals? What does that mean exactly?

I find that I am usually making wild guesses at the price estimate. Is there any kind of rule or guideline for estimating costs? Is it important to be the low bidder?

I find that there is usually not enough information in the RFP. What is the best way to get more information?

Sometimes the client limits the number of pages I may use, and I have trouble with that. Any ideas about handling this?

Does it help to have the proposal typeset, printed, and bound formally? How can I reproduce very large drawings without going to more expense than I can afford?

All these questions have been addressed, to at least some degree, in the general discussions of earlier chapters, but it will be helpful to focus additionally on the most commonly experienced problems and provide suggestions for coping successfully with them. Let's take these up, one by one, as well as several other problems that are likely to trouble you now or in the future, and you will see that the picture is not as bleak as you may fear.

The (Apparent) Problems of Smallness

It's quite common, if you are an independent consultant or have a small consulting organization to see your small size as a handicap instead of recognizing the ways in which being small offers advantages. And smallness does offer advantages, even in the marketing of your services. You can take advantage of being small when you write your proposals. But we must understand the problem before we can solve it. First, let's examine the reasons you see smallness as a drawback and consider generally some of the benefits of smallness.

First understand that the image of smallness as a weakness in your competitive position as a consultant manifests insecurity. It's born entirely out of fear—fear of what appears to be the overwhelming advantage of your large and (apparently) well-established and entrenched competitors.

Cost Advantages and Disadvantages

The humans employed by your large competitors are no less fallible than you and, in all probability, no more talented or experienced generally as individuals. Their advantages are primarily in having some kind of track record—experience and other resources to draw on. In some cases they can offer a cost advantage as a result of size. (The cliché here is "economies of scale.") Where and when that is the case, it is almost always because there is an optimum size for an organization, that size at which it can operate most efficiently and that usually means at lowest overhead rates.

On the other hand, the direct rates—principally the direct cost of all labor, before overhead enters the cost picture—tend to run considerably higher in larger organizations than in small ones, especially in the case of independent consultants. That tends to counterbalance any overhead advantage the large organization might have, so that as a small organization you can usually be cost competitive. In fact, if you are an independent practitioner, you can afford to make some sacrifices, such as working overtime without charging yourself for it, as one means of competing. This is a special advantage when you are in an early stage and need such special advantages to get started and begin to build your own track record.

The Importance of Costs

In ordinary circumstances, the very fact that a prospective client requests proposals, rather than quotations or bids, indicates that cost is not the first or most important consideration, but competence, reliability, and other such factors are. However, if cost is not always the most important consideration, it is never unimportant. Moreover, when and if two or more proposers are judged about equally attractive in all other respects, cost is likely to suddenly become the decisive factor. So do try to be as cost competitive as you can be without taking unacceptable risks.

Probably the most important message with regard to costs is don't be greedy. Yielding to the temptation to win a few extra dollars of profit costs many proposers assignments that they could otherwise have won. Do price to cover all costs and produce a reasonable profit; you are not only entitled to that, but you must have it to survive. However, be satisfied with that unless you are willing to lose many bids you might have otherwise won or have some special benefit to offer a client that you believe is worth more than the normal market price.

On the other hand, waste no time or tears lamenting the bids you lost where you priced properly. You lost a bid that would have cost you money, and you should have no regrets about that.

A Few Ways to Handle the Smallness Issue

One of the major advantages of smallness in marketing via proposals is being able to point out tactfully to clients that what is a small and not very important project to a large corporation is a very important project to you. (This is the "Small enough to serve you properly, but big enough to get the job done efficiently" argument.) Therefore, while the large organization would likely not assign its most experienced and most qualified professionals to the projects, you would give the project your full and undivided attention and see to it personally that every detail is attended to properly.

That latter argument, properly handled, can be a telling blow in your own behalf. And "properly handled" means getting the point across effectively to the client while being tactful. That means avoiding giving the appearance of making a direct attack on competitors. (You can compare yourself favorably with your competitors, but it is always a bad tactic to openly knock competitors and best never to mention them by name.)

An excellent way of making this statement diplomatically is to point out that there is an optimum size for handling the project in question and make the technical arguments for this view. Explain the potential hazard of a relatively small project becoming lost among large projects. That is the point at which you explain that this cannot happen with you because your operating philosophy is to focus on small, highly specialized projects. When you put the argument this way, the client will get the point quickly enough.

You can also use the successful approach made popular a few years ago by the car rental firm, Avis: We're Number 2, so we try harder.

But your concern may go well beyond smallness in general. You may be concerned about that more specialized problem of pursuing a contract that requires a half dozen consultant professionals, while you have only yourself or only one or two others on staff or even as associates. But even so, it is possible to make lemonade of this problem, to actually finesse the problem by seizing it and making a strength of the weakness. Let's first try to get a more insightful look at this problem than appears on the surface.

Defining and Redefining the Problem

Two Very Hot Problems

Consider the case of our space program, in which reentry was an early problem that appeared insurmountable to some. There was (and is yet, at least so far as we know today) no practicable way for a space vehicle to reenter the earth's atmosphere at any but extremely high speed. That means almost unimaginably great friction, with the resulting heat great enough to melt and even vaporize any metal or alloy we know of, not to mention what such heat would do to the interior of the vehicle and its occupants.

Since we did not know of any way to avoid this problem of speed, friction, and heat, our choice was to give up the program or find a way to succeed in spite of the problem. That is, we had to accept the great heat as a condition to live with, if the program were to continue.

Once we accepted that, we changed the nature of the problem: Instead of being a problem in how to avoid the heat, it became a problem in finding a way to shield the vehicle and its interior from the heat. And that quest resulted in the ablative heat shield—a ceramic shell on the surface of the reentry vehicle (ceramic tiles on the space shuttle) deliberately designed to burn off during reentry.

Charles Kettering faced a similar problem in designing an automobile self-starter. He knew, as every automotive engineer did, that any starter motor large enough to crank an automobile engine would overheat if it were not as large as the engine. Making it that large was impractical, but he had already decided that he must and would create a workable self-starter. He therefore changed the problem from one of trying to design a practicable self-starter that would not overheat to a problem of how to design a practicable self-starter that could endure overheating without being destroyed by it. Of course, he did so successfully, as we all know today.

The Insoluble Redefined

Remember the earlier admonition that a true problem definition itself points to the solution or to more than one possible solution? That means that if the problem is insoluble as defined, it must be redefined. Redefining the problem means first accepting any condition that is unavoidable, even if it appears to be a barrier to solution. Then create a new definition that accepts the unavoidable condition, but points to a solution that is workable despite the given condition! If you go back and reread the two examples of how to solve the "insoluble" with this in mind, you will see how problems were solved by first redefining them and then attacking the solution that the new (and true) definition pointed to. Now, apply this idea to some of the proposal problems.

In the case of not having enough key people on staff or as associates to handle the proposed project properly, there are several possible ways to approach this, each way based on redefinition of the problem. The original problem is conceived as being one of appearing to be totally unqualified for the project as a result of being disastrously understaffed. The fact of not having the necessary staff on board is the unavoidable condition that must be accepted.

The redefinition is simple enough: The problem must be redefined to become one of how to appear well qualified in spite of not having the necessary staff on board. And, aside from "hanging paper"—an act, practiced by unscrupulous proposers, of misleading the client by offering resumes of people you don't even know and haven't talked to, pretending that they are on staff or associates—you have only these alternatives: proposing to hire new people after award or proposing to seek out other consultants to act as subcontractors or associates, offering resumes and letters of agreement from such people to verify that they are professional associates and will work on the project with you. That, however, might still be regarded as an expedient, to compensate for a weakness in staffing capability. Something less defensive in appearance is needed to solve the problem satisfactorily. Otherwise, these expedients appear to be just that, and they appear also to be apologies for not being fully qualified, a suicidal approach to marketing.

Defensiveness is always a tactical mistake, for it is an admission of weakness, and you can win only by attacking from strength. You must take the bull by the horns and say, in effect, "Here is what I am going to do for you," as you finesse the problem. Here is one way that has worked well in turning this apparent weakness into a strength: State boldly that the special nature of the requirement indicates to you a need for certain specialists. You have therefore sought out the most notable and outstanding such specialists in the field and gotten their agreement to work with you on this worthy program. Of course, you must do more than make that kind of general statement. You must prove your case with suitable technical arguments, and you should indeed have an understanding with those specialists you name as staff members.

In general in all such situations, never appear to be apologetic and defensive, and never lie about real conditions. In this case, you need never admit that there is only you or you and one or two others, for you never address the matter of the size of your permanent, in-house staff at all. Instead, you bore in aggressively with resumes of these highly specialized new associates and their letters of agreement to work on the project with you. And if the question of your staff and its size does come up at any time, you can easily say that you handle all projects with handpicked associates because a significant feature of your consulting is exactly that: seeking out and employing in behalf of your clients the precisely right specialists. In fact, you can make that kind of positive argument in your proposal, if you wish to make an issue of it there and establish it as a basic premise upon which you base your entire approach to satisfying requirements. That would be a direct attack and probably a novel approach.

Questions of Experience

There are two kinds of experience in question when writing a proposal: the direct and personal experience of any whose resumes are offered and the experience of the proposing organization. If you are an independent consultant working alone, there is a certain ambivalence about this. On the one hand, the client wants to know about your experience and achievements as an independent consultant serving clients under contract. On the other hand, all your "organization" experience is your personal experience. Practically, they are the same. Technically and philosophically, they are not. Serving your employer's clients, with your employer bearing the ultimate responsibility, is not quite the same as winning the assignment on your own and being totally responsible in all respects for the work. So if you are only recently established as an independent consultant, you are in short supply of that latter kind of qualifying experience as an "organization."

Many consultants get around this problem by careful wording that does not specifically claim individual experience as organization experience, but encourages the reader to so interpret it. That is an expedient that works for many who are skillful enough and careful enough in writing to bring the idea to reality.

A second approach, which I am convinced is more effective and should be used whenever practicable, is to meet the issue squarely, head on. Argue the case of fresh ideas, an open mind uncluttered by conventional ideas, technology transfer resulting from your diverse earlier experience, and other such bold tactics, as they fit your own experience. And if your earlier experience included working with some prestigious firm, a university, or other impressive reference, by all means capitalize fully on it.

Again, avoid at all costs any appearance of defensiveness, apologia, or other self-deprecation. Those are defeatist tactics, and defeat is the result of using such tactics.

The same philosophy applies to those cases where you are in pursuit of a contract to do something a bit out of your usual field, but something you are sure you can handle well, despite your inability to point to directly related experience. In such cases it is important to dwell at length and in detail on your specific program designs and plans. Demonstrate the technology transfer or whatever basis on which you have built your program strategy. Show, in as much detail as possible, exactly what the technology transfer is and why it is not only appropriate, but advantageous to the client. Remember in all cases that the client's number one concern is what he or she thinks is in his or her own interest. The more your offer appears to be in the client's direct interest, the less proof of anything else you need to offer. Always seek the argument that indicates what you propose as best for the client's direct interest. In this milieu, nothing is good or bad in absolute terms, but only good or bad in terms of the client's interest. It is therefore bad for the client's interest to have the project put on the back burner or assigned to junior personnel by the large consulting organization, as it is good for the client to have the project get the full, personal attention of a fully qualified professional.

How "Professional" Do You Have to Be?

When I gave up my own costly suite of offices in downtown Washington in favor of a comfortable office and conference room in my own home, I did so with some trepidation. The move was very much in my own interests in many ways, but I feared its psychological effects on some of my clients. Particularly, I had misgivings about how one particular client would react to this move. This was a prominent and prestigious corporation with approximately 20 companies, very well known in the business and financial worlds, and I was dealing with people very near the top of the corporation. So it was with some hesitancy that I announced the change to the corporate vice president with whom I had most of my direct dealings.

To my relief and pleasant surprise, the reaction was along the line of "Cutting overhead, eh? Great idea. Smart move." They approved!

In the years since, I have worked with people from this corporation and others in my own home conference room, although the nature of my consulting work is such that I do not often have need to receive clients in my own office. Having my office and conference room in my home, in a quiet residential neighborhood near a shopping center, has never proved a disadvantage or, as far as I can tell, caused me any loss of respect by my clients.

I do not believe that it is necessary to be located in an office building, as far as it concerns your credibility, image, or prestige as a consultant. You may have very good reasons for renting space in an office building, but image and prestige are the wrong kind of reasons to do so. Nor should you ever fake it by using someone else's office. To do so is not only deceit that will harm your image—who will trust you after discovering that subterfuge? (and it will eventually be discovered)—but is totally unnecessary.

On the other hand, if you have your office at home or in a suburban business district and must meet and confer with a client in town, it is perfectly legitimate to make temporary arrangements. But don't deceive the client; be up front about it, and you'll suffer no harm for it. In fact, most clients will be appreciative of your action in making things more convenient for them.

On Incorporating

Incorporating yourself is today extremely easy to do. In most states you can do so for $50 to $75 by filling out a simple form or two. (In Maryland the form is a single page, and the fee when I incorporated there was $40 plus $6 for a certified copy of the approved form.) It is so easy to do, in fact, that for that reason alone there is no special prestige attached to being a corporation. There are good reasons for many consultants to be incorporated, but gaining prestige is not one of them. It will not make your proposal more impressive and should never be done for that reason.

Very much the same philosophy applies to the name you choose for yourself. One executive I know who reviews capability brochures and proposals quite often has remarked more than once, "The bigger the name, the smaller the company," whenever he encounters a lengthy company name in his reading. He smiles when he murmurs this because he is amused by the effort to be impressive via the route of a lengthy and pompous name.

The same philosophy applies to the personal titles you bestow on yourself and others. Of course, you are the president and chairman of the board of your own corporation, but you gain nothing but perhaps an amused smile by making a major issue of it in your proposal.

Here are the names of a few of the most prominent and successful consulting companies, and this is probably the best answer to the question of how helpful is a lengthy and "impressive" name:

Arthur Andersen
Ernst & Young
Price Waterhouse
KPMG
Deloitte & Touche
Coopers & Lybrand

How Elaborate the Proposal?

Proposals ought to be professional—neat, clean, grammatical, spelled correctly, well organized. Composition by most modern computer printers is almost the equivalent of typesetting and is the popular way to compose proposals today. They may be printed in an offset print shop, but duplication by modern office copiers is as good and quite acceptable. They can be bound in printed covers, but binding in a patent report binder is quite acceptable.

Those admonitions found in many RFPs about "excessively elaborate" proposals refer to a day when the Department of Defense was spending billions recklessly (although that does not appear to have changed very much) and defense contractors were going to such extremes as binding multivolume proposals in morocco leather with specially built cases to hold the several volumes and printing illustrations of the ultracostly process-color type, à la *National Geographic* magazine. *That* is "excessively elaborate." That, however, is no bar to composing, duplicating, and binding according to normal commercial standards. Most offices are now equipped to do production that is the equal of that done by commercial print shops.

Production Problems

Until now we have been discussing tactical problems, problems of proposal content, except for the question of what is excessively elaborate in a proposal. That latter is a production matter, and you may encounter a few production problems.

Production refers to all the details of making up the physical proposal, in whatever is the required number of copies, for delivery to the client. At the low end of the scale, where only a single copy is required and, especially, where that is an informal letter proposal, you need make only a single file copy for yourself and probably require only the simplest kind of graphics, if you need graphics at all. (It is likely that you will not, in such cases.)

On the other hand, as the proposal becomes more formal and larger, the practical production requirements change considerably, and related problems may arise. This is especially the case if you are an independent consultant with typically limited resources.

Reproduction

Today, with the ease of using modern office copying machines and the high quality of the work most produce, it has become common practice to "print" the required number of copies in this way. In fact, even photographs may be reproduced with fairly good quality on many modern office copiers.

In terms of cost, it is usually less expensive to reproduce proposals by office copier than it is to print them because proposals are usually produced in only a handful of copies. (The economies in offset printing are not realized until the number of copies begins to mount up into hundreds.)

Photos

If you wish to include photos in your proposal, you may be able to make reasonably good copies on an office copier. That failing, or if you are not satisfied with the admittedly less than perfect xerographic reproduction of a photograph, you can scan the photos (scanners are quite inexpensive now) and produce very good copies on your computer printer.

Line Drawings

You can, as noted already, prepare most and possibly all your own graphics with the aid of suitable desktop publishing software and achieve professional quality in doing so. Or, if you prefer, you can hire someone to prepare your graphics, either a freelance illustrator or a local graphic arts shop.

One problem that arises is that of large drawings. If you do develop functional flowcharts and other such drawings, they can easily grow to sizes well beyond that of a single page. The usual practice for using such drawings is to make foldouts of them—lengthy drawings folded down to page size, with a binding edge left free so that the reader can extend the drawing to its full size. And such drawings can easily become several feet long, which poses a special kind of problem: How can it be reproduced inexpensively, as it must be when you must deliver more than one copy of your proposal? (In any case, even when you need deliver only one copy, you still need a file copy for yourself.)

PRINTED COPIES

The alternatives are (1) have a printer print several copies for you; (2) reproduce the drawing in sections, on an office copier, and paste the sections together to make complete drawings; and (3) use another process, such as ozalid copying.

The first alternative is sometimes used by large corporations turning out major proposals that require a large number of copies. It's an expensive alternative because a large printing press is required, and a large negative and plate must be made. Moreover, it is not always easy to get the job done quickly this way, and that alone is often a bar to using this method, given the tight, often seemingly impossible schedules that are typical of proposal requirements. The second alternative is tedious, time-consuming, and not too pleasing aesthetically.

OZALID COPYING

The third alternative is often the most practical approach. Ozalid is a process used by most large blueprint shops. Most shops of this type can make copies of a large drawing economically and quickly.

The process is such that it can copy anything drawn on a transparent or translucent medium, such as vellum and mylar. If possible, have your original drawing on such a medium. Otherwise, a negative of the original must be made first. (Most large blueprint shops are equipped to handle that for you, however.)

BINDING

The question of where to bind foldout drawings in a proposal arises. Conventional practice regarding placement of graphics in publications of this type is to have the illustration follow the first text reference to it as closely as possible, which in this case normally means on the next page. For foldouts, however, this can create another kind of a problem: You may wish to make numerous references to the drawing, and it becomes quite awkward for the reader to flip pages back and forth, folding and unfolding the illustration.

A way around this problem is to bind all such drawings at the back of the proposal. This permits the reader to leave the drawing folded out for easy repeated reference.

Page-Limited Proposals

It has become a fairly common practice of government and some other proposal requesters to ease the burden of reviewing and evaluating large formal proposals by limiting their size. Without such controls, the sizes can vary wildly, from a few dozen pages to thousands of pages. The client, in such cases, makes a judgment as to a proper size—the number of pages in which a proposer ought to be able to make his or her presentation—and mandates that as a limit.

When an RFP mandates a page limit, it usually specifies minimum type size (usually 10 point, expressed as 12 pitch for a typewriter or printer), spacing (whether the pages are to be single- or double-spaced), and the size of margins. Frequently, such RFPs except certain elements of the proposal from the limitation. It is not unusual, for example, for the RFP to except resumes, some front matter, and sometimes appendixes from the restriction. On the other hand, the RFP may fail to state specifically whether there are any exceptions. Or it may warn that appendixes and exhibits are included in the limitation and will not be reviewed or taken into account in the evaluation if they exceed the page limit.

Most often this is a general and overall limitation, but not always. In one recent case the RFP limited the proposal on an element-by-element basis, calling out maximum page counts for the executive summary, the resumes, the discussion, and the other major elements.

This is a problem to many proposal writers, but it is also a problem to your competitors and therefore offers you a special and additional opportunity to excel. In fact, such a limitation can be made to work to your advantage by compelling you to do what you should do anyway in writing a proposal. It therefore ought not to be a major problem, nor should it require any subterfuge to overcome. For one thing, experience has shown that the clients' estimates of what is necessary to make an adequate presentation are usually quite sound. For another, it is in your own interest to keep your proposal as tight as possible, which would be the result of good writing and editing practices, in any case. There are two major points to be made here, both guidelines to follow when responding to any proposal request, regardless of whether it is page-limited:

1. Use graphics effectively, and you will eliminate many pages of text by that measure alone. Be conscious of this possibility in reviewing and editing draft, judging where the presentation could be made more efficient with a graphic illustration. Then generate those illustrations to reduce verbiage.

2. Don't attempt to limit your writing in first draft, but get it all down. Then edit it down to size. That alone should, in the typical case, boil out about one third of the text as extraneous, redundant, covering trivia, or otherwise easily dispensed with.

(If you still have too much, reduce the copy by eliminating the least important material that is not specifically required by the client.) Properly, you should not write a proposal to satisfy a page limitation; you should edit the proposal to comply with that limitation.

In my own experience, these measures have proved to be effective in every case, achieving compliance with the size limitation without compromising the effectiveness of the presentation.

Packaging

Packaging refers to physical and cosmetic characteristics of the proposal package you will deliver. Usually, there are at least three elements in the package: the technical proposal, the cost proposal, and the letter of transmittal.

Even in those cases where the client does not mandate that the cost proposal by physically separate from the technical proposal, it is a good idea to separate them to encourage review and evaluation of your technical proposal as objectively as possible.

The original letter of transmittal is normally in a separate business envelope, accompanying the package of technical and cost proposals.

Binding may be done in many ways, of which these three are probably the most popular and most commonly used:

- Side stitching—stapling the sheets and cover together
- Three-hole binder, either a hard ring binder or a report binder
- Spiral binder, using plastic spines

Spiral binding requires special equipment to punch 18 or 19 rectangular holes in the sheets and install the plastic spines. (The number of holes depends on the model of binding equipment you use.) But such binding does offer the advantage of the proposal lying flat when opened, and the client may appreciate that convenience.

Three-ring binding offers this same advantage, when a hard three-ring binder is used rather than one of the stationery-store report binders with its metal clips. However, repeated handling of a document in a three-ring binder almost always means that some of the pages become detached.

It is possible to buy hard binders to accommodate those 18- or 19-hole sheets and so combine some of the better features of each alternative. There are also some other types of jiffy binders that are easy to use without any special equipment or special preparation and are usually suitable if your proposal is a small one.

CHAPTER 13

Miscellaneous Important Information for Proposal Writing

The New Questionnaire

Other consultants' views, ways to overcome some inherent handicaps to proposal writing, ways to find more proposal opportunities, and several references may help you write your proposals more easily and effectively.

In researching and preparing to write the first edition of this book, I sent out a brief questionnaire to a large number of consultants, most of them small companies and/or independent practitioners. My purpose was to surface common problems in proposal writing, to be able to report factually to you on what other consultants do and how they feel about proposal writing, to validate my own opinions and experience in this field, and to validate (or amend) my own judgment as to what information and guidance should be included in these pages for you. The questionnaire petitioned the consultants' responses to a series of questions, some calling for factual reporting, some for opinion or speculation, and others for identification of concerns and perceived problems. Additionally, respondents were invited to make any comments they wished to and to send copies of proposals or related materials they use.

In preparing to write the second edition of this book, I went back to a number of those originally polled, as well as to others to determine whether any purpose would be served by instituting a new questionnaire and survey. I found that changes I would report and changes that would affect what I had written a few years earlier would have little relationship to what my questionnaire had produced, and so I chose to reproduce the original questionnaire and results, and just add a few notes and comments. For this, the third edition, however, there is no question that some of the changes that have taken place have had revolutionary effects on proposal writing and related functions of marketing. They justify assembling a new round of reports and opinions from a representative sample of independent consultants.

Figure 36 is a reproduction of the new questionnaire. In fact, it is only slightly changed from the original one, but the changes in the questionnaire are keyed to the changes I perceived in the proposal environment. I mailed many directly to consultants known to me, but many more responded to a copy of the questionnaire I mailed to others, consultants I did not know personally. I enlisted the help of several individuals to do this, as well as choosing many respondents at random from their print and online appearances.

The Survey Results

A tabulation of results, by percentages, is included here for the factual items reported in each category, with accompanying explanations, observations, and remarks, as necessary and appropriate. As almost always occurs in surveys of this type, there is a large element of "opinionaire" to the survey, so there are a few anomalies. Still, I hope to provide at least some insight and guidance from this admittedly limited survey of the field.

Respondent Specialties

Before presenting those figures, it is useful to have a look at some of the various consulting specialties represented here, since consulting as a profession and industry (it is both) is remarkably diverse, which itself accounts for many of what may appear to be anomalies in the results of this survey.

The survey did not require respondents to identify themselves; nevertheless, some respondents did, although many did not indicate clearly what their consulting specialties are. However, here is a list of some of the specialties that were identified. (Many consultants function in more than one of these fields.) Some are general categories with many specialties within the field.

QUESTIONNAIRE

USE OF PROPOSALS IN MARKETING:
[ ]Never [ ]Rarely [ ]Frequently [ ]Always [ ]Only when requested
[ ]Whether requested or not [ ]Other: _____

HOW OFTEN REQUESTED:
[ ]Usually [ ]Occasionally [ ]Rarely [ ]Other: _____

SUCCESS WITH PROPOSALS:
[ ]Over 75% [ ]50–75% [ ]25–50% [ ]Under 25% [ ]Other: _____

TYPE OF PROPOSAL USED AND FREQUENCY:
Informal/letter: _____% of time   Formal: _____% of time

PROPOSAL PRACTICES:
[ ]All original material [ ]Parts boilerplated [ ]All boilerplate
[ ]Quotation plus standard brochures and letter
[ ]Other: _____

SECTIONS/MATERIALS NORMALLY INCLUDED IN PROPOSALS:
[ ]Statement of problem/need [ ]Technical discussion [ ]Resume(s)
[ ]Qualifications [ ]Descriptions of deliverables [ ]Schedules
[ ]Facilities and resources [ ]Price [ ]Letter of transmittal
[ ]Other (e.g., special measures):_____

MARKET RESEARCH AND LEAD DEVELOPMENT:
[ ]Online _____%   [ ]In person _____%   [ ]Other _____%

PROPOSAL DELIVERY:
[ ]In person [ ]Online [ ]Other (how?) _____

COMMUNICATIONS IN RE PROPOSAL DEVELOPMENT:
[ ]E-mail _____%   [ ]Fax _____%   [ ]Telephone _____%
[ ]Writing _____%   [ ]Other _____%

PROPOSAL PROBLEMS, NEEDS, COMMENTS:
_____
_____
_____
_____

Additional comments are invited.

Figure 36 Questionnaire form.

Web site design	Internet training
Java programming	Training
Management	Computer systems and software
Financial services	Business plan services
Marketing	Proposal writing
Digital systems design	Polling and surveying
Engineering specialties	Dress-for-success consulting
Conference management	Direct-response marketing
Seminar production	Theatrical productions
TV productions	Small business management
Personal grooming	Modeling/models agency
Advertising and promotion	Business/personal image management
Medical-secretary training	Health care
Telephone marketing	Mailing-list management
Communications	Commercial real estate

I want to thank a few of the respondents publicly here, although I will not try to connect their names, listed below, with their individual responses and comments. I will list their Web sites and e-mail addresses, in some cases, as appropriate:

Ron W. Kaye, a writer and editorial services provider

Richard N. Coté, a busy book doctor and ghostwriter of books for clients throughout the world: dickcote@bookdoctor.com, site at http://www.bookdoctor.com/legacy/memoirs.html

Jeff Senne, of The Senne Group, an international speaker and consultant: jeff@sennegroup.com with a site at http://www.netincometactics.com

Steve Wilson, an Alexandria, Virginia, based proposal consultant, who is also a technical writer and general writing consultant: wilsonsr@erols.com

Shel Horowitz, a freelance business writer and publisher, who also runs a Web site dedicated to ways and means of getting the most value for your dollar and writes on that subject: shel@frugalfun.com, site at http://www.frugalfun.com

Edward J. Stone, President, EJS Marketing Communications

Paul Shivery III, Webmaster, Bellicose Industries, Senior Project Director and Webmaster: the one@bellicose.com, site at http://www.bellicose.com

Peter Meyer, The Meyer Group, who speaks, writes, and consults with clients on how to get more results from less time, fewer people, and less money, and with other consultants on how to deliver more client satisfaction while earning higher fees and getting more fun from their practices

Thomas Warner Zoss, Zoss Communications, Inc., who furnished very useful input for another of my recent books, *The Consultant's Guide to Getting Business on the Internet* (John Wiley & Sons, 1997): tzoss@zoss.com, site at http://www.zoss.com

Kaye Vivian, ABC (Accredited Communications Consultant), kvivian@cloud9.net, site at http://www.cloud9.net/ ~ kvivian/

Use of Proposals in Marketing

The tabulated results of the questionnaire are as follows (numbers rounded off):

Rarely:	25%
Frequently:	50%
Always:	12%
Only when requested:	00%
Whether requested or not:	25%
Other:	One significant response: "I refer to my proposal as a 'Summary'; it includes a blueprint for the project and the contract terms. I only develop one after I have had an Executive Overview session with the key decision makers to define and outline the project."

Note, first, that no one checked off "Never," and fewer than 7 percent indicated any rate of use less than "frequently." However, there is one apparent anomaly: It would be reasonable to expect that the people checking off "Whether requested or not" would be those who also checked off "Always." Mysteriously, that is not the case: Many of those who checked off this item also checked "Frequently," with no explanation for this apparent inconsistency. Those checking off "Other" used this as an occasion to make a remark to explain that they used something as an alternative to a proposal, similar to the response given by Jeff Senne and quoted here.

How Often Requested

Usually:	25%
Occasionally:	27%
Rarely:	00%
Other:	00%

Success with Proposals

Over 75%:	72%
50–75%:	13%
25–50%:	31%
Under 25%:	00%

Type of Proposal Used and Frequency

About 50 percent of respondents reported using informal and letter proposals more than half the time, with others reporting such usage as approaching 100 percent, and a few as actually reaching that figure. Twenty-nine percent reported the reverse orientation, usually using formal proposals. The remainder tended to about an equal or near-equal division of formal to informal proposals.

Proposal Practices

Some respondents checked off more than one item in this category, and the results are by frequency of appearance, with no attempt to make correlation:

All original material:	25%
Parts boilerplated:	60%
All boilerplate:	00%
Quotations plus standard brochures and letter:	25%
Other:	Comments supplied, such as the following: Varies a lot. Formal proposals (1–3/year) usually focus on client needs and my qualifications. Informal proposals are mostly one of a series

of one-page standard boilerplate letters with a little customization and focus on services available (especially writing). Most of my consulting comes in either through PMA-L or word of mouth, so I don't need to write many proposals.

Sections/Materials Normally Included in Proposals

Respondents were expected to check off several items in this category, and responses are reported by frequency of occurrence, with no attempt to make correlation:

Statement of problem/need:	75%
Technical discussion:	65%
Resumes:	3%
Qualifications:	3%
Descriptions of deliverables:	75%
Schedules:	25%
Facilities and resources:	13%
Price:	88%
Letter of transmittal:	25%
Other:	25%

"Other" was used to make qualifying remarks. Example: "Includes standard info package and contract with terms."

Market Research and Lead Development

Online:	52%
In person:	33%
Other:	70% Comments: From speaking engagements. Target mail blitz. Referral and phone. Greatest success comes from in-person presentations.

Proposal Delivery

In person:	35%
Online:	50%
Other (how?):	13%, FedEx, and phone, followed with contract.

Communications in re Proposal Development

E-mail: 75% use e-mail to varying degrees, reported as from 20 to 40%.

Fax: 75% report using fax in 10 to 40% of cases.

Telephone: 75% report using telephone in 30 to 75% of cases.

Writing: 25% use written proposals.

Other: 13% use other, unspecified methods.

Proposal Problems, Needs, Comments

Among the comments invited at the bottom of the questionnaire form are many of special interest. A few rather typical ones are quoted here:

- "Occasionally difficult to obtain timely feedback (approval/ rejection) to facilitate scheduling."

- "Writing proposals helps get the project organized from the get-go, and also helps clients understand exactly what's involved. However, it is possible to limit one's options with a proposal, and some flexibility is lost. Changes in situation and inaccurate predictions of labor time result in having to approach clients with new requirements, or simply taking the loss."

- "Most of my past business has come via personal referrals. That establishes some credibility immediately, and so my proposals are less extensive than they would otherwise need to be. Always follow up a phone conversation with a letter summarizing what was said and proposed. It's a good reminder to the potential client, who may otherwise forget to get back to you in the rush of a packed schedule. Some busy clients require more than one letter."

- "Potential clients appreciate thoroughness of presentation, attention to detail, and professionalism. It is best to talk with potential client, as many are not quite sure what they want or need. That's particularly true for smaller businesses. Proposal has a better chance of success if you and potential client agree beforehand, in phone conversation, exactly what client needs. You can't write a proposal without those specifics, in any event."

- "Proposals should be tailored to client's working style and personality. Not everyone is comfortable going through a long proposal. Editors are generally comfortable reading detailed proposals; entrepreneurs may not be. As you know, my style is to do an informal proposal that summarizes an already completed agreement. My proposal always includes the Success Criteria that the client and I have agreed on, in addition to deliverables. Also, costs included are total costs, not just my fees. More importantly, my proposals are mechanical procedures that summarize everything already agreed to. They tend to get read quickly and signed. They do not get scrutiny, and rarely do they result in negotiation. The purpose of a proposal, in my model, is to confirm the project that the client and consultant have already agreed to. No stress."

- "The worst position for a consultant to be in is when you think you are done with a project and the client doesn't agree. This almost always results from a relationship where you begin the work before the client and provider have agreed upon a definition of the work to be done—the endpoint. That's why a proposal is so important, and that it be in writing so it has "legs" and can be shared with the others you will be working with in the client organization."

- "I find that stating my view of the situation and how I would apply my skills to addressing that situation, and a clear statement of the price range (I rarely quote an exact figure, but it's almost always accepted that way) helps people make a buy/no-buy decision of an intangible, which is hard to do for many people today. They just don't know what ideas are worth. The proposal and the quotation help them to see into the future."

A number of respondents had additional remarks to make in general about proposal writing and related marketing considerations.

A Few Other Comments

Tom Zoss added the following: "I think the idea of quoting a price range is important—it gives a worst case scenario but clearly communicates the fact that I'm selling time. If things go well, if they cooperate and help me with data and access to people it will help when billing comes. I often bill less than the quote. I regularly send partial bills."

Peter Meyer is one of a number of respondents whose marketing presentations depend largely on preliminary contacts, discussions, and understandings that make written presentations primarily confirmations or those sales and marketing activities. He wrote his responses to my questionnaire on the plane en route to a government agency in Washington, D.C., to work on a survey and design session that would be the first phase of a project. Peter said he had followed his usual proposal process, to which my questionnaire was of limited relevance. He remarked that although this was a government contract, he used the same method in pursuing contracts with private-sector corporations. He added, "If I don't follow my guidelines—that is, to meet the decision maker and define the project with him or her—the success ratio drops to 10%."

In all, I think these results definitely reflect the influence of the online revolution on proposal writing. They also reflect the growing consciousness of the proposal as a marketing instrument, but here we find a wide divergence in definitions of what constitutes a proposal. Communications consultant Kaye Vivian is a veteran of 15 years of writing commercial proposals for professional services firms and a participant in the popular proposal-writers mailing list, proposal-l@govsolutions.com. She makes the point clearly that the proposals she writes are "business proposals" and are quite different from the proposals with which most others on the list are familiar. The latter are large, formal, and highly structured presentations, usually in pursuit of large government contracts, whereas she writes much simpler and less formal proposals. That illustrates an important difference: Government RFPs and proposal/contract requirements are subject to public law and the FAR (Federal Acquisition Regulations), whereas the organizations in the private sector are not so hemmed in by detailed requirements but may do pretty much as they please in soliciting bids and proposals and in evaluating those received. Writing proposals for private-sector organizations is thus far less regimented than writing those that must comply with extensive controls and public statutes.

Using Other Media in Presentations

Until recent years, it was taken for granted that a proposal would be delivered as a paper-and-ink document, although occasionally a contractor might supply a videotape or audiotape as an ancillary or appended element where there seemed to be a compelling reason to do so. Variations of that conventional approach are more common today. Today, proposals may be oral presentations, may be delivered via e-mail or fax, may be on disk, and may even be Web presentations. Or, as an increasingly common requirement, the client may ask for a disk presentation of all or part of the proposal, and some proposal specialists have speculated in an e-mail discussion of proposal writing on why clients would request proposals on disks.

The reason for using fax or e-mail as a transmission medium is simple enough: They are convenient and speedy delivery methods. Reasons for requesting presentation by disk may vary. In some cases, clients may simply want a convenient means for printing out additional copies of the proposal or some part of it, or even for duplicating the entire proposal easily by making copies of the disk.

Whatever the clients' reasons for this request, most participants in the discussion agreed that it is a good idea to be sure to place a copyright notice on your disk and a clear statement that the content of the disk must be used without changes of any kind.

The Proposal Library

There are two common problems in proposal writing for most consultants: One, it is almost always an ad hoc effort—one improvised as an interruption to regular daily activities, special and nonroutine. Important though proposal writing is as a marketing and business necessity, it is difficult not to regard it as an unwelcome disruption of our daily routine, activity for which we never seem to be wholly prepared.

The second problem is that there is never enough time to do the job: Proposals are almost invariably written in haste against a pressing and all-but-impossible schedule, and the need seems to always fall most inconveniently at a time when it interferes with our busy efforts to get some important project completed. Consequently, even when we get the proposal-writing job done, we often have the feeling that we didn't do as well as we should have and would have, had we had just a bit more time.

Corporations that do custom work and rely on proposals for all or nearly all their business often establish permanent proposal-writing departments or, if they have a technical writing group, assign proposal responsibility there and make that staff proposal specialists. You may not be able to do this as a practical measure, but you can do something else to offset some of the difficulties: You can create your own special proposal-development resource: a proposal library.

Unless you write or plan to write a proposal only once in a great while—and the fact that you are reading this book suggests that that is not the case—you are working under an unnecessary handicap if you do not have a proposal library. The efficiency and effectiveness of your proposal efforts will be greatly increased by a well-stocked and well-thought-out library of proposal resources. It will give you an organized basis for your proposal writing and make it a considerably less impromptu or improvised effort. Even more important, it will enable you to continuously improve the quality and success of your proposals.

A first requisite is a collection of reference books pertaining directly to your own career field and those technical/professional activities in which you specialize. As a consultant, however, you are in the somewhat ambiguous position of all consultants, compelled to be the master of both your technical/professional specialties and the technical and business skills and resources required for your consulting services. And included among those latter required resources are reference and other materials that normally constitute a proposal library.

The term *library* is used here in a rather special sense, referring to more than a collection of books, although it certainly includes those. But a properly stocked and well-organized library also includes many other kinds of on-the-shelf resources to make it easier to write proposals and to make it possible to write better—more effective—proposals. It can do this in several ways: by speeding up the process, an important consideration in most proposal efforts, through organizing useful materials and making them readily accessible; by placing the special materials—those of proven merit—conveniently at hand; and by providing ready access to materials that will contribute to the bid/no-bid analysis and decision making and to the evolution of a suitable approach and strategy.

To these ends, your proposal library ought to include at least these general classes of resources that are relevant:

- Books
- Periodicals

- Special reports about your field, consulting, and proposal writing
- Your own past proposals
- Your own brochures and other promotional literature
- Copies of competitors' proposals
- Copies of competitors' brochures and other promotional literature
- Swipe files

There are at least three general classes of reference books that you can put to good use in your proposal library. One is, of course, those dealing with your technical/professional specialties. A second class is that rather small collection of books that deal specifically with proposal writing and a much larger collection of books about sales and marketing, especially as they relate to proposal writing. And a third and possibly largest class is that of general reference books that will save you a great deal of research time by their ready availability.

The need for a five-foot shelf of reference books is considerably less today than it was a few years ago because a great deal of the information of interest is available in the convenient form of computer files, both on disks in your office, and accessible online in other computers around the world. Nor are all these simply books on disks; many are programs that will do much of the work of proposal writing for you. The following are some of the general types of material that may be paper and ink, disks and data files, or software programs:

- Books/disks/programs dealing with consulting skills generally and your field especially
- Equipment and software catalogs relevant to your field
- Directories, general and specialized
- Relevant how-to manuals/disks
- Proceedings of relevant conferences and symposia
- Periodicals
- Newsletters, print and electronic

There are an estimated 30,000 newsletters published in the United States and a large number of other periodicals—magazines, journals, tabloids, and other publications. Today, there are great numbers of newsletters online, often referred to as *electronic* or *digital* publications. Most are free, published by consultants and others for whom the newsletters are marketing tools.

Trade Journals and Related Periodicals

Even the most completely stocked newsstand does not carry on its shelves most of the periodicals published as trade journals and other specialty publications. A great many of these, especially the trade publications, are distributed free of charge to qualified applicants, as controlled-circulation publications. The qualification required is to be part of or have direct business interests in the industry addressed, such that you are a reasonable customer prospect for those whose advertising appears in the periodical.

Even more prominent by their special appeals and targeting are the many periodicals published by profit and nonprofit associations and corporations of many kinds. These are addressed to members, clients, and anyone with a special interest in the field. There are thousands of these publications, ranging from simple newsletters and tabloids to slick magazines in full process color.

The resulting ability to address the publication almost entirely and exclusively to those who are good sales prospects for those advertising in the publication makes it worthwhile for the publishers to give free subscriptions to those so qualifying. With the circulation figures verified by an audit agency, as is the case with controlled-circulation periodicals, the publisher is able to command premium advertising rates, making the venture worthwhile. (Those who do not qualify for free subscriptions are usually permitted to purchase subscriptions, if they wish to.)

There are several directories that list these publications. (A few will be listed here in the reference lists of publications.) Some of the directories are rather expensive, but it is not necessary to buy them, for most well-stocked libraries have reference copies available for your use, and librarians are quite helpful in guiding you to such public library resources. Moreover, you can use the search capabilities of Internet programs to help you find what you wish as part of the enormous amount of information available free of charge in the worldwide net of computers that make up the Internet.

The usual requirement for a free subscription to those periodicals that are distributed without charge may be merely an application on business stationery and/or a business card, although most will require you to complete a simple questionnaire.

Past Proposals

You should have an inventory of your own past proposals, especially those that were successful. They are useful in more than one way: Reviewing them may uncover a previous proposal that has many points of similarity with your current effort and so can save you a great deal of time in all phases of the effort, from research to final writing. You may also be able to save yourself a great deal of time and expense by reusing some of the graphics and other materials from earlier efforts. Keep a tight rein on these; the loss of even one file copy of your past proposals may be a disaster. And "loss" may even mean merely mislaying it; nevertheless, that is a true loss, at least for the moment. You should probably never dead-file old proposals generally, and certainly not old successful proposals. (Of course, your file copies can be and should be—are most effective assets—in your computer or on floppy disks.)

Brochures and Promotional Literature

As you read in reviewing the results of my questionnaire-survey, many consultants utilize standard brochures and other sales literature as parts of their proposals. This reduces proposal-writing time and enables them to develop and submit a greater number of proposals than they would otherwise be able to handle. But even if you do not incorporate the actual brochures and other materials—sales letters, reprints of articles by and/or about you, your own newsletters and reports, and other such material—they are often handy time-savers for the creation (pasteup) of rough drafts. And many, especially reprints of articles but not confined to those, are useful as enclosures—appendixes and exhibits—to your proposals. (Pasteup today is electronic, of course, done easily in computer files.)

Competitors' Material

From time to time you get opportunities to acquire copies of competitors' proposals. One way, if your competitors do business with the federal government, is by requesting copies of winning proposals under the Freedom of Information Act. But copies can come into your hands by other means, too, such as via new employees who are eager to contribute what they can to your success.

Competitors' general literature—brochures and other items—are relatively easy to acquire, especially at trade fairs, national conventions, conferences, and other such events.

Such material is valuable through all phases of proposal development, from the initial bid/no-bid analysis and decision making to the development of written arguments.

Swipe Files

Anything and everything in your proposal library is potentially useful to actually borrow (swipe) and use in your new proposal. But for most cases it is only after spending much time to review many things in your library that you uncover such useful materials and decide that they can or cannot be used without, or almost without, change—readily modified for a new use, that is. On the other hand, there are usually certain items that fit so well into most of your proposals that you find them reusable again and again, with little or no change necessary to adapt them to the new uses. That is likely to be true for milestone charts, schedules, labor-loading matrices, tabular/text descriptions of past projects, and lists of resources, for example.

It should not be necessary to spend a great deal of time tracking down such universally useful materials; since they will be used again and again, they ought to be made readily accessible. To achieve this, it is necessary only to make master copies of such material and store them in special files, suitably indexed for quick search and location.

Filing Methods

A conventional library consists of books arrayed on shelves, periodicals arrayed in some suitable stand, and other materials on shelves and/or in filing cabinets, with suitable indexes or catalogs to make search and retrieval possible. Today, index cards are passé, even in public libraries, replaced by computer indexes, the most efficient and convenient way to store and gain access to indexes.

You will find it advantageous to have as many of your files as possible on disks, either floppies or hard disks. That applies to most of your text files, which you may have originally created: your past proposals, articles, reports, and other data. The ease and speed of summoning files, examining them on-screen, and making changes to update or modify them, if necessary, are the benefits of disk storage.

There is no point in keeping paper copies of that which you have already magnetically filed on disks, although it is wise to always have two copies of anything important, so that for safety your library copy is backed up with an archived copy, a second disk, or a tape backup. (Data on disk is durable, normally, but can be destroyed. Backup copies are a sensible precaution against losses of disk files.)

Swipe files should likewise be on disks. You can create these easily by copying from your various proposal and other files any materials you expect to be able to use frequently and repeatedly. Then set up special files for these materials, along with suitable indexes. (There are many catalog and indexing programs available to help you create suitable indexes to facilitate searches and retrievals.) Full-page scanners are readily available and inexpensive today, so it is relatively easy to make an electronic copy of any material you wish to copy to disk and store in your computer system or on a floppy. You can, of course, easily and swiftly make a copy of anything in your disk files. In fact, you need not and should not alter or modify the original copy in your files. Make an exact copy, and make your changes to that copy. (And if you run into difficulties or make mistakes that are troublesome to correct, don't even spend the time to do so; just make a new copy and start over.) Also, always consider, when you modify a copy of master files to create something new, whether it might not be worthwhile to add that new item to your swipe files as another original or, perhaps, whether the new material is such an improvement over the old that you might wish to replace your original with a new original. In this manner your files grow, not only in their abundance, but in their inherent quality, with resulting benefits in your future proposal efforts.

Federal Government Business Opportunities

Figure 37 lists some of the typical consulting requirements of government agencies. In fact, these are probably the most far-ranging kinds of requirements to be found anywhere in the world. There are few products or services the U.S. federal government does not buy, and a great many of these are custom services, designed for the federal agencies' specific needs (although the government is trending to buying more products commercially, off the shelf, than was the case in the past). Services, especially consulting services, tend by their nature to be custom work, and the increasing complexity of so much in our lives today stimulates the steady increase in requirements for services, mostly consulting despite their listing under a variety of other headings in the *Commerce Business Daily* (CBD) and other government publications.

The CBD does not list all government requirements (more than $200 billion annually), unfortunately. In fact, it lists only about 10 to 15 percent of all requirements. The requirements that are estimated to cost less than $25,000 are not listed. The other resources for uncovering RFPs include filing the federal government Form 129, Application for Bidders List, which is available from any government contracting or procurement office and can be downloaded from the Internet at www.hud.gov/forms/formwrhs.html. With the way procurement is trending, however, the 129 form is of decreasing importance. There are many other ways now to get information online about procurement by government agencies.

Before the online revolution, I advised readers to visit the nearest Government Printing Office bookstore and to write or visit the Small Business Administration, the Department of Defense, and many other agencies. Today, you can get all the information and a great deal more online, without leaving your desk, through the Internet and the many electronic bulletin boards. You may also make an informal request via e-mail to be placed on a mailing list for notices of requirements. NASA, for example, offers this.

A principal activity for pursuing government business is reading the CBD, where you find the requirements of various agencies published in synoptic form, advising you of the next step to take to pursue the contract. Today, the CBD is available online, at various places on the Web. One of these is a site of the Government Printing Office, another a site of the Loren Data Corporation, and still another at the Federal Marketplace Procurement Data Warehouse site. These are found at the following URLs (*uniform resource locators,* the Web addresses):

http://cbdnet.access.gpo.gov/index.html

http://www.ld.com/cbd/today/

http://www.fedmarket.com/

B—CONSULTING SERVICES TO DEVELOP SHORE INFRASTRUC-
TURE METRICS SEAPORT/AIRPORT CAPACITY SOL N00244-98-
Q-0025 DUE 111497 POC Bid Officer (619) 532-2690 or 2692
FAX (619) 532-1088 or 1089 WEB:http://www.sd.fisc.navy.mil.
Click here to obtain more information regarding FISC San Diego,
E-MAIL: Click here to contact the Contracting Officer via e-mail,
joan_balazs@fmso.navy.mil. FISC San Diego has a requirement
to procure consulting services for CINCPACFLT to develop shore
infrastructure metrics Seaport/Airport capacity required for the
year 2006. You may request a copy of the RFQ from the Bid Officer
by FAXING your request to (619) 532-1088 or 1089. (0302)

R—EMPLOYEE COUNSELING SERVICES SOL 1443RP509098001
DUE 121897 POC Point of Contact—Contact Point, Kimberly
Washington, 404/562-3163 Contractor shall provide employee
counseling services and employee assistance program for approximately 1,542 Southeast Region locations/employees. The contract
will cover a period of five years. This will be a firm-fixed price
contract. The technical proposal will be evaluated on technical
evaluation criteria which will be contained in the solicitation.
The solicitation will be available on or about November 18, 1997.
No telephone request. Written requests only. Fax number (404)
562-3256. This procurement is totally set aside for small business.
(AC1103001-01) (0307)

R—CONSULTING SERVICES FOR TACTICAL AUTOMATED MIS-
SION PLANNING SYSTEM SOL N00421-98-R-1005 DUE 112897
POC Christina A. Roach, AIR-2.5.5.1.1B (301) 757-9071 E-MAIL:
Inquiries may be sent via e-mail to address, each_Christina
%PAX9B@MR.NAWCAD.NAVY.MIL. Advisory and Assistance
Services SOL N00421-98-R-1005. POC: Christina A. Roach, Contract
Specialist (301) 757-9071. The NAVAL AIR WARFARE CENTER,
AIRCRAFT DIVISION, PATUXENT RIVER, has a requirement for the
procurement of Advisory and Assistance Services in support of the
Tactical Automated Mission Planning System (PMA-233). These
services include, but are not limited to: analysis of engineering and
technical systems, and management support. The period of perfor-

Figure 37 A few consulting needs synopsized in the CBD.

mance shall commence on or about 24 January 1998 and will consist of a base year of 12 months with a 6-month option period. In accordance with Federal Acquisition Regulation (FAR) 6.302-1 only one responsible source and no other Supplies or Services will satisfy agency requirements; therefore, the Government shall negotiate an indefinite delivery/indefinite quantity contract on a sole source basis with Brandes Associates Incorporated (BAI) 1417 Crestline Drive, Santa Barbara, CA 93105. BAI has supported the TAMPS program since 1992 and has the resident program management expertise and technical knowledge necessary to provide the continuation of services and ensure there will be no service degradation in the support of several critical milestones and events. All responsible sources may submit a proposal which shall be considered by the agency. Capability statements may be faxed to Christina Roach at (301) 757-2628. See Note 22. Requests for information may be e-mailed to the following address. All Internet responses must provide the return Internet address, a Post Office Mailing address, and a phone number within the body of the response. Internet responses without the aforementioned addresses will not be recognized.

Figure 37   *(Continued).*

Notices in the CBD once always advised you to request a copy of the solicitation from some office, often naming the individual in the office. Many of the notices still do that, but a great many today state that the notice you are reading is the entire solicitation, although it may also cite FAR (Federal Acquisition Regulations) that apply.

Figure 37 offers examples of typical notices, two of which specifically call for consulting services as such, although a great many requirements called for under a wide variety of other names are, in fact, consulting services, even if not so named, so study the nature of the services required rather than what the notice calls them.

Most federal agencies today have their own Web sites and electronic bulletin board systems (BBSes) and offer all kinds of information, including that pertaining to procurement actions, needs, and procedures. For that information, go to the Federal Acquisition Jumpstation at http://procure.msfc.nasa.gov/fedproc/home.html.

This, together with the *Commerce Business Daily,* is the door to virtually all government procurement information. From the listings at this site you can find much more government purchasing information than you can use. In fact, one problem will be determining which areas of procurement and which agencies are the best prospects—you can't cover them all.

There are other Web sites that should be of interest. One is that of an association of proposal specialists, the Association of Proposal Management Professionals (APMP), whose home page is at http://www.apmp.org/. Another is the home page of OPTYM Professional Services, a proposal support service at http://www.govsolutions.com/, where you will find information of interest. An especially useful site will be found at http://www.fedmarket.com/, where you will find a number of convenient links to related facilities and various items of procurement-related information.

State and Local Governments

Most of what is true about doing business with the federal government is true about doing business with the thousands of state and local governments. There are about 80,000 of these government entities, according to the U.S. Census Bureau, and within many of these state and local governments, as within the federal government, there are large numbers of subordinate agencies and bureaus that may buy your services independently and that often solicit proposals. In the aggregate there are at least a half million or more prospective government clients, and that is a conservative estimate. Many of these governments, especially the state governments and the larger city and county governments, publish substantial literature describing their procurement systems and policies and listing dozens and dozens of local government agencies, bureaus, and establishments, so that these too offer a large contribution to your store of information resources.

Most of these governmental entities urge contractors to visit their purchasing offices to become personally acquainted with the various buyers in these offices and to learn at first hand how the systems function. The central purchasing offices and purchasing officials are located in the state capitals, the county seats, and the city or town halls. You can get a complete listing at the State and Local Procurement Jumpstation, http://www.fedmarket.com/statejump.html.

Fortunately, you may now visit most of the state and local governments via the Internet. All or virtually all now have their own Web sites, publish their requirements online, and permit you to register online. One excellent resource for finding these is provided by the periodical, *Government Computing News,* at its Web site, http://www .gcn.com/, which also provides a lengthy list of BBSes in government offices at http://www.gcn.com/links/chart2.htm. Other sites that provide information for accessing various government offices and information are listed and can be reached at or via links from http://www.fedworld.gov/.

Most of the state and local governments have their own forms for registering with their procurement agencies as a supplier, and many require that you file that form with them to qualify for bidding or proposing to them. Many also have literature for prospective contractors. Many also emulate the federal government socioeconomic programs with programs of their own, offering loans, loan guarantees, and other kinds of special assistance and preference to small business, to minority entrepreneurs, to women entrepreneurs, and to handicapped individuals. And many state and local governments offer some preference to local suppliers, although all will do business with anyone who qualifies. Together, these many governments represent a vast market, estimated at more than $660 billion annually, with a substantial portion for consulting services. (The figure depends on how you define consulting, but it is estimated that about 20 percent—more than $132 billion annually—is used to buy a variety of technical and professional services.) Like the federal government agencies, state and local governments and their agencies tend to perceive many of their needs as unique, which therefore require special consulting services to satisfy.

On the other hand, state and local governments do not have an equivalent of the federal government's *Commerce Business Daily* in which to announce their requirements and solicit inquiries. Maryland, however, does announce at least some of its requirements in the official *Maryland Register,* the state's equivalent of the federal government's *Federal Register,* and occasionally a local government has some official publication it can use for this purpose. But for the most part, state and local governments use their bidders lists but rely primarily on local newspapers to announce their requirements, synopsizing them in classified advertising columns under the heading "Bids and Proposals," but often running large display advertising to solicit bids and proposals. State and local laws generally mandate that requirements be advertised in whatever is the leading daily newspaper in the locality of the procurement office. (For example, the city of Washington, D.C., and most surrounding Maryland and Virginia counties and municipalities advertise their requirements in the *Washington Post.*)

State and local governments have their own small-purchase laws and permit procurements defined as small purchases in their procurement regulations to be made under limited competition and, for the smallest classes of such procurements, often without competition. Therefore, many small projects are never advertised at all, but are let through direct negotiation, usually following submittal of an informal letter proposal and/or an unsolicited proposal, formal or informal. They almost unanimously urge suppliers to visit personally and meet the various buyers.

Recommended Publications

The following is a partial list of publications I believe will be helpful additions to your proposal library, and I stress both partial and recommended because a great deal depends on your special interests and needs, especially with regard to periodicals. There are, in fact, relatively few publications that bear directly on the subject of proposal writing, but there are some that cover relevant subjects, such as marketing, writing, editing, and publications processes.

Books

Anatomy of Persuasion, The: How to Persuade Others to: Act on Your Ideas, Accept Your Proposals, Buy Your Products or Services, Hire You, Promote You, by Norbert Aubuchon, NTC Business Books, 1997

Careful Writer, The, by Theodore Bernstein, Atheneum, 1965

Elements of Style, The, by William Strunk and E. B. White, Macmillan, 1995

Handbook for Writing Proposals, by Robert J. Hamper and L. Sue Baugh, AMACOM, 1995

How to Create and Present Successful Government Proposals: Techniques for Today's Tough Economy, by James W. Hill (editor) and Timothy Whalen, IEEE, 1993

How to Succeed as an Independent Consultant, third edition, by Herman Holtz, John Wiley & Sons, 1993

How to Write Winning Proposals for Your Company or Client, by Ron Tepper, John Wiley & Sons, 1990

Net Income: Cut Costs, Boost Profits, and Enhance Operations Online, by Wally Bock and Jeff Senne, Van Nostrand Reinhold, 1997

Persuasive Business Proposals: Writing to Win Customers, Clients, and Contracts, by Tom Sant, AMACOM, 1992

Successful Business Writing: How to Write Effective Letters, Proposals, Resumes, Speeches, by Lassor A. Blumenthal, Perigee, 1985

Words into Type, 4th edition, by Henning Helms, Prentice Hall, 1998, Byte Books, 1985

E-zines

Electronic publications, magazines, and newsletters are referred to by some as *e-zines,* the initial "e" standing for "electronic." They are also known as *online publications,* because they exist only online, except as one chooses to print them out, for that is possible.

Many of these exist only in e-mail forms, but others are on Web sites in full typeset and full-color regalia of tricky typography, line illustrations, drawings, and photographs. A few—*Inc.* magazine, the *New York Times,* and *Government Executive* magazine are online editions of paper-and-ink publications. Most e-zines are free, although there are a number that charge subscription fees. Both http://www.dominis.com/Zines/ and http://www.ezines.com/ (especially the first of these) will present you with lists of all existing e-zines that are far from complete but are, nonetheless, quite comprehensive.

A Few Relevant Sources on Internet Web Sites

Previous pages offered you suggested formats for your proposal and various proposal elements. There are, of course, many other formats possible and used by others. Following are a few sites on the Web that offer suggested formats and other information that may be of interest and use to you to supplement what you have read here. They cover several kinds of proposals, including grant proposals and unso-.licited proposals.

> PETC (Pittsburgh Energy Technology Center) Home Business Guide for the Submission of Unsolicited Proposals, http://www .petc.doe.gov/petctext/business/unsol.html
>
> Writing the Proposal, general grant and proposal-writing tips, from Texas A&M, http://tlrc.tamu.edu/grants/grantpro/writprop.htm
>
> Proposal Writing Workshop from the Capital Health Authority of Edmonton, Alberta, Canada, http://www.cha.ab.ca/commdev
>
> The Online Communicator: Proposal Writing Short Course from The Foundation Center, http://www.communicator.com/writprop .html
>
> A Proposal Writing Short Course from The Foundation Center, http://fdncenter.org/2fundpro/2prop.html

Some Suggested Standard Formats

You can save a great deal of time on and orientation of any help you use in proposal writing by standardizing both the overall format of your proposals and the formats of items you use in all or nearly all your proposals. Some of the kinds of items exemplifying and suggested for this have been presented earlier in these pages. There also appeared a few items designed to guide and help you in requirements analysis and development of approaches and strategies. The following is a list of such items, and the list is then followed by examples of additional items designed to help you. It would probably be useful to compile a set of copies of these in a master file to be used in each proposal effort. If you are working with a computer, these can be entered as computer or word processor files, for even greater flexibility.

You may use these items in and for development of your proposals without change, choose one from among several where alternatives are offered, or modify and adapt them to your own needs, as you prefer.

Items That Have Appeared in Prior Pages

First steps in devising strategy	Figure 1
General proposal format	Figures 2 and 19
Exercise sheet: consulting specialties	Figure 3
Bid/no-bid analysis reporting form	Figure 4
RFP requirements checklists	Figures 5 and 6
Functional flowcharts	Figures 7–10 and 30
Value management (FAST) diagrams	Figures 13–16
Resume format	Figure 21
Typical organization chart	Figure 22
Schedule, as table and as milestone chart	Figures 23 and 24
Format for task/labor estimates	Figure 25
Format for and sample of response matrix	Figures 26 and 35
Pictorial diagram	Figure 27
Block diagram	Figure 28
Simple network	Figure 29
Standard drawing templates	Figure 31
Sample of computer-generated clip art	Figure 32
Logic tree	Figure 33
Sample title page	Figure 34

A Few Additional Offerings

MODULAR RECENT-PROJECT PRESENTATION FORMAT

To provide efficiency and flexibility in furnishing references and information on your current and past performances you ought to modularize your project descriptions so that they can be fitted into the general format suggested here (see Figure 38), while being reorganized (most relevant projects first) readily for each new proposal.

COST SUMMARIES

Small projects are usually quoted with either a fixed price for the job or a consulting rate with, usually, an estimate of consulting time

---

CURRENT AND RECENT PROJECTS

PROJECT TITLE OR FUNCTIONAL NAME	CLIENT ORGANIZATION
Summary description, highlights size ($$, labor hours, time, or other measure), record of performance with regard to schedule and budget, most impressive accomplishments	Contact: Name, address, telephone number of purchasing agent or other individual(s) responsible for monitoring project and able to furnish information

(Next project description)

Figure 38 A modular format for describing other project experience.

(hours, days, weeks, or other time unit) required. However, where the project is to be a large one, it is not unusual, especially in the case of government agencies, for the client to ask for some details on how the cost estimate was established. Government agencies, especially those of the federal government, usually provide a standard form for this. But even in those cases where clients do not provide such a form or prescribe the format, they ask for essentially the same information. In general, the form shown in Fig. 39 serves the purpose quite well.

This form is predicated on the assumptions that there is no significant amount of materials required (those businesses that are heavy in the materials area tend to have separate overhead rates for materials), that the accounting system does use a general and administrative (G&A) indirect expense pool to accommodate certain types of indirect costs, and that the overhead rate includes fringe benefits. Of course, if your own accounting system does not conform to this—it does not include G&A and/or you list fringe benefits as an item separate from the overhead pool—you will modify this form to reflect that. If your fee is a flat figure and not a percentage, change that also.

G&A, by the way, is a rate that is applied to all costs that appear above it on this form. The same is true for the fee or profit rate.

Direct labor:

_____ _____ @ $_____ = $_____
(functional title) (hours)   (rate)   (subtotal)

_____ _____ @ $_____ = $_____ $_____
                                                     (direct labor total)

Labor overhead:

$_____ @ _____ % = $_____
 (direct labor)   (overhead rate)   overhead total)

Other direct costs:

_____ $ _____
   (itemize)

_____ $ _____ $_____
                                                       (ODC total)

General and administrative cost: _____ % $_____
                                (rate)

Fee or profit: _____ % $_____

Grand total: $_____

Figure 39   A general form for breaking down cost estimates.

This format and detail need be used only when the client demands it and you are willing to reveal your various cost centers and burden rates. In most cases the government will require it for any project running more than a few thousand dollars—above $25,000, which is the small-purchase rate today. Commercial clients are less likely to demand this, but those who do government work and subcontract to consultants tend to emulate government methods and sometimes are even required by their government contracts to subcontract according to federal procurement methods. Today, even purely commercial organizations are tending to impose this requirement for large contracts.

If it happens that you do not know precisely what your overhead rate is—and it is not uncommon for circumstances to create that uncertainty—the usual practice is to estimate it as a *provisional* rate, subject to subsequent audit and adjustment. But that audit and adjustment is generally applied only to contracts of at least $100,000, if then.

EXPERIENCE AND QUALIFICATIONS (RESUMES) SUMMARY

For many projects, the individual qualifications of the proposed staff are of primary concern to the client. Figure 40 offers an efficient

PRO- POSED (Name)	EDUCATION (Degree/Univ)	AREAS OF TRAINING/EXPERIENCE				
		(Item)	(Item)	(Item)	(Item)	(Item)

Figure 40   Format of qualifications and experience summary matrix.

means for organizing that individual experience and qualifications record into a single, concentrated summary—a matrix, in fact.

The cells of the matrix are developed according to the individual requirement. Each item, for example, will be a given discipline, special skill, educational major, or specific experience, such as data processing, budget control, training, or writing. The set of items should, of course, represent all the qualifications required, and the candidate names proposed will represent the professional and key staff offered for the project.

SAMPLE SELLING HEADLINES AND CAPTIONS

The point was made earlier that in proposal writing every opportunity to drive home a sales message—make positive and persuasive arguments—must be exploited and that one of the most neglected areas for doing this is that of titles, headlines, and captions. Here, to illustrate this more clearly through a few for instances, are some before and after examples (see Figure 41). However, even these are generalized and generic, and can be further sharpened and made even more positive by expressing them in the specific terms of the requirement. For example, instead of "Proposed Ways to Cut Costs," a specific proposal to develop or revise a computer program might caption or title this, "A Tighter Program to Cut Operating Costs." Or, if the schedule is a tight one and there is some evident concern on the client's part about capability for meeting the deadline, the schedule item might be phrased, "How (your name) Will Deliver (the end item or service) by March 15." The idea is to concentrate on the client's worry items, as a reminder of them, and in so doing make references to and reinforce those worries, the benefits you promise, and the proofs that you can and will deliver on those promises. It raises the client's concern about others' assurance of on-time delivery, and so is a competitive strategy. Those titles, headlines, and captions should be a series of reminders of the most important elements of your strategy and theme.

Guidelines to Cure Bad Writing and Maximize Credibility

1. Avoid this common writing mistake of starting to write too soon. Too many proposals don't make it beyond the initial reading by the client because the writer began to write before he or she fully understood the requirement and never did bother to perfect his or her knowledge of what the client wanted. The requirement rarely appears quite the same after a half dozen readings of the RFP as it did after the first reading.

2. Spend at least as much time in studying, analyzing, planning, researching, and otherwise preparing to write as in writing itself. It will be time well invested and will save you enough false starts and rewriting to more than compensate for the time it takes. Your ability to do all the other things listed here depends upon your first doing what is urged on you here.

3. Don't allow yourself to wander aimlessly. (Many proposals are of the "river raft" type: They drift from one place to another, with no apparent destination.) Draw up specific objectives—all the major points you must make in your proposal. Know in advance exactly where you wish to go and march to your destination.

4. Don't have vague ideas about how you will reach or achieve each objective. Draw up your subordinate objectives so you know your itinerary in advance—the route you plan to take to get there and the milestones you must reach along the way.

5. Don't try to work from plans in your head or even from a generalized philosophy. Develop an outline in which all major points and objectives are specified—not an outline of what you will *talk*

BEFORE (generic/passive referent)	AFTER (focused selling point)
Costs	Cost Consciousness
Cost Considerations	How This Program Will Cut Costs
Schedule	Objectives That Will Be Met
Milestone Chart	Milestones Marking Success and Progress
Functional Flowchart	How All Problems Will Be Solved and Objectives Reached
Qualifications and Experience	Proof That (your name/organization) Can Do the Job
Qualifications Matrix	Array and Correlation of Capabilities
Understanding of the Requirement	Essence of the Problem
Discussion	Specific Steps to Successful Planning and Completion
Proposed Program	How We Will Deliver the Result We Promise
Our Facilities and Resources	Resources We Will Place in Your Service for This Program

Figure 41 Examples of selling titles, headlines, and captions.

about in your proposal, but an outline of what you will *say* in your proposal.

6. Don't expect to write a good first draft. Expert writers become expert writers because they know that first drafts are rarely as good as second and third drafts. Plan to do some self-editing and rewriting.

7. Examine everything you have written, in your self-editing, and judge whether each sentence, paragraph, and other element achieves its objectives and whether it not only can be understood, but cannot be misunderstood—that is, is not only clear, but is unambiguous. (If it can be misunderstood, it will be. You may rely on that.)

8. Don't be elegant, subtle, clever, or humorous in your writing style. All such characteristics are misplaced in proposals, which are read by busy people who probably do not enjoy reading at all, much less analyzing what they have read to see if they understand it correctly. (In fact, if what you have written brings from the reader a chuckle, that is probably ominous.) Focus only on meaning. Think about your reader and no one else, not even yourself.

9. Offer as much detail as possible in the areas that you believe are most important in influencing the client. Anyone can generalize and philosophize, and being able to do so suggests that you are glib, but it does not prove that you are in command of the subject or possess the necessary capabilities. The ability to plan and describe in details—to specify—on the other hand, indicates complete command of the subject and competence, both technical and managerial. It makes such a proposal infinitely more credible than the one that is full of glib, general assurances.

10. Be sure that you do have a clear-cut strategy, rather than a vague idea or hope that the client will see you as superior to everyone else. Without such a clearly understood strategy underlying your proposal, it is difficult for your proposal to have a positive tone; it almost inevitably comes across as a defensive plaint. And without a clear strategy, properly implemented, you are not even partially in command of the situation.

11. Be sure that your proposal has a theme. The theme should be linked closely to the strategy and should, in effect, reinforce the strategy on almost every page of your proposal. (If, for example, your strategy is based on low cost, your theme might well be along the lines of "Efficiency and Cost Consciousness," and this could even be a running head or foot appearing on each page to remind the client of your promise.)

12. Finally, be sure that you have been absolutely explicit, both qualitatively and quantitatively, about what you promise to deliver and communicate distinctly what you offer without making it appear to be a plea.

Computer Software

The most basic computer software that you need is, obviously, a modern word processor. You probably have one already that you are familiar with and favor, but for the sake of discussion, take note that the two most popular word processing programs in this age of almost universally used Windows software are WordPerfect™ and Word. WordPerfect had become the leading word processor for DOS before most of us began to convert to Windows, but Microsoft's Word has been a strong contender as a word processor in the Windows environment. Both are entirely adequate for most purposes, but many proposal writers advocate—even insist on—FrameMaker™ or Page-Maker™ as necessary to turn out the most professional product, and there are still other programs, such as Corel™, favored by many proposal specialists. Many users advocate using Adobe Acrobat® for creating files that include forms in any copy to be viewed on-screen because that will ensure that the form will appear the same on every system.

Acrobat™ is a group of programs by Adobe Systems. Any given presentation on the Web may vary somewhat in appearance because each browser may see it a little differently. Acrobat software creates the PDF (portable document format) files that will appear the same to each viewer, regardless of differences in browsers. It must be read with the Acrobat Reader, but that is free and may be downloaded from many sites, including the Adobe Web site at URL http://www.adobe.com/, where you can gain more information about Acrobat software. I used Acrobat, for example, to download and print out a copy of Standard Form 129, Application for Bidders List, that is exactly like the government's printed version in all respects.

Index